The Legend of
Guardian
Industries

President and CEO William Davidson

The Legend of
Guardian
Industries

Jeffrey L. Rodengen

Edited by Debra Kronowitz
Design and layout by Dennis Shockley

Write Stuff Enterprises, Inc.
1001 South Andrews Avenue
Second Floor
Fort Lauderdale, FL 33316
1-800-900-Book (1-800-900-2665)
(954) 462-6657
www.writestuffbooks.com

Publisher's Cataloging in Publication

Rodengen, Jeffrey L.
　　The legend of Guardian Industries/ Jeffrey L. Rodengen. — 1st ed.
　　　p. cm.
　　Includes bibliographical references (p.) and index.
　　LCCN 00-136038
　　ISBN 0-945903-78-2

1. Guardian Industries Corporation— History.
2. Glass trade — United States — History.
II. Title.

HD9623.U47G83 2001　　338.4'76661'0977432
　　　　　QBI21-79

Library of Congress
Catalog Card Number 00-136038

　　ISBN 0-945903-78-2

Completely produced in the
United States of America
10 9 8 7 6 5 4 3 2 1

Also by Jeffrey L. Rodengen

The Legend of Chris-Craft

IRON FIST:
The Lives of Carl Kiekhaefer

Evinrude-Johnson
and The Legend of OMC

Serving the Silent Service:
The Legend of Electric Boat

The Legend of Dr Pepper/Seven-Up

The Legend of Honeywell

The Legend of Briggs & Stratton

The Legend of Ingersoll-Rand

The Legend of Stanley:
150 Years of The Stanley Works

The MicroAge Way

The Legend of Halliburton

The Legend of York International

The Legend of Nucor Corporation

The Legend of Goodyear:
The First 100 Years

The Legend of AMP

The Legend of Cessna

The Legend of VF Corporation

The Spirit of AMD

The Legend of Rowan

New Horizons:
The Story of Ashland Inc.

The History of American Standard

The Legend of Mercury Marine

The Legend of Federal-Mogul

Against the Odds:
Inter-Tel—The First 30 Years

The Legend of Pfizer

State of the Heart:
The Practical Guide to Your Heart
and Heart Surgery
with Larry W. Stephenson, M.D.

The Legend of
Worthington Industries

The Legend of IBP, Inc.

The Legend of
Trinity Industries, Inc.

The Legend of
Cornelius Vanderbilt Whitney

The Legend of Amdahl

The Legend of Litton Industries

The Legend of Gulfstream

The Legend of Bertram
with David A. Patten

The Legend of
Ritchie Bros. Auctioneers

The Legend of ALLTEL
with David A. Patten

The Yes, you can of
Invacare Corporation
with Anthony L. Wall

The Ship in the Balloon:
The Story of Boston Scientific
and the Development of
Less-Invasive Medicine

The Legend of Day & Zimmermann

The Legend of Noble Drilling

Fifty Years of Innovation:
Kulicke & Soffa

Biomet—From Warsaw
to the World
with Richard F. Hubbard

NRA: An American Legend

The Heritage and Values
of RPM, Inc.

The Marmon Group:
The First Fifty Years

The Legend of Grainger

The Legend of
The Titan Corporation
with Richard F. Hubbard

The Legend of Discount Tire Co.
with Richard F. Hubbard

The Legend of Polaris
with Richard F. Hubbard

The Legend of La-Z-Boy
with Richard F. Hubbard

The Legend of McCarthy
with Richard F. Hubbard

InterVoice:
Twenty Years of Innovation
with Richard F. Hubbard

Jefferson-Pilot Financial:
A Century of Excellence
with Richard F. Hubbard

The Legend of HCA
with Richard F. Hubbard

The Legend of Werner Enterprises
with Richard F. Hubbard

The History of J. F. Shea Co.
with Richard F. Hubbard

True to Our Vision
with Richard F. Hubbard

Albert Trostel & Sons
with Richard F. Hubbard

TABLE OF CONTENTS

FOREWORD

BY
PROFESSOR B. JOSEPH WHITE
UNIVERSITY OF MICHIGAN BUSINESS SCHOOL

THE DEVELOPMENT OF Guardian Industries over the last half-century from a small, struggling local company in Detroit, Michigan, to a leading giant in the global glass industry is a remarkable and compelling business story. It is also a story of the entrepreneurial and visionary leadership of William (Bill) Davidson, Guardian's owner, chairman, and chief executive.

It is perfectly consistent with Bill Davidson's modesty and self-effacing personality that the legend presented in this book is of the company and its people, not of Bill himself. This is as it should be. But this foreword seems to me the right place to note that without Bill's great leadership, there would be no company legend to tell.

I love business and its job-creating, wealth-producing, and individual-empowering effects. I admire the risk taking required to build a business. I believe deeply in the stimulating environment created by competition and in the market's brutally effective process of sorting out winners and losers. I appreciate the vital role that innovation plays in advancing companies, industries, and human welfare. I value business leaders who can integrate the hard edge required for competitive success with a deep and sincere belief in the valuable contributions every employee can make to that success. All these elements and more are present in abundance and recounted in a highly readable fashion in *The Legend of Guardian Industries*.

I became personally acquainted with Guardian Industries and Bill Davidson during the decade I served as dean of the University of Michigan Business School, of which Bill is a graduate. As a result, I got glimpses of the glass business and came to appreciate its technology, risk characteristics, and innovations.

I remember visiting Guardian's float glass plant in Thailand. I was struck by the extraordinarily high stakes involved in investing the vast capital in and taking on the operating costs of every new glass plant, of which Guardian now has many around the world. I was amazed to learn that when a new glass plant is fired up, because of the complexity and highly "tuned" nature of the production process, Guardian's presumption is that the plant will operate continuously, around the clock and throughout the year, year after year, whatever the demand and market prices for glass. I had never before encountered anything quite like this in business.

I came to appreciate the remarkable strides in glass technology that have occurred in recent years and to which Guardian has made substantial contributions. Progress in the safeness, environmental friendliness, quality of coatings, and other features of glass that are little appreciated by the average person have nonetheless saved many lives and much energy and made the architectural applications of glass nearly limitless.

Perhaps most importantly, I came to appreciate Bill Davidson as an extraordinary business leader and a wonderful human being. Bill introduced me to many fine people, among them the late David Hermelin, one of Bill's closest friends, another graduate of the Business School, and a man I came to cherish as a mentor and a friend. David and Bill had known each other most of their adult lives. I asked David how Bill had been able to make the enormously consequential business decisions, fraught with risk for the company and himself, that are described in this book. David told me that Bill Davidson was the most quietly self-assured human being he had ever met, and I have found this to be true. I would venture a guess that this is not only because his own instincts and judgment are very sound, but also because he recruits and appoints outstanding people to key positions, listens to them very carefully, challenges their thinking, and then backs them strongly once a direction is set. Thus are great business decisions made and executed successfully.

Because this book is about Guardian Industries and its growth and development, there are dimensions of Bill Davidson that are either omitted or given very little space, but are nonetheless essential to a full understanding of him as a business leader and human being. He is avid about athletics, from the football and basketball teams at the University of Michigan to his own Detroit Pistons. I think his enthusiasm is rooted in his love of competition, talent, and individual excellence combined with great teamwork, and in his desire to challenge people to achieve their personal best. Bill has broad-gauged business interests which are reflected in his ventures in manufacturing, entertainment, and athletics. He is a generous philanthropist who has quietly and magnificently supported great causes: young people in his hometown of Detroit, the development of business in emerging market economies through the Davidson Institute at the University of Michigan, the perpetuation of Jewish values in America through the Jewish Theological Seminary in New York, and the restoration and preservation of antiquities for all to appreciate in Israel. Bill is interested in art, especially glass art, and as a result, Guardian Industries' headquarters displays one of the world's great collections of work by the pioneering glass artist, Dale Chihuli. Finally, Bill Davidson is a very private man and a loving husband and father.

I want to take this opportunity to congratulate the people of Guardian Industries on more than a half-century of remarkable business achievement. What is most exciting about the Guardian story is that the company continues to be a work in progress with its best days most likely still ahead of it. Guardian Industries has the scale, the global reach, the momentum, and the leadership to thrive in the years ahead. If history is an indicator, there are sure to be some surprises, new ventures, and unexpected developments that will both challenge and inspire the people of the company as the future unfolds.

I expect that no one hopes and believes more fervently than Bill Davidson that the best is yet to come for his company. At every age and every stage, Bill has been one to look ahead, focus on the future, and do what is required to make Guardian Industries a great company. He continues to do so today. I wish Bill and the other members of the company a next half-century as remarkable and productive as the one recounted here in *The Legend of Guardian Industries*.

ACKNOWLEDGMENTS

MANY DEDICATED PEOPLE ASSISTED IN the research, preparation, and publication of *The Legend of Guardian Industries*.

The principal research and assembly of the narrative time line was accomplished by research assistant Barbara Koch. Executor Editor Debra Kronowitz oversaw the text and photos from beginning to end, and the graphic design of Art Director Dennis Shockley brought the story to life.

A number of key people associated with Guardian Industries lent their efforts to the book's completion, sharing their experiences, providing valuable oversight for accuracy, and helping guide the book's development from outline to final form: Bill Davidson, president and CEO; Peter Walters, group vice president; Jeff Knight, group vice president and chief financial officer; Bob Gorlin, vice president and general counsel; and Gayle Joseph, director of communications.

Many other executives, employees, retirees, and family members enriched the book by discussing their experiences. The author extends particular gratitude to these men and women for their candid recollections and guidance: Frank Abissi, Richard Alonzo, Roy Anderson, Ken Battjes, John Bedogni, Howard Benedict, Jack Borgits, Alton Brown, Joe Bruce, David Clark, Warren Coville, Chuck Croskey, Bruce Cummings, Paul Dix, Russ Ebeid, Wilson Farhat Jr., Duane Faulkner, Oscar Feldman, Ken Forbes, Albert Franck, Tom Gaffney, Ralph Gerson, Claude Gishlar, Mike Gluckstein, Robert Goebbels, Tony Hobart, Paul Janisse, Dusty Kozloff, Mark Lacasse, Glen Longardner, George Longo, Vinay Modi, Jim Moore, Fernando Moretti, Mike Morrison, Antonio Herrera Munoz, Ann Newman, Ron Nadolski, Dusit Nontanakorn, Wally Palma, Mike Panther, Drew Peslar, Dr. C. K. Prahalad, Paul Rappaport, Arnie Rife, Lu Rimar, Rich Rising, Sandor Rocskar, Dave Rose, Chuck Shipp, Jack Sights, Ken Silverman, Franky Simoens, Ross Steggles, Karl Straky, Scott Thomsen, Chris Treadaway, Don Tullman, Bill Valk, Ajit Vashi, Claire Wagner, Ann Waichunas, Pat Weatherholt, Mary West, and Jordan Wright.

Special thanks is also extended to the staff and associates at Write Stuff Enterprises, Inc.: Amy Bush, Mickey Murphy, and Stanimira Stefanova, senior editors; Kevin Allen, copy editor; Sandy Cruz, senior art director; Rachelle Donley, art director; Mary Aaron, transcriptionist; Barbara Koch, indexer; Bruce Borich, production manager; Marianne Roberts, vice president of administration; Sherry Hasso, bookkeeper; Amy Major, executive assistant to Jeffrey L. Rodengen; and Lars Jessen, director of worldwide marketing.

Finally, a special thanks is extended to Bob Gorlin of Guardian Industries for his tireless efforts on this project.

Guardian Glass Company Inc.

MANUFACTURERS OF GUARDIAN SAFETY GLASS

PHONE CADILLAC 5346
1734 W. LAFAYETTE BLVD.
Detroit 16, Mich.

GUARDIAN PROTECTED

January 26, 1950

Withdrawing all previous quotations, we are pleased to quote the following prices, terms and conditions on Bent Herculite and Bent Duplate, subject to change without notice:

NAGS NO.	BLOCK SIZE	PART NO.	MAKE OF CAR	YEAR	PRICE PER LIGHT
			Lincoln Zephyr	1940	$ 5.90
			Chrysler-DeSo-Dodge	1940	5.90
XXX1	14x34	06H-7342006	Plymouth	1940-41	5.60
XXX2	14x34	848283	Dodge	1940-42	
			Plymouth	1940-48	4.77
XXX3	14x32	848054	Chev-Olds-Pont.	1940	6.23
			Buick-Cad-LaSa-Olds-Pont.	1940	5.46
XXX4	12x34	H-71791	Cadillac	1940	6.19
XXX5	14x40	H-71072	Hudson	1940	6.48
XXX6	12x40	F-30150	Packard	1941-42	3.85
XXX7	14x36	141334	Packard	1941-42	4.31
XXX8	14x38	357150	Cadillac	1940-42	6.51
XXX9	10x28	357602	Cadillac	1941-49	7.28
XX10	10x36	F-31190	Cadillac	1941-42	8.30
XX11	12x40	F-31843	Cadillac	1941-47	7.23
XX12	14x40	H-76014	Cadillac	1941-49	
XX13	16x38	H-76181	Buick	1941-48	6.23
XX16	16x38	H-75152	Olds-Pontiac	1941-42	
			Buick	1941-42	6.45
XX17	14x40	H-71072	Olds-Pontiac	1941-42	
			Buick	1941-48	5.90
XX18	14x38	H-75974	Chev-Olds-Pont.	1841-48	5.44
			Ford-Mercury	1940-48	5.90
XX19	14x34	11A-7042016	Lincoln Continental	1941-42	
XX20	12x36	06H-5742006	Lincoln Zephyr	1947-48	27.15
XX21	14x34	06H-7342006	Lincoln	1941-42	7.60
			Chrysler	1941-48	6.48
XX22	18x50	892679	Chry-DeSo-Dodge	1941-48	7.35
XX23	16x40	892195	Chry-DeSo-Dodge-Ply.	1941-48	6.78
XX24	14x38	901818	Chry-DeSo-Dodge	1941-47	7.69
XX25	14x44	901819	Hudson	1941-48	6.78
XX26	14x40	148629	Nash	1941-48	4.48
XX27	18x36	4325154	Nash	1941-46	5.94
XX28	14x40	4325155	Studebaker	1941-42	
XX29	10x34	274204	Studebaker		
XX30	12x40	274373			

The Guardian Glass Company, in Detroit, Michigan, supplied automotive replacement glass at very reasonable rates, as this partial 1950 price list shows.

CHAPTER ONE

A FAMILY AFFAIR

*After only a couple of years of practicing law, I decided I wanted to
represent myself, not others.*

—Bill Davidson

THE COMPANY THAT LATER became Guardian Industries was born in a place and during an era that epitomize both the triumphs and challenges of modern American capitalism: Detroit of the 1920s and 1930s. The original founders were a group of family and friends who seized the opportunities open to those with entrepreneurial spirit during the boom times of the late '20s. They created a new business based on the promise of the emerging automotive age and initially prospered. During subsequent decades of its earliest history, however, Guardian vacillated between growth and disaster as it experienced the Great Depression, World War II, the postwar boom and, common to many family businesses, internal dissension and lack of stable and decisive leadership. By the mid-1950s, Guardian was at a critical crossroads and facing possible extinction. The person who came to the helm of the company at that moment was Bill Davidson; he would lead it from disaster, through and beyond bankruptcy, and eventually into the modern era of its history.

The Birth of the Automotive Age

By the early 1920s, the United States was a fully mobile society. In many ways, this was not a sudden development. Visionaries in Detroit and elsewhere had been working for more than two decades to realize this goal.

In another sense, however, the Age of the Automobile signaled a profound and sudden shift in American life. With tens of thousands of cars rolling off assembly lines in Detroit, Americans quickly learned to think of their vehicles as necessities instead of luxuries. While cries of "horseless carriage" and "devil wagon" faded into background noise, the American public spent the heady 1920s cheerfully driving into the Age of the Automobile.

This new enthusiasm had as much to do with manufacturing techniques as it did with changing consumer attitudes. During the automobile's earliest development, cars were generally built by hand, with parts individually fitted to each vehicle. It was a trade dominated by skilled artisans and tradesmen rather than an efficient, modern manufacturing process. But as early as 1901, the tide had begun to turn. Industrialization was rapidly sweeping through American factories, pushed along by thinkers like Frederick Taylor, inventor of the modern efficiency study and the concept of "scientific management."

Automobile production, a painstaking process that involved manufacturing and assembling

Guardian's logo was originally created to represent the security and protection against wind, weather, and debris that Guardian's windshields gave to drivers and passengers of vehicles.

The Age of the Automobile signaled a profound and sudden shift in American life. Americans believed their vehicles were a necessity, not a luxury. *Courtesy of Walter P. Reuther Library.*

thousands of parts time after time, was ripe for mechanization and standardization. Around the turn of the century, Ransom E. Olds, founder of the Olds Motor Works, hired several outside companies to supply standard components for his cars, which were produced on a makeshift production line.[1]

Seven years later, Henry Ford began famously experimenting with advanced production techniques. He believed that interchangeable parts and the use of a moving assembly line and overhead conveyors could improve efficiency. As history has shown, Ford was right. His innovations were incorporated at Ford Motor Company's Highland Park, Michigan, assembly plant in 1913, and production soared.[2]

But assembly was grueling work. In 1913, turnover at Ford was as high as 400 percent. A year later, to attract and keep workers, Ford took the unprecedented step of doubling wages to $5 a day. Eager for the high-paying work, immigrants and southern laborers poured into Detroit. Between 1910 and 1920, the number of auto industry workers in the city increased from 15,000 to 160,000.[3]

Laborers weren't the only people lured to Detroit during this boom. Entrepreneurs also were migrating there in great numbers. Among these newcomers was Chicago native David E. Hokin, who moved to Detroit from Indianapolis in 1916. A former jewelry store owner, Hokin had hoped to make his fortune selling scrap metal to automakers. Instead he started a steel company and became wealthy in a variety of businesses.[4]

A Clear Opportunity

During the recession of 1921, however, Hokin's enterprises suffered greatly. Fortunately, through a friendship with Ford Motor Company's director of purchasing, Fred Diehl, Hokin learned of another lucrative opportunity: Ford needed a windshield supplier. Hokin and his partner, salesman Max Unger, devised a plan to import Czechoslovakian glass through Canada, thus avoiding the United States' 50 percent duty on European sheet glass. The glass was brought into Windsor, Ontario, just across the

Detroit River from Detroit, cut, and packed for shipment. Since fabricated glass was subject to only a 10 percent duty, Hokin and Unger managed to save their clients 40 percent on duty taxes.[5]

The company expanded in 1928, the year Ford introduced the laminated glass windshield as standard equipment on the Model A.[6] Laminated glass consisted of two layers of glass bonded by low heat and pressure to a plastic interlayer. Its use in automobiles greatly improved safety. If laminated glass broke, the pieces adhered to the plastic. If a person hit the laminated windshield during a car accident, the glass broke safely, reducing serious injury.[7] Hoping to continue getting Ford's business, Hokin established a new company, Laminated Glass Manufacturing Company, which produced laminated glass using a process developed in Czechoslovakia.[8]

By 1929, Laminated Glass Manufacturing Company and service stations also owned by Hokin were reaping the rewards of America's newly mobile society. That year, American auto production reached a peak. The flux of used cars created demand for replacement windshields, and Laminated, tapping another booming market, supplied them.

Unfortunately, the good times were not to last much longer. Just as Hokin's new laminating business seemed poised to take off, the stock market crashed, and the economy quickly descended into the Great Depression. The effect was traumatic. Throughout the country, farmers defaulted and farms were repossessed, local banks folded, the dollar plummeted in value, manufacturing activity screeched nearly to a halt, and—perhaps worst of all—the unemployment rate approached a staggering 25 percent. Like everything else, auto production stagnated, and demand for Hokin's windshields plunged.

It was not uncommon to see long lines at soup kitchens across the country during the Great Depression. *Courtesy of National Archives.*

Guardian is Born

To make matters worse, in 1932 new technology rendered Laminated's windshields obsolete, and its biggest customer, Ford, stopped buying them.[9] Unable to pay his suppliers, Hokin was forced to liquidate his business.[10] Yet despite the dismal economic outlook, Hokin's business attorney, David I. Hubar, believed in Laminated. Hubar gathered a group of investors to reorganize Laminated Glass, and in February 1932, new owners acquired the beleaguered company, renaming it Guardian Glass Company and adopting a logo incorporating a big G surrounding a knight on a horse.[11] The logo represented the security and protection against wind, weather, and debris that Guardian windshields gave to drivers and passengers of vehicles.

Hubar, through his brother-in-law Julius Lipman, held the largest block of stock. The second largest block of shares was held by Barney Wetsman.[12] The oldest son among six children of Ukrainian Jewish immigrants, Wetsman had been the successful owner of a clothing store, a construction company, and a theater.[13] His family was involved in several businesses, primarily theaters, and they all shared in the profits.[14] With construction down during the Depression, Wetsman was open to a new business venture.

In addition to Hubar and Wetsman, Guardian's rescuers included Alexander C. Nixon, a chemical engineer and a former officer and employee of

Barney Wetsman, left, an early financial rescuer of Guardian Glass, and Bert Root, right, the company's president, stand on the steps of the Saint Jean Avenue plant, circa 1934.

Laminated, who became Guardian's general manager; Walter Sorensen, a former partner of Hokin's in the Arrow Steel Corporation; and Horace E. Allen, one of Hokin's associates. Frank Handler, a cousin of Wetsman's and owner of a Buffalo, New York, brokerage firm, also sat on the board.[15]

At the time of the reorganization, the company's assets were minimal. Located in a dingy plant along St. Jean Avenue on Detroit's Lower East Side, the company employed about 20 people and produced fewer than 100 windshields a day. Its only equipment was a press used for laminating glass to the interlayer; all other work was done manually.[16] Sales during the new company's first year totaled just $130,000.[17]

Bert Root

In 1934 and 1935, Wetsman and Hubar bought out all the other partners except Handler. By 1936, only three officers and directors remained—Wetsman, Hubar, and Handler—in addition to Bert Root, who had joined the company as president two years earlier.[18]

Root was a former vice president and general manager of Libbey-Owens-Ford, a glass company based in Toledo, Ohio. In 1938, he set up a modern plant for Guardian in a former sign factory at 1734 West Lafayette Boulevard in Detroit. New equipment, including a high-pressure autoclave, improved the quality of the company's products.[19]

Barney Hertzberg

In 1938, Root convinced Barney Hertzberg, glass shift foreman at Ford Motor Company's Dearborn glass plant, to join Guardian. Hertzberg had worked at Guardian in 1934 but went to Ford because he felt Guardian's plant was too small and poorly equipped to be successful. When the company moved to the Lafayette location, however, Hertzberg agreed to come on board as plant manager.[20]

Hertzberg had worked in the glass industry since leaving England in 1912 at the age of 15. While attending school in New Jersey, he worked for an uncle, replacing broken windows in ships in a New Jersey harbor.[21] When his family moved to Detroit, Hertzberg took a job in Fisher Body's glass department, where he worked for 15 years. He returned to New Jersey to become plant manager of Triplex

Bert Root relocated Guardian Glass Company to 1734 West Lafayette Boulevard in Detroit in June 1938. The modernized plant used new equipment that improved product quality.

Safety Glass Company, one of the first companies to make laminated safety glass for automotive use. When another glass manufacturer bought that company, Hertzberg returned to Detroit, where he worked first at Laminated, then at Ford.[22]

Solid Footing

Wetsman and Hubar managed the company's finances and left the technical side to Root and Hertzberg. Under the four men's leadership, the company prospered. Guardian was producing original equipment and replacement windshields for cars, trucks, and buses, and safety glass for other applications.[23]

As Guardian Glass began to find itself on more solid financial footing, Wetsman turned his interest to other ventures. During the 1930s, he invested in a Spanish railroad, a Canadian mining company, and various real estate ventures. He also marketed a breakfast cereal and opened a women's clothing store and a distillery.[24] Eventually he bought out Hubar to become Guardian's biggest stockholder with 51 percent interest. Frank Handler held the remaining 49 percent.[25]

In 1940, with the Depression ebbing, Wetsman revived his construction company and began build-ing an apartment complex in Flint, Michigan. The job quickly consumed him, and he relinquished many of his executive responsibilities at Guardian to Handler, who had moved from Buffalo to Detroit.

Tragedy

The feverish pace that Wetsman maintained throughout his working years finally took its toll in 1940. That year he suffered a severe heart attack and died a month later at the age of 52. Since Wetsman had never married, his shares were placed in a trust for his mother, Bessie Wetsman.[26]

After his death, Wetsman's siblings looked after the family's interest in Guardian Glass. Brother Frank was named treasurer, and he and brothers-in-law Ralph Davidson and Morse Saulson oversaw the company, along with their other holdings. But just 10 months after Barney Wetsman's death, tragedy once again struck the family as Davidson and Saulson were killed in a dreadful car accident.[27]

Devastated by the magnitude of their loss in recent months, the Wetsman family now turned to Frank Wetsman, 45, the only remaining male family member, to look after Guardian Glass. Frank Wetsman's interests did not lie in the glass business, however. He and his partner were successful

theater owners. Wetsman had no choice but to leave Guardian Glass in Handler's hands.[28]

It was a difficult position for the family to be in. The Wetsmans didn't trust Frank Handler to control the business. He had moved to Detroit in 1939 after serving more than three years in prison for swindling customers of his Buffalo brokerage firm.[29] In a Wetsman family history, author Phillip Applebaum described Handler as a "caricature of a tycoon."

He could be captivating and charming. Most of the time, though, his family regarded him as an arrogant, blustering boor. To them, he had grown infatuated with his image as vice president of Guardian Glass.... He strutted, jabbed the air with a big cigar when he spoke, domineered, demanded. His attitude could be summed up in one of his usual lines: "I'll do what I goddamn please."[30]

Limping Along

Nevertheless, strong family ties prevented the Wetsmans from excluding their cousin from the business. With Root and Hertzberg handling the company's technical side, Guardian limped along until World War II, when the business of war stoked business in Detroit, which came to be known as the "Arsenal of Democracy." While automakers and auto suppliers produced guns, aircraft, and military vehicles, Guardian turned out laminated windshields for jeeps and trucks and enjoyed its most prosperous

Upper left: The "Guardian Girls," the company's version of "Rosie the Riveter," pose in front of the Lafayette Boulevard plant in Detroit. During World War II, Guardian supplied millions of square feet of glass for military vehicles. Middle: The Guardian Glass Company's workforce photo was taken around 1933. Bottom right: The employees of the White Room pose together in 1940, wearing the brown and white uniforms of the day.

years since 1929.[31] "They made a lot of money in the war years," recalled Bill Davidson. "Basically the profits were in laminated flat glass."[32]

Unfortunately, however, the rejoicing was short-lived. Bert Root died in 1944, and business dropped off after the war.

Family Secrets

Frank Wetsman strongly believed that the company's poor financial position was the result not only of external economic factors but also of Handler's pilfering. He suspected that company profits were being used to pay Handler's gambling debts.[33] Consequently, Wetsman made it a habit to examine Guardian's books whenever Handler wasn't around, and though he found evidence of dishonesty, he could not bring himself to confront his cousin. The stress of keeping his family's secrets may have caught up with Wetsman, who suffered two heart attacks during the mid-1940s.[34]

Bill Davidson

With a family history of heart disease and his own cardiac condition, Wetsman decided it was time to train the next generation to manage the family enterprises. In the early 1950s, he began grooming his oldest nephew, Bill Davidson, son of the late Ralph Davidson and Wetsman's sister Sarah. In 1953 he hired another nephew, Saul Saulson, to collect evidence against Handler. Handler caught on to the scheme, and Saulson quit after a difficult year.[35]

Davidson tried to persuade his uncle to do something about Handler. At age 30, Davidson was already a shrewd businessman. Born in Detroit in 1922, he had been trained as a Navy storekeeper and served in the Pacific during World War II. He

then earned a business degree from the University of Michigan in 1947 and a law degree from Wayne State University in 1949.[36] At 6 feet 1 inch and 200 pounds, Davidson was also an avid athlete.[37] While attending high school, he had broken the record for the half-mile and had helped the 880-yard relay team win a city championship. He also had played football and run track during his freshman year at the University of Michigan.[38]

Following his graduation from law school, Davidson worked in a private law firm. In 1951, he bought the Frank W. Kerr Company, a bankrupt wholesale pharmaceutical company, which he revived. Davidson soon found that he liked business better than law, and in 1951 he gave up his law position.[39] "After only a couple of years of practicing law, I decided I wanted to represent myself, not others," he once told a *Detroit Free Press* writer.[40]

In 1952, Davidson bought Rupp & Bowman, a failing surgical supply company, and nursed it back to health.[41] Not surprisingly, Wetsman considered his nephew to be an able steward of the family businesses. Although Davidson could not persuade Wetsman to remove Handler from Guardian, Davidson did agree to become more involved. He was appointed treasurer in 1955 so he could get greater access to the books and records of the company.[42] At the same time, Davidson continued to run his other businesses.

Rescuing Guardian

The 1950s should have been prosperous years for Guardian. The company emerged from World War II with half a million dollars in cash.[43] When the war ended, 16 years of deprivation and sacrifice also ended for American families. As servicemen returned home, married, and started families, America renewed its love affair with the automobile.

Many of these young families started their new lives in new homes in suburban housing tracts. Road construction boomed as families moved away from cities. Some found they now needed two cars—

Bill Davidson, with a track record of saving failing businesses in the early 1950s, took control of Guardian Glass and led it out of bankruptcy.

The television was introduced in the 1950s, adding another dimension to the new landscape of America. For a short period of time, Guardian's glass was used in television screens. *Courtesy of Walter P. Reuther Library.*

one to take Dad to work and a second for Mom to drive the children to school or to shop.

A new landscape soon sprang up along suburban roads. Supermarkets, shopping centers, malls, fast food restaurants, and drive-in banks were built to accommodate the suburbanites. As record numbers of children were born, additional schools were built. All of this commercial and residential construction, as well as auto production and a new entertainment phenomenon—the television— created an unprecedented demand for glass products.[44] Guardian's glass was used in windshields, school buses, phone booths, and for a short time, television screens.[45]

Opportunities

Between 1945 and 1955, the number of cars on America's roads doubled, reaching 52 million.[46] Immediately following the war, automakers pro-

duced models that looked much like prewar models, but within a couple of years, longer, sleeker designs rolled out featuring innovations such as curved windshields. An ad for a 1949 Lincoln stated, "Big picture windows and wide windshields let you see more ... and more easily."[47] Hertzberg saw an opportunity in the new styles. Solely responsible for Guardian's technology since Bert Root's death, he recommended purchasing new machinery to produce curved laminated windshields.[48] In 1956, Guardian bought a plant on Campbell Avenue in Detroit from U.S. Radiator.[49] Built in the late 1800s, it had operated as a radiator foundry and machine shop.[50] When Guardian moved in, production of curved laminated windshields began.[51]

Deeply in Debt

Yet despite the high demand for Guardian's products, the company teetered on the verge of bankruptcy. When they examined the books, Wetsman and Davidson discovered that trips to Las Vegas, custom-made suits, and plumbing expenses for Handler's home had been charged to Guardian. In addition, Handler had put his son, Frank Jr., and brother-in-law on the payroll with no discernible duties. Handler also assigned Guardian employees to work at another of his businesses and charged wages to Guardian's payroll. Again Davidson sug-

gested that his uncle confront Handler, but Wetsman did not do so. Then in the spring of 1956, the Wetsman family and Guardian Glass experienced another tragic loss when Frank Wetsman died of a heart attack.[52]

Deeply in debt, Handler immediately claimed that he was majority shareholder of Guardian Glass. Although he actually owned only 49 percent of the stock, he claimed that Barney Wetsman had

The six-acre Detroit windshield plant on Campbell Avenue was used as Guardian's corporate headquarters until 1971. It was closed 10 years later. In the background is General Motors' Fisher Body plant.

given him 2 percent before his death. Handler put Guardian up for sale.[53]

Hertzberg had thus far remained neutral in the battle between Handler and the Wetsmans, but he could not stand by as Handler attempted to seize the company. He alerted Davidson whenever a potential buyer visited Guardian. Davidson would come to the plant and ask the buyer to leave.[54]

Buying Out Handler

Davidson consulted with his family and their attorneys and decided to try to buy out Handler to remove him from the company once and for all.

Guardian executives gather to tout their HiTest Safety Glass at a trade show. From left are Les Weller, unidentified, Murray Yudin, Bill Davidson, Alton Brown, and Barney Hertzberg.

But Handler proved stubborn and did not easily relinquish his shares of Guardian.[55]

Phillip Applebaum described the confrontation between Davidson and Handler:

Davidson, as majority owner representative, confronted Handler in his office at Guardian and told him he was fired. He ordered Handler to pack his things and leave at once. Bill then went to Frank Jr. and told him the same thing.[56]

Getting Handler to sell his shares was another matter altogether. After months of wrangling, Handler conceded in 1957 and sold his interest in Guardian Glass for $175,000. Finally, Guardian Glass was solely in the hands of the Wetsman family. That same year, Bill Davidson agreed to take over as president on a full-time basis,[57] which was the start of what would become five decades of extraordinary leadership.

"He worked very hard," remembered Ann Newman, who joined the Frank W. Kerr Company in 1952 and would remain an executive of the company for decades. "He was at Guardian all day, and he came at night to see what was happening at Kerr."[58]

Davidson placed Guardian in Chapter 11 bankruptcy, which allowed him to reorganize the company and negotiate with creditors.[59] He hoped to turn Guardian around as he had with Frank W. Kerr and Rupp & Bowman.

The Road to Recovery

The fact that Guardian had survived despite Frank Handler's practices was a testament to the inherent strength of its business position and people. Now, with the Wetsman family's support, Davidson's management skills, Barney Hertzberg's technical expertise, and a dedicated workforce of 200,[60] Guardian Glass had a clean slate. Under the guidance of Davidson, with his know-how in resuscitating troubled businesses, the company would have a real shot at achieving its rich potential.

By the time Handler was finally ousted from Guardian Glass, the family feud had reverberated to the company's bottom line, and sales had declined.

To boost business, Davidson opened a wholesale distribution center for replacement windshields in Detroit in 1958. The next year, Guardian opened a second laminating plant in Fort Lauderdale, Florida.[61]

As Guardian's new leader, Davidson found himself in a frustrating position. On one hand, he wanted to expand Guardian into the original equipment market. On the other, domestic glass manufacturers made it difficult to obtain raw glass.[62] However, a strike by glassmakers that began in 1958 and carried over into 1959 proved fortuitous for Guardian. The 18-week Glass Workers Union strike halted glass production at nine U.S. glass plants, including Toledo glassmaker Libbey-Owens-Ford.[63] Automakers generally relied on large glass companies to supply their original equipment products, and Libbey-Owens-Ford was a supplier to American Motors (AMC). With AMC in need of windshields, Davidson quickly made his move to supply it with Guardian's product.[64]

Barney Hertzberg later recalled how AMC helped the company recover from bankruptcy.

[AMC] gave us an order for 1,200 windshields a week. That was just the order we needed to really get us going. We went to work on it immediately. And after the strike was over, we continued to supply American Motors for many years.[65]

During some three decades of existence, Guardian Glass had experienced and weathered the challenges of the Great Depression, World War II, postwar expansion, and personal tragedies befalling its senior managers and owners. As it prepared to enter the 1960s, Guardian now was, at last, under the leadership of an individual who would provide it with vision, stability, and direction for many decades to come.

Around the time he took control of Guardian Glass Company, Bill Davidson launched a photofinishing business with Warren Coville.

CHAPTER TWO

GUARDIAN PHOTO

We were delivering to drugstores in the area on a daily basis. Photofinishing was a natural adjunct to that.

—Bill Davidson
on the founding of ABC Photo

T HE GLASS INDUSTRY WOULD ultimately become the principal arena for Bill Davidson's business vision and accomplishments, and it is primarily in this and related industries that the legend of Guardian would take shape. As he initially assumed control over Guardian in the 1950s, however, Davidson had no intention of limiting himself to the fledgling glass industry. Rather, he was a classic entrepreneur, always seeking out new opportunities. By this time, he had already acquired control of and injected new life into the Frank W. Kerr Company and Rupp & Bowman. In 1955 a new opportunity presented itself when he and Warren Coville, a local photographer and Detroit native, founded ABC Photo, a photo processing firm that eventually became one of the nation's largest. While Guardian would ultimately sell this business segment in 1991, its history forms a direct and important part of the Guardian story and played a major role in Guardian's growth and success.

ABC Photo

Coville first became interested in photo processing when he was a student at Detroit's Central High School. Later he served as an aerial photographer with the Eighth Air Force during World War II. After his discharge from the service in 1945, he opened a portrait studio in Detroit that specialized in children's photography.[1]

His business did well, but he soon realized that it would be difficult to support his growing family on a photographer's salary. "I felt I was really limited in what I could do," Coville said. "I decided to sell the studio and pursue other areas."[2]

Then in 1954, the government handed him an opportunity. That year, Kodak signed a consent decree to settle an antitrust case. Under the terms of the decree, Kodak was forced to allow independent companies to process its market-leading Kodachrome and Kodacolor film. Before that, Kodak had insisted that all color film processing be done in its own lab in Rochester, New York. Kodak also was ordered to stop pricing its film to include the cost of photofinishing. With the door to the $100 million film-developing market thrown open, entrepreneurs rushed to beat Kodak at its own game.[3]

This was exactly the kind of opportunity that Bill Davidson liked. When he was introduced to Coville through a mutual friend, he still was running the

Warren Coville, Guardian Photo's original president, remained with the group through its rapid growth years in the 1970s and into the 1980s.

Frank W. Kerr Company and saw a chance to piggyback photofinishing onto the pharmaceutical business. "We were delivering to drugstores in the area on a daily basis," said Davidson. "Photofinishing was a natural adjunct to that."[4]

Davidson and Coville opened ABC Photo in the same building as Kerr. The first year, the company processed 55,000 rolls of black-and-white film and took in $56,000.[5] In 1959, ABC expanded into color print processing. In 1960, it moved to a larger plant in Detroit, and in 1961 it began processing color slide film.[6]

Throughout this period of growth, ABC Photo remained separate from Guardian Glass. In 1968, however, as part of Guardian's overall reorganization as it went public, ABC Photo was merged with the newly created Guardian Industries Corp. and became a division operating under the name of Guardian Photo. At the time, the photo business accounted for some $3 million in sales—about 15 percent of Guardian's total.[7] Also that year, Guardian Photo moved to a new plant in Novi, Michigan, a western suburb of Detroit. The plant occupied 30,000 square feet of a 70,000-square-foot building it shared with Kerr and was considered the most modern photofinishing plant in operation.[8] Warren Coville continued to lead Guardian Photo, which by then developed and processed film for large department stores, discount and drug chains, and independent stores.

Guardian Photo Takes Off

As a part of Guardian Industries, the photo company took off. In 1970, sales jumped 35 per-

Top: In 1966, ABC Photo (soon to merge with Guardian) broke ground for the photo plant in Novi, Michigan. E. Ross Steggles, vice president of manufacturing, and Oscar Feldman, secretary and company director, are left. Guardian President Bill Davidson, wearing a striped tie, is in the center. Warren Coville is on the far right.

Left: Guardian Photo received extensive publicity when this picture was taken of Warren Coville and other employees fishing at Guardian's water treatment plant. The pond was constructed to eliminate pollution and purify water flowing from the plant into nearby streams in Novi, Michigan. Fish from the stocked pond were safe to eat, proving the purity of the water.

Warren Coville, left, president of Guardian Photo, looks over a roll of enlarged Kodachrome prints with Dan Steinbach, a supervisor in photo processing.

cent from 1969 levels. Then in 1971, the photo group reached a milestone when it processed 100,000 rolls of film in just one week. Later that year, Guardian Photo expanded outside the Detroit area when it opened a joint glass distribution center and photofinishing plant in the Chicago area. The new, 33,000-square-foot plant was expected to capture a significant share of the photo processing and distribution market in Illinois, northern Indiana, and southern Wisconsin[9]—a market considerably larger than the Michigan/Ohio market served by the Novi plant.

At the same time, the photo group increased sales as new products and manufacturers came into the amateur photography market. In 1971, Guardian became an exclusive distributor of Fuji film.[10] This was an important development that foreshadowed the shape of things to come. At the time, Kodak still dominated the photographic paper market, but competitive forces were already beginning to wear down its dominance. Fuji and AGFA were making inroads into the film and paper markets, pricing their products below Kodak. In response, Kodak continued to develop new products, such as the Instamatic camera, which used unique film cartridges designed to increase sales.[11] While this approach often worked over the short term, Kodak's inability to compete on price in its

major markets would eventually signal the end of the company's outright dominance of the film, photographic paper, and processing markets.

Other forces were also changing the film and image industry. Super 8 movie cameras were becoming more prevalent. These primitive devices allowed consumers to shoot rough home movies, usually without sound. In the early 1970s, Guardian became one of the first photofinishers in the country to process Super 8 movie film. In 1972, Guardian also introduced Colorsilk prints, a silk-finish, borderless print with rounded corners. Borderless prints were a relatively new photofinishing product and gave customers a 25 percent larger image area for a comparable price.[12] By 1973, about 20 percent to 25 percent of prints produced nationwide were borderless.[13] Borderless prints required new equipment to mask and cut them, and Guardian Photo technicians developed a machine to do the job. Called the Posi-Mark, the patented machine was sold to photofinishers throughout the United States and in 35 countries.[14]

In 1974, the photo group formed Guardian Professional to service the professional photography industry. The new operation offered portrait-quality prints, special mountings, wedding albums, and novel finishing techniques like double and framed exposures.[15]

Left: Guardian's borderless Colorsilk prints represented a new level of sophistication and quality for photo prints. Cheryl Thayer, left, inspects prints using the Kodak 2610 computerized printer. Dan Steinbach, senior supervisor, middle, and Basil M. O'Neill, marketing manager, right, look on.

Below: Checking enlarged color prints as they are finished at the Guardian Professional Color Lab. The facility opened in 1979 at Guardian Photo's main plant in Novi, Michigan, to serve professional photographers.

Technology, meanwhile, continued to develop. Film processing, like many other facets of American life, was rapidly becoming automated. Automatic printers "looked" at every negative and determined how best to print it. "Auto pacs" cut and bagged orders, inserted matching negatives, and counted the number of pictures printed. A satellite computer facilitated billing.[16]

Using this kind of technology allowed Guardian Photo to increase its volume dramatically. During the summer of 1973, for example, it processed 1 million prints, 400,000 slides, and 16,000 rolls of movie film per week.[17] Guardian had become the largest and most automated photo finisher in the Midwest and one of the 10 largest in the country.[18]

Then Guardian captured an even larger share of the market when it acquired Howard's Photo Laboratory of Fort Wayne, Indiana, in 1974. The facility served Indiana, Michigan, and Ohio and had sales of approximately $4 million. The company had been in business for 47 years and operated an up-to-date lab similar to Guardian's. The acquisition doubled the group's sales volume.

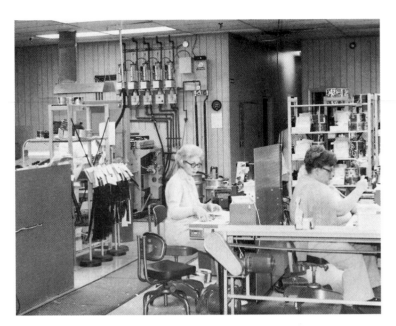

Above: In 1974, Guardian acquired Howard's Photo Laboratory in Fort Wayne, Indiana. This major acquisition moved Guardian into new markets and doubled sales volume.

Below right: The industry's patterns began to change when photo developing kiosks appeared, offering fast photo processing. The Hudson's Photo Hut did business at Detroit's Northland Shopping Center.

The Drive-Thru Option

As technology gradually made photofinishing faster and more automated, it began to change the industry. Beginning in the mid-1970s, new photofinishing options competed for customers' dollars, and Guardian Photo was part of the game. Through Fast Foto, Guardian offered mail-order photo processing, which by 1975 was the second-largest market for photo processing, according to *Photo Marketing* magazine.[19] In 1976, Guardian launched a marketing campaign with the Automobile Association of America (AAA). The giant auto organization enclosed Fast Foto self-mailers in maps it sent to its clients and offered special promotions in its monthly magazine.[20]

Soon another option emerged: drive-thru photofinishing.[21] Guardian and other photo processors built these free-standing kiosks in parking lots of high-traffic shopping areas, such as malls, so that customers could easily drop off film and pick up their photos. While the exact number of photo kiosks in 1975 is unknown, the industry leader, Fotomat, operated some 2,000 units.[22] Guardian opened its first kiosk in 1975 in Waukegan, Illinois, and added more booths in the Midwest during the late 1970s.[23]

K Photo

By 1976, Guardian's three labs were processing 50,000 rolls of film a day. Guardian constantly updated its equipment and provided excellent quality and service. Ninety percent of orders were processed and delivered in one day. The division serviced more than 1,500 accounts in Michigan, Illinois, Indiana, and Ohio. In addition to independent drug stores and camera stores, Guardian served chain stores such as Kmart, J. C. Penney, Revco, and Meijer Thrifty Acres.[24]

In 1977, Guardian moved beyond the Midwest when it purchased K Photo in Pennsylvania. K Photo serviced customers in New York, Pennsylvania, New Jersey, Maryland, Delaware, Virginia, and Washington, D.C. Guardian also acquired K Photo retail outlets in eastern Pennsylvania and New Jersey. A year after the acquisition, Guardian moved the Philadelphia-based operation into a new, state-of-the-art, 63,000-square-foot plant in Allentown, Pennsylvania.[25] Guardian added a number of new

This 1979 photo shows envelopes of finished prints ready for pickup. At this time, Guardian had just completed the acquisition of GAF Corporation's photofinishing business, thereby adding a number of plants to its growing roster.

accounts through its Allentown plant, more than doubling its sales in a year.[26] Increasing its service area from four states to 10 was a significant move for Guardian Photo. The Allentown plant served one of the country's most heavily populated areas, including New York City and Philadelphia.

In 1978 Guardian Photo took an even greater step forward when it acquired the photofinishing business of GAF Corporation, almost tripling Guardian Photo overnight. GAF, with annual sales of $47 million compared to Guardian's $26 million, operated 17 photofinishing plants in 13 states and employed 1,300 people. But GAF's plants were suffering heavy losses, leading it to announce in February 1978 that "the best interests of the corporation" lay in getting out of the photofinishing business.[27] When the GAF operations were put up for sale, Guardian was initially interested in only a few key facilities but eventually agreed to purchase all 17 plants for $6 million. After Guardian completed the transaction, it jumped into a close competition with Fox-Stanley for the number-three position (behind Kodak and Fotomat) among U.S. photo processors.[28]

Updating GAF

It would not take long for Guardian to discover why GAF was so eager to part with 17 plants for a mere $6 million. Unlike Guardian, GAF had not kept up with the rapidly advancing technology, and to make matters worse, the photofinishing industry was skeptical of Guardian's ability to turn the business around. In an interview with *Photo Marketing* magazine, Photo Group President Warren Coville described Guardian's challenge in the GAF acquisition:

> *The fundamental problem was that GAF didn't spend any money updating the plants and keeping up with the state-of-the-art. Not only was the equipment not modified and kept up-to-date with the industry, but this also had a psychological effect on all the employees. They saw that GAF was not putting anything into it and a lot of the employees were just turned off.*[29]

Coville's solution was to renovate the plants and update the equipment, revamp management and personnel, acquire new accounts, and release less-profitable ones.[30] It was a long, challenging process.

In the end, Guardian spent $12 million updating, closing or consolidating the former GAF plants. Two years after the acquisition, Guardian Photo operated plants in Michigan, Massachusetts, Pennsylvania, North Carolina, Indiana, Illinois, Kansas, Iowa, Texas, Arizona, California, Washington, and Oregon.[31]

During the integration, Guardian did not neglect its existing plants. The flagship Novi plant expanded in 1976 and again in 1979. The Chicago and Kansas City plants moved into expanded facilities in 1979. Guardian also built a 16,000-square-foot plant in Slippery Rock, Pennsylvania, in 1980.[32]

Competitive Challenges

After the GAF acquisition turned Guardian Photo into a national company, a reorganization became necessary. The photofinishing plants were grouped into three regions, each headed by a regional manager. Every plant handled its own processing, but only one plant per region produced reprints, enlargements, prints from slides, and other special orders.[33] Guardian dropped less-profitable accounts, and in July 1978, *Photo Marketing* magazine reported that many in the industry believed Guardian was "reaching across the country and taking the best accounts in several markets—at the expense of the small and medium-size photofinisher."[34]

"There are some good, strong finishers and there always will be," Coville responded. "There's always room for a good, small operation in any business. [But] there is a certain fallout that is taking place in the finishing business right now. It's been happening for the last 10 years and I think it's going to continue. Some of the smaller labs are going to suffer and the larger ones will certainly get larger."[35]

Competition was in fact heating up, driven by advancing processing technology and the entry of minilabs into the business. New technology, such as Instamatics, Polaroids, and disc cameras, would offer customers ever more options in photography. The relatively new minilabs had begun to erode the traditional photofinishing business, changing the economics of the industry. Located in retail stores, minilabs processed color film onsite in as little as an hour. Many photofinishers believed customers would avoid

Photofinishing is a process in which negative film is transformed into finished photographic prints. After the film is developed in chemical solutions, images from the film are printed onto unexposed sensitized paper. These images are then processed to a finished state by a paper processor, such as the high-capacity unit shown here, being monitored by a production supervisor and operator.

minilabs because they charged more than overnight photofinishers. But Guardian did not ignore the new competitors. It solicited business from the minilabs for types of processing the minis could not handle, such as black-and-white film, slides, and enlargements. Warren Coville, president of Guardian Photo, told *Photographic Processing* magazine, "Let's face it. The minilab is here to stay. Rather than close our eyes, we should be getting a piece of the action. In a sense, the minilab phenomenon has heightened the public's awareness about photography, and that benefits all of us."[36] Guardian was determined to stay relevant in its challenging and consolidating market.

In 1985, the photofinishing unit added new options. While most of its marketing had focused on low price and fast service, Guardian recognized that some customers preferred higher-quality prints, even if they took longer to produce. To accommodate these customers, Guardian introduced H.Q. Processing, a new service that gave each print indi-

vidual attention. Although the process took longer and was more expensive, some customers preferred the higher quality. Another option, Color Guard II, gave customers two prints from each negative and used the marketing slogan "One to keep and one to share."[37] In addition to the new print processing options, Guardian offered disc film processing, although sales of the new-format cameras were disappointing for their manufacturer, Kodak. Also in 1985, Guardian launched a nationwide program to identify and return missing children by inserting missing child flyers in the film bags processed for Kmart and other retailers. The flyers were produced in conjunction with the Lost Child Network of Kansas

In 1983, Guardian Photo processed film for amateur photographers in two major formats—35 mm and disc. In 1985, *Photographic Magazine* named Guardian "Photofinisher of the Year."

In 1985, Guardian launched a nationwide program to identify and return missing children by placing flyers in the film bags it processed for its clients. These flyers were produced with the help of the Lost Child Network. In 1985, Frank Abissi of Guardian Photo, right, was joined by Kansas Attorney General Rubert Stephan, left, and John Walsh in announcing the Lost Child Network. Walsh had helped create the network following the abduction of his child.

City, Kansas, which was known for placing missing children's pictures on milk cartons.[38]

By late 1983, Guardian had completed the consolidation and upgrading of the former GAF plants, purchased in 1978. The division had 12 plants nationwide, to which it added Tru-Foto, a Dayton, Ohio, wholesale photofinisher serving the Midwest, in 1984, and Mando Photo, of Minneapolis/St. Paul, Minnesota, in 1986.[39]

Guardian Photo reached a milestone in 1985, when its sales exceeded $100 million for the first time. Also in 1985, Warren Coville retired as CEO of Guardian Photo and Frank Abissi was named the new president and CEO. That year, *Photographic Processing* magazine named Guardian "Photofinisher of the Year" and featured the group in a 10-page article in the magazine.[40] The article described Guardian's efficient production process and pointed out that Guardian had always been in the forefront of new photofinishing services. It had been one of the first processors to produce borderless prints in 1972. In 1981, Guardian had introduced guaranteed 24-hour service, and in 1983, seven-day-a-week service.

The End of the Line for Guardian Photo

Between 1985 and 1990, Guardian Photo grew more slowly, and the business essentially stagnated. The company's revenues stood at about $109 million in 1991, leading Abissi to recommend that Davidson sell the unit. A search was conducted, and eventually Guardian Photo was sold to Qualex, a competitor owned by Fuqua Industries and Eastman Kodak.[41] "It had played out," said Davidson. "The industry was changing. It was becoming more difficult to compete with instant photofinishing outlets and the prospects of new digital technology. We thought selling was the right thing to do, and it worked out well for Qualex and for us. They were being threatened by Fuji and were very eager to get into the retail end of the business. For our part, we obtained a very advantageous price for the business—one that we would not likely have matched if we had held on to Guardian Photo much longer."[42]

A Success Story

While overshadowed by the phenomenal growth of Guardian's glass business, especially after 1970, the history of Guardian Photo is itself a remarkable success story. From the humblest of beginnings, through a combination of internal growth and acquisitions, Guardian Photo had become one of the largest photo processing companies in the world. Even standing alone, it was a stunning accomplishment, especially considering the value it brought when the business ultimately sold in 1991. It is to the glass business, however, that one must return to grasp the full extent of the Guardian legend.

Guardian President Bill Davidson, left, and Richard Alonzo, right, manager of engineering, prepare to light the furnace at the Carleton facility prior to its opening in 1970.

CHAPTER THREE

THE GLASSMAKER: AN UNINVITED GUEST

Bill and I first met with Pilkington in St. Helens, England, near their world headquarters, but the fact of the matter is that they refused even to consider us.

—Attorney and long-time Guardian director
Oscar Feldman on the attempt to obtain
a float glass license from Pilkington

IF THERE IS ANY ONE DEFINing moment in Guardian's history, it is undoubtedly its entry into glass manufacturing. This is a story of entrepreneurial vision, careful planning combined with risk taking, perseverance bordering on stubbornness, and the dedication of many people coming together with a common purpose. It was in the late 1960s that the modern day Guardian was established and the foundation laid for its future growth and prosperity.

Guardian Enters the 1960s

Guardian Glass in 1960 was still a small and fairly troubled company. Frank Handler was gone, and the company emerged from bankruptcy protection that year. Davidson was determined to turn the company around and establish his reputation in the community as a reliable and sound businessman; while Guardian could have made only partial payments to its creditors, it paid its debts in full, thus positioning itself to concentrate on growth.[1] Guardian Glass enjoyed steady if not spectacular growth in sales and profits during the '60s, but it retained its character as one of many small companies operating in a much larger glass industry dominated by a few major players. It was this disparity in size and power that Bill Davidson would later seek to remedy.

During this period, Davidson also rapidly expanded the automotive glass distribution business that he had started in 1958. Between 1960 and 1968, he established distribution centers in New York, Georgia, Massachusetts, Illinois, Texas, Washington, D.C., Kansas, Michigan, New Jersey, and California,[2] and each center distributed all types of automotive glass and carried more than 10,000 parts.[3] The distribution centers were closely linked to the manufacturing capabilities of Guardian Glass. In fact, by the late 1960s, some 70 percent of the automotive windshield production of Guardian Glass went to Davidson's distribution centers for resale, with the remainder going to original equipment manufacturers.[4]

The Glass Market in the 1960s

More and more glass used in the United States was coming from overseas, where it was less expensive to manufacture.[5] However, a tariff imposed by President John F. Kennedy in 1962 stabilized imports

This mold was used to produce windshields. Throughout the 1960s, Guardian was a fabricator of other companies' glass. At that time, automotive glass replacement accounted for most of Guardian's revenue.

Guardian managers assemble in 1964 for their annual meeting.

at about 25 percent of U.S. flat glass consumption.[6] At the time, although there were countless glass fabricators like Guardian, there were very few domestic glass manufacturers. This meant that fabricators had to rely on overseas supplies for their raw material, which they would then process, coat, laminate, and turn into thousands of products. As a result of this reliance on overseas suppliers, Guardian was sometimes unable to obtain enough glass to meet its demand for windshields.

At the same time the supply of raw glass was squeezed, the demand for fabricated glass products was rising. In the United States, new applications and technologies were pushing glass into wider usage, in both the automotive and the architectural markets. Between 1966 and 1969, the amount of glass used in automobiles increased 20 percent, and this figure was expected to keep growing in the coming years.[7]

Demand for architectural glass was also on the upswing. The post–World War II building boom continued through the 1960s, and commercial and resi-

dential design demanded more glass. Glass offered a number of advantages over concrete or steel in building construction. Not only was it less expensive and easier to maintain, it also took less construction time.[8] Double-glazed windows improved energy efficiency and increased glass usage. Residential design called for sliding doors, shower doors, and large windows. Commercial architects and engineers now preferred a more aesthetic look, and new offices, schools, and public buildings utilized "curtain wall construction," in which exterior walls were made primarily of glass.[9]

Guardian, like other U.S. fabricators, found itself in a squeeze between the tightening supply of raw glass and the rising demand for its products. Yet unlike other glass fabricators, Guardian would do something about its predicament. To Bill Davidson, it was becoming increasingly obvious that the only way to guarantee a good supply of quality glass, and to open a whole new range of opportunities, was to move into glass manufacturing. As Davidson later recalled, "This was the only path available for us to achieve independence of action and significantly enhance our potential for growth."[10]

The Float Process

The jump from fabricator to manufacturer was a long one, made more challenging by the economics of glassmaking and the changing nature of the business. Through the 1960s, glass manufacturing underwent a revolution that made it not only less expensive but more adaptable. Until then, just two types of flat glass were manufactured. Sheet glass was made by drawing molten glass in a taffy-like state out of tanks. This glass was clear but had an uneven, wavy surface. Plate glass was made by passing molten glass through rollers. Since the rollers marred the surface, the glass had to be ground and polished on both sides, which made the product very expensive.

In 1959, Pilkington Brothers of Great Britain introduced the float process, which produced a glass product comparable in cost to sheet glass and superior to plate glass in quality. It represented a giant leap forward in glassmaking, bringing the cost of high-quality glass down at the same time that it yielded nearly perfect glass. The float method produced a better quality glass and eliminated the expensive grinding and polishing that plate glass required.

"It was a tremendous technological improvement, but the initial idea for it came about by accident," remembered Oscar Feldman, a lawyer and friend of Davidson's since their college years at the University of Michigan and whose close involvement with Guardian began in the mid-1950s.[11] That relationship has continued into the next century.

According to one description of how Alastair Pilkington developed the float process:

Oscar Feldman was a close friend of Bill Davidson. He began a relationship with Guardian in the mid-1950s that would continue into the 21st century.

Like many other inventors, the solution to the problem dawned on him when he was not actually attending to it. One day in June 1952, while helping his wife wash dishes in the kitchen, he was struck by what he saw. The idea that a flat, polished finish could be produced by floating molten glass on a liquid surface came to him as he watched the grease solidify on the water in the sink. To pour molten glass onto a bed of molten tin was a direct corollary to that.[12]

According to some accounts, it took seven years and the expenditure of some £7 million to commercialize the process.[13] After perfecting the process, Pilkington obtained numerous worldwide patents covering the manufacture of float glass and undertook a very tightly controlled licensing program. When Davidson "made the determination that we had to go into the float glass business" in the late 1960s,[14] he naturally wanted to use Pilkington's float process.

Davidson's Plan of Attack

Entry into glass manufacturing at this time was a daunting undertaking. In America, the float glass manufacturing business was dominated by PPG Industries (which had been making glass since 1883), Libbey-Owens-Ford (L-O-F), and Ford Motor Company.[15] Clearly, these companies would not welcome another glassmaker in their backyard, and in fact no company had entered the glass manufacturing business in the United States since Ford in 1920. Guardian's entry into the business threatened to break the long established "old boys' club" and would meet with stiff resistance.

Davidson's plan to break into this entrenched industry proved to be multifaceted, extraordinarily ambitious, and fraught with risk. To be successful, Davidson needed to carry out a campaign on numerous fronts. First, he reorganized his various business interests into one consolidated company, Guardian Industries, which he took public in 1968. He used the new liquidity of Guardian's stock to acquire businesses that would help support glass manufacturing. He recruited the talented and motivated people necessary to construct and operate Guardian's first glass plant at Carleton, Michigan. He overcame seemingly immovable obstacles in acquiring the technological capability to enter the float glass business. Finally, he somehow raised the substantial

Bill Davidson, center, buys the first 100 shares of Guardian Industries stock, traded on the American Stock Exchange. Oscar Feldman, left, secretary of Guardian, and James Maguire, member of the board of governors of the exchange, look on.

amount of money required to see the expensive float glass project through to a successful conclusion. Each of these paths contained obstacles that would have caused ordinary people to quit, but Davidson persevered and overcame them all. He realized that while the obstacles were indeed high, the incentives and rewards for success were great. A fabrication company like Guardian that pushed its way into the glassmaking business would find a whole universe of opportunity, and he was determined to seize it.

Guardian Goes Public

The linchpin of Davidson's broad plan was the decision to consolidate many of his various business interests under one new company—Guardian Industries Corp.—and to take that company public. On November 7, 1968, the original Guardian Glass Company that had been established in 1932

was merged, along with Guardian Photo, Inc. (formerly ABC Photo, Inc.) and 10 automotive glass distribution centers owned by Davidson, into the new Guardian Industries Corp. Immediately after these transactions, a public offering of Guardian shares was made on the "over-the-counter" market. The shares sold in the public offering came from several Wetsman family descendants. As a result of these transactions, ownership of the newly constituted Guardian Industries broke down as: William Davidson, 45 percent; new public shareholders (including employees), 26 percent; and shareholders (other than Davidson) of the original constituent companies, 29 percent.[16]

These corporate transactions served a number of purposes related to Davidson's strategic objectives. First, he realized that his plan to expand into flat glass manufacturing required a company with far greater financial substance than was possessed by the old Guardian Glass Company alone. Merging the glass fabricating company with ABC Photo and the previously independent distribution centers created an entity with a substantially larger income statement and balance sheet and did not require any outlay of cash. This would facilitate the raising of capital later when major resources were needed to pay for the Carleton float glass plant.

Second, going public created a liquidity outlet for individuals who had ownership interests in the three component companies. Davidson, for his part, did not sell any of his Guardian Industries stock at this or any other time during the nearly 17 years that Guardian was to remain a public company. He had decided to tie his own future to the growth and prosperity of Guardian Industries and never hedged his bets about whether that company would succeed.

As he later recalled, "I always felt that Guardian was the best place to invest my money, and I turned out to be right."[17]

Third, while Guardian Industries itself did not raise money for the future float glass plant or at any time later by offering shares of common stock to the public, the new business structure and public market at least made this a viable option. Further, the stock itself would be used to make acquisitions that advanced Davidson's objective of entering glass manufacturing.

Finally, going public provided a vehicle for employee ownership of the company and direct participation in its success. In the "President's Message to Shareholders" for 1968, Davidson made a point of noting that, as a result of the public offering in November 1968, approximately 175 employees had become stockholders of the company.[18] The growth of this participation was to be an enduring point of pride throughout Guardian's years as a public company.

Guardian Acquires Permaglass

The newly consolidated Guardian Industries had sales of about $19 million in 1967 and $22 million in 1968.[19] Guardian immediately focused on using its increased size and now liquid stock to leverage the acquisition of other companies with downstream operations that consumed significant quantities of float glass. Davidson had concluded that investment in a float glass plant would be feasible only if Guardian's fabricating operations themselves could generate demand for a significant portion of the output of the manufacturing plant. As a

Above: An original stock certificate issued to Bill Davidson. In 1969, the stock was listed on the American Stock Exchange.

Left: The officers and directors of Guardian Industries in 1968. Seated from left to right: Oscar H. Feldman, secretary and director; Bill Davidson, chairman and president; Byron Gerson, director. Standing left to right: William Wetsman, treasurer and director; E. Ross Steggles, vice president, manufacturing and director; Warren Coville, president, Guardian Photo Inc. and director; Reymont Paul, assistant secretary and director. Officers not pictured include Barney Hertzberg, vice president, marketing; and David Best, controller.

The Ambassador Bridge, linking Detroit with Windsor, Ontario, provided an international setting for this 1960s promotional photo. Guardian's Canadian subsidiary, Permaglass Industries, in Ajax, Ontario, sold tempered automotive and architectural glass and became a major supplier to the Canadian farm equipment market.

glass fabricator, Guardian produced primarily laminated glass for the automotive industry. Other glass fabricators produced a variety of laminated, tempered, and coated glass, all of which required basic float glass as their primary raw material. Each of these three types was based on a different technology and had different uses, although tempered and laminated shared certain architectural and automotive applications.

Laminated glass, two sheets of glass with a plastic sheet between them that holds together when broken, was ideal for windshields. Tempered glass was heat-treated to produce a strong, break-resistant product four to five times more shock resistant than ordinary glass.[20] When it did break, tempered glass was less likely to cause personal injury.

Guardian's focus on laminated glass limited the scope of its opportunity even within that product category. Windshields, for instance, were made from laminated glass, but side windows (side lites) and rear windows (back lites) used tempered glass. Similarly, most architectural applications used tempered glass. Many customers wanted to buy both products from the same source. "Not being in tempering meant that we were losing some of the laminated business," recalled Davidson.[21] Expansion into tempering, however, was primarily a means of increasing internal Guardian demand for the output of the float glass plant that Davidson intended to build.

In December 1969—after months of negotiation led by Davidson and his counsel, Oscar Feldman—Guardian entered the tempered glass segment of the glass market through acquisition of all the outstanding stock of Permaglass, Inc., in exchange for Guardian common stock. By the time the deal with Permaglass was concluded, Guardian's stock had risen significantly in value compared to the original public offering price, which made the transaction particularly advantageous for Guardian. "We bought Permaglass in order to have enough fabrication business to go into the float glass business because we did not have the fabrication volume that would have been required. But between what we had and what Permaglass had, it would generate enough work for a significant percentage of a float plant," Davidson recalled.[22]

With its principal offices in Millbury, Ohio, and several additional manufacturing locations, Permaglass produced tempered glass for automotive and architectural use.[23] The company owned more than 50 patents in the glass fabricating field and licensed manufacturers around the world. In 1969, Permaglass had sales of approximately $11 million.[24]

The acquisition increased Guardian's original equipment automotive sales to Chrysler, GMC Truck and Coach, Checker Cab, American Motors, White Truck, International Harvester, and other customers.[25] It also provided Guardian with entry into the architectural market. With plants in Millbury, Genoa, and Payne, Ohio; Torrance, California; and Fort Lauderdale, Florida, Permaglass expanded Guardian's U.S. presence. Permaglass also had a plant in Ajax, Ontario, and owned controlling interest in Permaglass of Sydney, Australia, thereby establishing Guardian's first international presence.

It was out of the original Guardian Glass business, the recently merged ABC Photo and the newly acquired Permaglass entities, that Guardian established its various business groups, which included Guardian Photo, Automotive Glass, Architectural Glass, International, and Glass Manufacturing. In addition, Guardian continued to maintain its glass distribution centers and a new research and development department.

Recruiting New Talent

While undertaking the going public transaction and acquiring the downstream operations that were central to his objective of becoming a glass manufacturer, Davidson also focused on attracting talented people who could execute his vision. His new team included a four-man group that had previously worked at Ford Motor Company's float glass operation. Their leader was Ed Sczesny, who became Guardian's new director of engineering and research.[26] Also part of the team was Richard Alonzo, a young engineer who recalled what first attracted him to Guardian:

Ford was a great company, and I know I would have had a good career there. The problem for me was that I could predict where I would be and what I would be doing many years down the road. This

Guardian entered the tempered glass market through its acquisition of Permaglass, Inc. The plant, shown after expansions, resides in Millbury, Ohio.

level of security and certainty can be very attractive, but at that time in my life I was ready for a different kind of challenge. Guardian was a place where I really felt I could make a difference. Just a few people were undertaking great things. There was plenty of risk involved, but the sense of optimism and the "can do" attitude made us all believers. I took the job at Guardian and never looked back.[27]

Alonzo would go on to a long and distinguished career at Guardian as the company's vice president of engineering.

The other members of the new team recruited by Sczesny from Ford were Bob Cobie and Karl Straky. Cobie had been at Ford's glass division for approximately five years before joining Guardian in early 1969. During construction he was responsible for engineering of the Carleton atmosphere generation systems, the batch house, and the furnace. He would become Carleton's first plant manager in 1970 and Guardian's "Employee of the Year" the following year.

Straky came to Guardian in 1969 after seven years in process engineering with the Ford glass division. Once the Carleton plant was under construction, he was given the responsibility of establishing the plant's production schedules and sales plans. He later became heavily involved in Guardian's coated glass business and was named "Employee of the Year" in 1982, thereby giving that distinction to all members of Sczesny's team who started with Guardian in 1968 and 1969.

Another new recruit at the time was Ken Battjes, who joined Guardian in 1969 as director of personnel. Battjes immediately focused on the need for improving communication among management, employees, and the plants. One of his innovations was the *Guardian Newsletter,* which was first published in September 1969 and was renamed *Guardian World* in June 1971. This publication would chroni-

cle the major events in Guardian's history for all its employees. Battjes would also be a pioneer in launching employee-related programs that focused on health and safety. His career at Guardian would last almost 30 years.[28]

Guardian and Pilkington

The next element of Davidson's plan to enter glassmaking focused on obtaining the necessary technological capability and legal rights to build and operate a plant. The logical place to turn for expertise and legal validation was Pilkington. Since deciding to build a glass manufacturing plant, Davidson had occupied himself with how to obtain a license from Pilkington. If successful, Guardian would become the fourth manufacturer to be licensed in the United States, following PPG Industries, licensed in 1963, L-O-F in 1964, and Ford in 1966.[29] None of these com-

---

Below from left to right: Ed Sczesny, Guardian vice president and "Employee of the Year" in 1970, helped Guardian build the Carleton plant. Sczesny was a veteran of Ford Motor Company, where he had worked in glass technology. Richard Alonzo had a long and distinguished career at Guardian as the company's vice president of engineering and was "Employee of the Year" in 1978. Bob Cobie was a Ford veteran before joining Guardian in 1969. He was Carleton's first plant manager and was named "Employee of the Year" in 1971. Karl Straky came to Guardian in 1969 after spending seven years at Ford's glass division. He became heavily involved in Guardian's coated glass business and was named "Employee of the Year" in 1982. Ken Battjes joined the team in 1969 as director of personnel. He focused on communication between management and employees and founded the *Guardian Newsletter*, which later became known as *Guardian World*. He was "Employee of the Year" in 1981.

THE FLOAT PROCESS

THE FLOAT GLASS PROCESS IS A COMplicated, ingenious, and vastly superior process for making high-quality flat glass. First, raw materials consisting of sand, soda ash, dolomite, limestone, salt cake, carbon, rouge feldspar, and recycled glass are mixed in a 14-story storage structure. The mixture is fed into a refractory brick-lined furnace approximately 190 feet long by 35 feet wide. Temperatures inside the furnace reach 2,900 degrees Fahrenheit.

Molten glass is discharged from the furnace onto a molten pool of tin. The glass floats on the tin's surface for approximately 200 feet. As it moves across the two-inch-thick bath, it cools from about 2,000 degrees to about 1,100 degrees. This temperature is hot enough to assure a smooth flow.

Tin is the only metal suitable for this process because it won't chemically react with the glass and can tolerate the varying temperatures without vaporizing or hardening. The tin's high density supports the glass, and gravity causes the molten glass to spread out over the tin's surface, creating a perfectly smooth and even product. The tin also functions as a conveyor belt, pulling the glass forward. By the time the glass reaches the end of the bath, it has hardened enough to permit movement by rollers. The faster the ribbon is pulled through the bath, the thinner the glass.

As it leaves the bath, stainless-steel rollers pull the glass ribbon into an annealing lehr, a cooling oven approximately 400 feet long and 15 feet wide. The glass is gradually and uniformly cooled inside the lehr to about 120 degrees. This controlled cooldown prevents residual stress.

Depending on the thickness of the glass being made, from 10 to 180 minutes pass from the time the glass enters the tin bath until it reaches the end of the line.

panies had been producing float glass for more than a decade, and there was considerable opposition to Guardian's entry into their industry. That opposition found a champion and voice in Pilkington's negative reaction to Guardian's overtures.

While Davidson prepared for the contingency that Pilkington would reject Guardian, he did undertake a good faith effort to negotiate a license for Pilkington's patents in the float glass field. As Davidson recalled, "I was perfectly willing to take one of their standard licenses, as long as we were treated like Pilkington's other licensees, but this turned out to be a moot point."[30]

The first meeting between principals of the two companies took place on January 20, 1969. As Oscar Feldman, who along with Davidson represented Guardian, recalled: "Bill and I first met with Pilkington in St. Helens, England, near their world headquarters, but the fact of the matter is that they refused even to consider us for a license."[31]

The stated reason for Pilkington's refusal was that it never had granted, and never would grant, a license to a company that was not already a glass manufacturer, and especially not to a relatively small, regional company.[32] To make matters worse, in a letter from Pilkington to Davidson dated January 28, 1969, Pilkington not only reaffirmed denial of a license but also declared that Guardian could not build a float plant without a license, accused several new Guardian employees of violating so-called confidentiality obligations to Pilkington, and threatened legal action.

It was now apparent to Davidson—who had set his sights on glassmaking when he first hired a manufacturing expert back in 1965—that the only way to build a float glass plant in the United States was to go ahead and simply do it. In 1968, he had retained patent and antitrust counsel to assess Guardian's rights and obligations. In February 1969, the attorneys informed Davidson that there was ample technical and legal room to build a float glass plant in the United States, even without permission from Pilkington. Weaknesses in its patent position made it risky for Pilkington to jeopardize its worldwide licensing program by taking legal action in the United States that might result in the invalidity of its

On June 13, 1969, officers broke ground for Guardian's first float glass plant in Carleton, Ash Township, Michigan. President Bill Davidson, center foreground, is joined on the left by E. Ross Steggles, vice president of manufacturing, and Frank Hawley, supervisor of Ash Township (shoveling dirt). To the right of Davidson is Earl Reeves, chairman of the Ash Township Planning Commission, and Ed Szesney, director of engineering and research.

patents. In that case, the existing and growing flow of royalties to Pilkington from its many licensees around the world would immediately dry up.

Moreover, the attorneys concluded that, in light of the concentrated nature of the existing glass industry in the United States and its history of antitrust infractions, if Pilkington were to challenge the efforts of a small company in Michigan to enter the field, Guardian could assert antitrust claims in return. While there were serious risks that Pilkington would attack, at least Guardian would not be defenseless.

Full Speed Ahead

Davidson's next step was to instruct the team of experts and engineers he had previously hired to go full speed ahead on the design and construction of a float glass plant in Carleton, Michigan. He had initially hoped to take a license and obtain the technical assistance from Pilkington that it typically gave to its licensees. He did not invite or welcome the cloud of uncertainty and added difficulties created by Pilkington's opposition and threats, but "I also felt there was no choice but to go forward in spite of them," he said.[33]

On March 20, 1969, Guardian publicly announced its plan to construct a new float glass manufacturing plant to be located at Carleton, Michigan. On the same day as the announcement, Davidson telephoned the news to a Pilkington executive in England and sent him a copy of the press release. On April 28, construction began, although the official groundbreaking ceremony was held at the site on June 13, 1969. A prominent speaker at the groundbreaking was Michigan's senior senator, Philip

Above: Construction continued in December on the "tin bath pit" for the new plant in Carleton, Michigan.

Above right: This southern view shows the interior of the building at the new plant.

Below: This progress photo of the new flat glass plant was taken in December 1969 and shows the exterior construction nearing completion.

For years, I've been counseling against this nation's growing concentration of economic power ... so it is very reassuring to me to see a new competitor entering a field that up to now has been closely controlled by very few corporations.[34]

Construction activity continued uninterrupted during the spring and summer of 1969 and then into the new year, while behind the scenes Guardian and Davidson dealt with an endless stream of new challenges.

A. Hart, who happened to be the ranking Democratic member of the Senate Judiciary Committee—one of the committees with responsibility for antitrust matters. Among the senator's remarks:

Paying for Carleton

An immense obstacle was, of course, the staggering $17 million needed to build a modern, state-

of-the-art float glass plant. This sum represented almost an entire year's revenue for Guardian in 1968, and was five times the company's equity. Guardian understood the tremendous difficulty in raising this amount from the financial community and continually downplayed the potential cost of the project so as to not scare people off. The official line was that the plant would cost "$10 million plus." Guardian believed that if it could raise this much in outside financing it somehow could cover the rest of the project cost from internal sources.

It is remarkable to look back on this period and note the absence of any sort of project financing that usually accompanies an undertaking such as Carleton. Normally, all of the financing required for a large project is firmly committed before anything goes forward; but this was not the case for the Carleton float plant. During the spring of 1969, as Guardian was moving forward to prepare for groundbreaking, it had received no commitments for long-term lending.

Over the years, Michigan National Bank had become Guardian's primary bank and was where Guardian first turned in trying to arrange financing in early 1969. However, even with the good relationship, Michigan National initially gave Guardian a cool reception. The bank understood the real cost of the project and considered it too risky. Sam Greenawalt, the loan officer at the time for Michigan National and a strong Guardian advocate throughout explains:

> The cost of the project was enormous for a company the size of Guardian; they had no experience in glass manufacturing, no license, and were under the threat of lawsuit by Pilkington, and there wasn't enough of a market for the glass that would be produced at the plant. On the surface, you would have to be crazy to take the credit risk for a single purpose project of this size.[35]

Guardian approached other banks in early 1969, but without success. Indeed, on April 23, barely a week before the construction was to begin, Chemical Bank turned Guardian down for a requested loan. Undeterred, Davidson decided to go forward and figure out later how to raise the money. In the meantime, the costs of the project would be funded with monies generated by ongoing operations, delaying payments to suppliers, loans from

This January 1970 photo shows a cullet tunnel in the foreground and "tin bath" and furnace building in the background at Guardian's new Carleton facility.

Kerr and relatives of Davidson, and the sale of an investment held by Guardian Photo. In 1966, the former ABC Photo had become a large shareholder in Revco, a drugstore chain that was its largest customer. Fortunately, the value of this investment in the market had increased threefold, to $4 million, and the sale of the stock provided critical resources for the construction of Carleton.

As construction proceeded, Guardian continued discussions with Michigan National. With the planned acquisition of Permaglass promising to result in a greater utilization of the glass plant's production, key personnel at the bank were getting more comfortable with other aspects of the project as well. The team members Guardian hired from Ford were impressive glass experts, and the risk of lawsuit by Pilkington was beginning to subside. Most importantly, Davidson's relentless determination was turning skeptics into believers. The amount needed was still too large for Michigan National to handle on its own, but in September 1969 it agreed both to lead the financing if it could find another bank to share the risk and to provide some limited short-term funding while working on the long-term deal. Guardian started to breathe a little easier, but the comfort would be short-lived. As Davidson and Greenawalt met with New York banks to discuss the financing, it quickly became clear that they had been intimidated by Guardian's competitors and would not participate for fear of losing business with the "old boys' club." As Greenawalt recalled:

> It was obvious that everyone was scared off by all the power aligned against Guardian. It was especially frustrating because we always felt we were fighting forces behind the scenes that we could never see.[36]

It was clear now that the major New York banks would not be the answer, so the search turned to regional banks who would not have relationships with the competitors. With time quickly running out, the group's efforts finally met with success. In December 1969, Franklin Bank agreed in principle to participate with Michigan National in a long-term loan covering roughly half of the actual project cost. Even with this agreement it would take several months to negotiate and finalize the definitive documents.[37] The loan agreement was not finally closed until late 1970, after the plant had started up.

During this period Bill Davidson had demonstrated once again that he would not be deterred. He was prepared to risk everything to see Guardian evolve from a fabricator to a cutting-edge glassmaker, and he was not going to let any obstacles,

especially those put in Guardian's path by members of the old establishment, stand in his way.

The "Uninvited Dance Guest"

Pilkington and the rest of the glass industry continued to keep a sharp eye on developments in Michigan. Their private and public reactions evolved as Guardian's determination began to convert the float glass project from a vision into a reality.

Significantly, in January 1970, after Guardian had completed the Permaglass merger and the Carleton project was well under way, Pilkington contacted Davidson and offered to discuss the possibility of licensing Guardian in float technology. Davidson expressed interest, and the parties began a round of negotiations that would last more than a year; meanwhile, what was actually happening on the ground in Carleton was never very far from the negotiators' minds. The first meeting took place at the Queen Elizabeth Hotel in Montreal, Canada. Pilkington representatives presented a draft license agreement to Davidson and Feldman. The draft was similar to the license that previous licensees had signed, although the financial terms as initially proposed were actually less favorable to Guardian. Virtually no progress was made because Guardian was insisting that it not be discriminated against vis-a-vis other United States manufacturers.

The next major meeting took place in London on April 29 and 30, 1970, and was attended by Sir Alastair Pilkington, yet the parties remained far apart.

In 1970, Guardian executives hosted a luncheon to celebrate the dedication of the company's new float glass plant, which signified its entry into the glass manufacturing industry.

The President
and
The Board of Directors
of
GUARDIAN INDUSTRIES CORP.
cordially invite you to attend ceremonies marking the dedication of the Company's new flat glass plant, and signifying the first entry by a new company into the glass manufacturing field in more than 50 years.

Monday, October 26, 1970, at 11:00 A.M.
1200 Will Carleton Road, Carleton, Michigan

Please RSVP   Luncheon
by card enclosed   will be served

Indeed, as Davidson recalled, "I told them that Guardian no longer needed the standard Pilkington license, which in addition to giving patent coverage also granted to the licensee Pilkington's know-how and trade secrets, because our Carleton plant was almost up and running and we had achieved this without any help from Pilkington."[38] Davidson insisted that Guardian pay a reasonable amount for the right to use Pilkington's patents and nothing more.

While the negotiations appeared to reach an impasse over this issue, work at Carleton proceeded on schedule. Heat up of the furnace started in August 1970, and the first Guardian glass was pulled later that month. At the official dedication on October 26, 1970, Davidson told the assembled industry, community, civic, and government leaders that:

It is Guardian's intention to truly be a glass company of the future, matching the properties of the

product to the needs of the people, and it is with this in mind that we are entering the glass manufacturing field.[39]

Above: One of many control panels in the 275,000-square-foot Carleton float glass manufacturing plant.

Below: Guardian's first float glassmaking plant in Carleton, Michigan, as it appeared in 1970, its first year of operation. The plant laid the groundwork for many more that followed.

The events at Carleton, Michigan, sent shock waves throughout the industry. "The U.S. flat-glass industry held its breath after the new plant started up in 1970, fully expecting Pilkington to crush Guardian with a suit for patent violation," commented *Fortune* magazine in 1982. To the established glassmakers, Guardian had acted unethically in building the factory without a license. "The top three companies looked upon Guardian as a pirate and Davidson as a maverick," recalled Andrew Wardrop, retired general manager of Ford's glass division. They also complained to Pilkington that it was not policing its license effectively.[40]

Glass Industry magazine reported the Carleton startup in a short note in its November 1970 issue: "Guardian Glass Co., Detroit, Michigan, late last month dedicated its new 275,000-square-foot float glass plant with a pull of 350 tons per day. So far, there is no license agreement, but rumor has it that negotiations are still in progress with Pilkington Bros., which developed [the] float process."[41]

The rumor was correct. Just weeks after the dedication, in November 1970, senior representatives of Guardian and Pilkington met for two days at the Princess Hotel in Bermuda. Davidson recalled telling Pilkington that "our only interest at that point in taking a license was to buy peace between our companies. Guardian was not interested in paying what other licensees had paid since Guardian had built its float plant without any technical assistance from Pilkington and did not believe it was infringing on any valid Pilkington patents."[42] While this was a major blow to Pilkington's worldwide licensing program, since Guardian was proposing a lower royalty rate than other licensees had paid and was also rejecting the need (and payment) for Pilkington know-how, Pilkington accepted Guardian's terms. On May 18, 1971, Guardian and Pilkington entered into a running royalty license agreement essentially along the lines proposed by Guardian in Bermuda.

"After that, we were home free," Oscar Feldman remembered. "Later, we met with Pilkington again, this time for the purpose of getting a paid-up license rather than paying a royalty. We had a wonderful trip to southern France and cemented our social relationships. We finally got a paid-up license."[43]

Guardian's license infuriated the other domestic glassmakers. Although the terms of the agreement were not made public, the competing glassmakers believed with good reason that Guardian paid less for the Pilkington process than they had.[44] "They fought us tooth and nail," Feldman said of PPG, L-O-F, and Ford.[45]

It is relatively easy to understand, with the benefit of hindsight, why Pilkington never sued Guardian over the Carleton plant, despite all the threats and despite the efforts of the established licensees to undermine Guardian's project. As a later writer for *Fortune* magazine noted, if Pilkington had lost in court, it might have lost its patents, along with its lucrative royalty payments. In addition, existing glassmakers were operating in the shadow of the 1949 consent decree between PPG and L-O-F. Guardian could have claimed that Pilkington was encouraging oligopoly in the United States by refusing to license Guardian.[46]

Davidson had calculated that Pilkington would not risk a lawsuit, and that even if it had brought a case, construction of Carleton would not have been stopped: "The chances of getting a court to say that Guardian had to pull down its plant were pretty limited. The most it would have said would have been, 'Go away and make an arrangement.' "[47] As Davidson further recalled, "We were fairly confident Pilkington wouldn't attack us, for antitrust reasons. We were reasonably safe as long as we were in the United States."[48]

Such hindsight observations, even as voiced by the participants, do not adequately recognize Guardian's boldness in going it alone against the wishes of the industry giant. Everyone else expected Pilkington to squash Guardian before it could ever get started. Davidson was risking legal action by an adversary with immense economic resources, although his calculation that Pilkington would not go to war in American courts proved to be uncannily accurate. But legal risk was only part of the equation. More importantly, he had stretched his and Guardian's finances to the breaking point in relying on a group of relatively untested Guardian employees to build a float glass plant without Pilkington's help and support, whether or not Pilkington sued. This was an unprecedented act of courage, determination, and confidence.

As *Fortune* later noted, "Guardian Industries strode into the float glass business with all the unruly determination of an uninvited dance guest."[49]

It was only after crashing the party that Guardian paid Pilkington for an admission ticket—and this at a discounted price. As events would show, however, life inside the dance hall—or glass industry arena—would present even more challenges for Guardian. And in keeping with his approach to business and to life, Davidson would not be satisfied with merely dancing in step with everyone else. His intention was that Guardian would eventually win the contest and be the last one standing when the evening was over.

A Guardian operator looks at the flame pattern through specially darkened glass. Flames alternate from side to side at 20-minute intervals, 24 hours a day.

CHAPTER FOUR

GROUNDWORK

*Customers loved us. We had great quality. The success of the Kingsburg
plant was, in effect, the shot heard round the world.*

—Russ Ebeid, 2001

FOR GUARDIAN INDUSTRIES,
the decade of the 1970s was as
full of challenges and accomplishments, if not fireworks and
drama, as the decade that preceded
it. Through extraordinary efforts, the
Guardian engineering and produc-
tion teams built a state-of-the-art float glass plant
in Carleton, Michigan, and began to operate it profitably. Early on, Guardian employees not only
learned the basic dance steps but also started to
choreograph their own unique way of running a
glass business. The decade also saw the continuation of downstream expansion into additional operations that would be consumers of Guardian's float
glass as well as profit centers in their own right.
Guardian also began to pursue opportunities in new
lines of business, such as building insulation. Finally,
Guardian successfully expanded its float glass manufacturing operations to new markets in California
and Texas, where the unique business philosophy
and values born at Carleton—to be known later as
the "Guardian Way"—were further developed and
refined and became firmly entrenched as the company's culture. By the end of the decade, Guardian,
led by Bill Davidson and a younger generation of
individuals, including many who had "earned their
stripes" in the battles to establish the Michigan,
California, and Texas plants, was a major player
in the North American flat glass industry and was
looking for new worlds to conquer.

The Beginnings at Carleton

The Carleton float glass
plant was built by Guardian
employees who were entirely on
their own and who were, moreover, besieged by the outside
world. Typically, as part of its licensing program,
Pilkington provided considerable technical support
to companies embarking on their first plants. At
Carleton, the engineering team led by Ed Sczesny
and Richard Alonzo could rely only on themselves
and a cadre of dedicated employees who were generally new, both to Guardian and to the task of con-
structing such a facility. Moreover, all the established
United States licensees—PPG, L-O-F, and Ford—were
large and financially stable companies for whom
obtaining funds to build their plants was a relatively
easy matter.

Guardian's effort at Carleton, on the other hand,
was a "hand-to-mouth affair, where we often did not
know where the next dollar to pay a supplier or contractor was coming from."[1] As Davidson later recalled,
"We had enough money just to get the float line up
and running. There were no bells or whistles or even

With completion of a second glassmaking line, Guardian's huge
manufacturing complex in Carleton, Michigan, produced more
than 750,000 square feet of glass each day.

Russ Ebeid was Carleton's first maintenance supervisor. He later became Kingsburg's plant manager and the 1979 "Employee of the Year," then went on to become Guardian's Glass Group president.

some things that are considered necessities to a float plant. We had on-line cutting, and that was it. We would add other parts later."[2] The same lack of specific float glass experience and relative isolation from outside assistance also applied to those charged with starting up the plant and turning it into a profitable business operation. Russ Ebeid was Carleton's first maintenance superintendent (hired from General Motors with no glass-making experience) and an instrumental figure in Guardian's future growth. He later reflected, "If those of us who started the Carleton plant knew then what we know today, we probably would have said, 'This will never work.' A tremendous amount of precision goes into glassmaking, but if you had told me back then to throw a sack of potatoes in the furnace to help make the glass, I would have tried it."[3]

All these formidable obstacles, difficult as they were to overcome in the short term, actually forced Guardian and its people to adopt attitudes and behavior that made them stronger over time. The experience of building and launching Carleton was a crucible from which Guardian's unique spirit and cultural values were forged. One need only look back at the issues of the *Guardian Newsletter* (later *Guardian World*), initially published monthly, to see the energy, excitement, initiative, "can-do" attitude, and teamwork developing among all the people associated with the Carleton project.

Their efforts were tested at the plant's start-up as reported:

4:20 p.m. August 20 [1970] was the BIG moment at the Carleton plant when the first glass came down the line, urged on by a crew of hot, tense, expectant, tired, proud equipment operators, engi-

neers, supervisors, plant managers, and maintenance personnel, plus a sizeable gathering of onlookers and well-wishers. Following the start-up of the "ribbon" came many days and nights adjusting the hot-end equipment and ... of programming the complex [cutting system]. ... Programming the cutting systems proved to be a real test of the stamina of the design and staff engineers, as well as the operating crews. There were lots of tired people, lots of broken glass, lots of cleanup—so close to being on-stream and still having to crush many, many feet of glass. Some staff and supervisory personnel worked 12, 16, 18 hours a day and then came back the next day to do it again.[4]

With the exception of the former Ford engineers, the Carleton plant workers were inexperienced in float glass manufacturing. Wayne Held, a maintenance worker at the plant, recalled the plant start-up:

What I remember most was the camaraderie. Everyone there was doing something new, and that created a bond between us. It didn't matter who you were or what your job was. Each and every one of us was there to do his or her part to get the plant up and running—whatever it took.[5]

Wally Palma, another member of the start-up team who went on to a long and valued career at Guardian, recalled the swirl of emotions attending the launch:

Many of us who joined the company to start the Carleton plant felt that we were embarking on a new career. We felt like we were at the start of something big, and the greatest thing was being in on the ground floor. We were filled with vim and vigor and ready to take on this new adventure. I remember working seven days a week for four months to get the plant on its feet. We endured many hours of electrical failures and equipment failures. While we had hoped the launch would go smoothly, it didn't—being our first plant, there were many things we didn't know or anticipate.[6]

After days of hard work and adjustments, the first usable glass was shipped to Guardian's Millbury, Ohio, plant for fabrication.[7] By October, Guardian's Detroit plant was using only Guardian glass to make windshields.[8] About half of the 350 tons of flat glass initially produced daily at the float plant would be used at Guardian's six North American fabrication plants. The rest would be sold to other glass fabricators.[9]

A New Operating Philosophy

At Carleton, Guardian attempted to recast the relationship between management and workers by emphasizing individual contribution and curbing bureaucracy. Davidson correctly perceived the tremendous energy, wisdom, and willpower in all of the employees, not just a handful of executives at the top, and wanted to liberate all that talent.

Guardian intended to remove artificial barriers between employees and the company, allowing workers to contribute their abilities and energies

---

When the first float glass line at the Carleton plant was fully operational, it produced 350 tons of glass daily, enough to supply Guardian and other glass fabricators.

directly. So, while the company was not hostile toward unions, they were not part of the operating plan. Instead, Carleton workers operated under guidelines hammered out by a group consisting of some 25 people, only six of whom were management employees. As *Guardian World* explained, this approach was:

> *... in line with the belief that the successful and profitable operation of the plant is the responsibility of all employees and further that creative problem-solving talent is widespread in the employee group.*[10]

The group met monthly to establish plant policies for safety, vacations, absenteeism, and tardiness.[11]

Plant safety quickly emerged as one of the paramount concerns of both managers and employees, and it would remain in the forefront of Guardian's operating philosophy. All plant personnel devoted considerable attention to safety matters, with very positive results.[12] This priority was emphasized on a company-wide level in January 1975, when Guardian instituted a year-long competition among plants to

show the greatest improvement in safety. The winner would be given the president's "Award of Honor" at the end of the year.[13] In later years, the plant with the worst safety record for the year would be awarded the "Golden Spike," an unwanted distinction that no plant would ever win twice in a row.

Production workers at the plant enjoyed good relations with management, who adopted Davidson's informal style, including the absence of suits and ties. All employees shared the same cafeteria; there were no reserved parking spaces in the parking lot. If a machine broke down, Bob Cobie, who had been recruited from Ford in 1969 and was promoted to plant manager in December 1970, was as likely as anyone to pitch in and help fix it.[14] In addition, all plant employees were salaried; there were no time clocks. Workers were on the honor system, and they didn't abuse it. Absenteeism dropped sharply during the years after the plant opened in 1970. Fringe benefits offered by Guardian were comparable to those at other glass industry plants. Workers were paid production bonuses based on performance and could participate in a stock purchase plan. To avoid burnout, workers would not be pigeonholed by restrictive job classifications and could be rotated to different jobs.[15]

After two years, 22 production or maintenance workers had seized the opportunities available to them and had been promoted to supervisory positions.[16] A quality technician described his experience at the Carleton plant in a 1972 *Guardian World* article:

I've never worked any place where I felt more involved in my job than here. I feel like I'm actually involved in making this plant a profitable business, not just doing a job. There is a tremendous difference between working here and any other place I've ever worked. Like the piped-in music and that the management people know you and talk to you. Everybody is on the same level, it seems, all part of the team. The open door policy here really works. I feel like I can talk to anyone about what's on my mind. I appreciate the steady, dependable nature of Guardian. I feel secure in my job.[17]

Keith Waldvogel, hot-end equipment operator, shared a similar sentiment:

You are treated like a person, treated fair, trusted, and believed. It's different all the way ... right up to the top management because they are for the workers in the plant. Being on salary and not having to punch a time clock is definitely a plus. I like my job because we rotate our assignments and that really makes it interesting. My earnings at Guardian are double what I was making as a machinist before.[18]

Another operator who had worked at Carleton during the launch stated that "the company... gives us a job to do and then [they] let us do it without looking over our shoulder every minute." Finally, a veteran operator observed:

We have a lot of variety in our jobs. Guardian is better than any other place I have ever worked. You are on your own. You have responsibility for doing your job, the company trusts you. Another thing is that we have contact with all the management people on a first name basis.[19]

These and numerous other testimonials confirmed that something unique and special was taking place at Carleton.

One indication of the success of Guardian's operating philosophy was the plant's response to early efforts of union organizers, who were always eager to add new manufacturing plants to their rosters. In 1971, the United Glass and Ceramic Workers held an organizing drive in Carleton. Not surprisingly, workers rejected the offer. Two years later, they overwhelmingly rejected bids by the UAW and the Teamsters unions to represent them.[20]

Expansion at Carleton

The Carleton plant had begun operations at a time when overall market conditions for flat glass were weak. The economy had slowed down and was in the throes of a long six-year slide; further difficulties came in the form of large inventories of foreign-supplied glass that were glutting the U.S. market. This downturn in the economy was just one more obstacle for Davidson and the Guardian team to overcome.

Despite the gloomy economic landscape, the Carleton plant was operating profitably just seven months after its start-up, and the plant continued

Guardian's stock opened on the New York Stock Exchange on January 23, 1973. The New York Stock Exchange Executive Vice President Francis J. Palamara, left, welcomed Guardian President Bill Davidson, center, to the trading floor. Stock specialist Milton M. Cohen is on the right.

to steadily increase its production. It was turning out nearly 350 tons per day by the end of 1971. The company's financial performance followed suit, and by 1972 Guardian's net income was more than triple what it had been three years earlier.[21] With the financial success of Carleton now solidified, Guardian was able to complete a major refinancing plan in 1972 that greatly improved its balance sheet and positioned the company for growth.

Guardian had weathered the financial storm of building Carleton. It was now ready to move on, and Wall Street was definitely taking notice. After initially trading in the over-the-counter market following the public offering in 1968, Guardian stock had moved to the American Stock Exchange for three years, and on January 23, 1973, made the big step to the prestigious New York Stock Exchange. Guardian was a high-flying growth stock during this period. Its initial trade on the NYSE was 15 times its original offer price just four years earlier.

The successful launch of the float line and Guardian's improved financial performance and position made possible immediate expansion on two fronts: construction of a second float line and installation of downstream tempering, and other

Looking over plans for expansion of the new float glass manufacturing plant in Carleton, Michigan, are from left to right: Bob Cobie, plant manager; Richard Hoffman, project engineer; Richard Alonzo, manager of engineering; and Ed Sczesny, vice president of engineering and corporate development.

fabricating capacity at Carleton. In April 1972, Guardian announced that it would construct a second float line at the plant at a projected cost of $20 million. The project was completed a year later. The new line could produce up to 450 tons of glass daily, more than doubling the plant's capacity. It also had the capability of producing clear glass as thin as 2 mm, an increasingly common requirement for automotive windshields.[22]

Simultaneously, with the success of line one and the construction of line two, Guardian took measures to greatly increase its tempering capacity, since the company's ability to supply its own needs for flat glass was now assured. The purchase of Permaglass in 1969 had been a shrewd move for Guardian, and not only because it had facilitated Guardian's efforts to build the Carleton plant. Demand for tempered products was skyrocketing. By 1971, 14 states had laws requiring safety glass (laminated, tempered, or wired glass) for doors and glass panels in commercial and residential buildings. Other states were expected to follow suit, and many architects and builders routinely used the safer product even if not required to by law.[23]

Builders often chose to use tempered glass because it was easier to handle and cost less than laminated glass. Tempered glass was made by heating glass to the softening point (approximately 1,100 degrees Fahrenheit) and then rapidly cooling it. As the glass cooled, its outer surfaces started to solidify and contract. When the inside began to cool, it contracted even more. The difference in tension between the inside and outside of the glass created permanent stress, which made tempered glass five times stronger than ordinary glass.[24]

During 1972–1973, Guardian added significant tempering capacity at Carleton to complement what it had acquired from Permaglass. The first phase of the expansion included a new fabricating building, where a large tempering furnace was installed. The next phases provided for the handling of large sheets of architectural glass,[25] adding a 240-by-720-foot warehouse and a new horizontal tempering furnace capable of producing 20 million square feet of tempered glass annually.[26]

The Carleton plant also installed a new insulated-glass assembly line for production of double-glazed glass, which was being used more frequently in heated and air-conditioned buildings.[27] The Arab oil embargo of 1973 had created an energy crisis in the United States, and Americans were suddenly scrambling to conserve energy. Architects and builders demanded energy-efficient glass in new construction to help lower air-conditioning and heating costs.

Acquisitions and More Internal Growth

At the same time it was reaping the benefits of internal growth, Guardian continued its acquisition program. The strategic purposes of the acquisitions were to broaden the company's product mix, expand its reach deeper into the various segments of the glass market, and provide a ready outlet for Carleton's growing float glass production. In 1972, Guardian bought two companies, Beachland Glass and Glass for Cars, which provided an entrée into the retail glass market. By the end of the year, through acquisitions and internal expansion, Guardian had assembled a total of 23 retail outlets. The retail operations offered auto glass installation, home and commercial glazing, storm door and window repairs, tabletops, mirrors, electric window repairs, and emergency board-up service.

Acquisitions also extended to the architectural market when Guardian acquired two fabricators, Sitelines, of Harbor City, California, and Glass Guard Industries, of Webster, Massachusetts, in 1974.

Sitelines, which became Guardian's Engineered Systems Group, designed, fabricated, and installed high-performance acoustical and environmental

Above: Standing in front of the furnace for Guardian's second glassmaking line at Carleton are, left to right: Russ Ebeid, production manager; Jon Greenawalt, director of personnel; Wally Palma, plant engineer; and Bob Cobie, plant manager.

Below: The Carleton, Michigan, plant after the expansion that added a second float line.

Above: Tempered glass is four to five times stronger than ordinary glass. Supervised testing of the break pattern is conducted regularly during the tempering fabrication process.

Below: A Guardian glass retail outlet in Orlando, Florida. By the mid-1970s, Guardian had more than 20 of these outlets, which supplied automotive replacement glass.

control window and curtain wall systems for commercial buildings. Its products had been used in Pepsi's world headquarters building, the administration building of the Dallas–Fort Worth Airport, and the lower level of San Francisco's Saint Francis Hotel.[28] Glass Guard was a tempering and insulating glass manufacturing company that sold architectural glass to approximately 450 East Coast customers.[29] The company had been founded in 1967 and had annual sales of $12 million. Prior to Guardian's purchase, Glass Guard had been one of the Carleton plant's largest customers. Its owner, Norman Shulman, became sales manager for Guardian's Webster and Carleton plants[30] and would later assume additional responsibilities for U.S. flat glass sales.

In 1974, Guardian opened a new laminating plant in Upper Sandusky, Ohio, increasing windshield and flat-laminated capacity by 75 percent. This plant marked an important step for Guardian's automotive business: it was the first plant outside Detroit built primarily for the automotive market.[31] Additional laminated glass capacity in the automotive market was becoming increasingly necessary. Auto designers continued to incorporate more glass into new models, and the energy crisis encouraged automakers to create lighter cars, so thin, lightweight windshields were in demand.[32] With its new capabilities, Guardian landed contracts with Chevrolet, Mack Truck, Kenworth Truck, Brockway Truck, Diamond Reo Truck, and Champion Home Builders (manufacturer of mobile homes).[33]

Overcoming Adversity

The fact that Guardian was able to grow through the 1970s was a testament to the company's determination, savvy, and leadership. Few decades have been as hard on American business, and few companies maintained Guardian's growth rate through this difficult decade. Economic conditions were disastrous throughout the period, characterized by high inflation, low growth, and major spikes in energy prices. The oil embargo imposed by OPEC beginning in October 1973 crippled U.S. energy supplies and resulted in a severe recession in 1974–75. Just as Guardian was hitting its stride as a glassmaker, the energy crunch and the recession crushed the two industries on which Guardian

Above: The Carleton plant engineering staff in 1975 included: front row, from left: Wally Palma, plant engineer; Ron DeBruin, cutting line; Dale Lehman, instrumentation; and Ed Hodgkiss, electrical systems. Back row, from left: Paul Block, material handling; Chuck Croskey, tin bath; Ed Beaumont, fuel; Jim Sabbadini, tin bath; Dean Hooks, cutting line; and Jim Dunmeyes, batch house.

Below: Workers repair the first float glass line at the Carleton, Michigan, plant in 1975. This photo was taken from inside the furnace.

relied—automotive and construction. *Business Week* summed up the state of the glass industry: "Of all the industries that have reported sales and earnings for 1974, few reflect the downturn in the U.S. economy more seriously."[34] *Business Week* also quoted Libbey-Owens-Ford President Robert G. Wingerter, who said, "Both auto and construction glass are in a state of depression, not recession."[35] Car, truck, and bus production declined 21 percent in 1974 and another 21 percent in 1975.[36] The value of residential construction was down 15 percent in 1974 and 8 percent in 1975. Commercial construction's decline began in 1975 with a 19 percent drop, then slid another 4 percent in 1976.[37]

None of this would stop Guardian's growth, and while profits declined marginally during the 1974–75 recession—the only years of decline during the period that Guardian was a public company—sales continued to rise each year. A significant milestone was reached in 1974 when sales exceeded $100 million for the first time. For Davidson and Guardian, this was a major accomplishment and sent a message that Guardian was here to stay. Indeed, by the mid-1970s, Guardian had diversified intelligently and developed new, profitable capabilities. Its revenue picture had changed dramatically from just six years before, when it was primarily a fabricator of windshields. By 1974, Guardian Photo accounted for approximately 18 percent of sales; automotive glass, 32 percent; raw glass, 27 percent; and architectural glass, 23 percent. Half the company's sales came from operations that hadn't even existed five years earlier. In 1975, *Financial World* ranked Guardian Industries 16th in earnings growth by a publicly held company. The award covered the period 1964–1974, when Guardian's annual earnings growth rate was 37 percent.

Investing for the Future

Despite the economic slump, Guardian continued to expand, preparing for the day when the economy would turn around. The first Carleton float line was repaired in 1975, a process that was then necessary approximately every five years. The $5 million project increased the line's capacity by 10 percent.[38] Carleton's staff helped devise a new system for producing single- and double-strength glass, allowing Guardian to produce windows for residential construction.[39] Three years later, in 1978, a new tempering furnace was added.

A view of the cutting line in Carleton's second float glass line is shown here.

In 1977, Guardian entered the reflective glass market through a partnership with Airco, a New Jersey–based company specializing in metallic coating processes. Airco built a multimillion-dollar plant adjacent to Guardian's Carleton plant. The Airco plant had the capacity to coat 10 million square feet of glass annually.[40] Under a five-year exclusive agreement with Airco, glass from the Carleton plant was coated by Airco and sold by Guardian under its own name. The new plant began production in the fall of 1977, a time when commercial construction was climbing.

"When you compare the performance of tinted glass to coated glass, the energy performance of the coated glass is so much better that the demand for this product just skyrocketed," said Karl Straky, director of commercial glass products.[41] The Airco technology was superior to the coating process being used by other glassmakers. Airco applied a thin metal film to Guardian glass, producing a gold, silver, or bronze coating. The process, known as sputter coating or sputtering, could be applied to raw, tempered, or laminated glass.[42] The glass rode on a continuous conveyor to be washed, then was fed through several vacuum chambers until it reached the coating process, which electrostatically deposited the film on the glass. This produced a microscopically thin coating that actually became part of the glass.[43] Guardian eventually took over the Airco plant and ran it for many years.

Building the Organization

Guardian's expansion and diversification required organizational change and, more importantly, the injection of new people with the skills and drive to manage and help lead escalating growth and complexity. This was accomplished steadily throughout the 1970s. In a careful manner designed to maintain Guardian's lean approach to management and to avoid the encroachment of bureaucracy, titles were added and new positions created to reflect changing times and requirements. But titles remained less important than the entrepreneurial qualities of people who succeeded by getting results and not worrying about organizational charts and where they fit in the so-called pecking order. The core senior leadership of the 1960s grew as the Glass Manufacturing Group became prominent and glass fabrication expanded in the early 1970s. Sczesny, who led the team that designed and built Carleton, became vice president of engineering and corporate development in 1971, while Murray Yudin, Alton Brown, and Norm Shulman handled marketing and sales. Future Guardian leaders also were emerging at this time from its infant glass manufacturing operations. Finally, Guardian reorganized its fabrication plants and gave important roles first to Bill Morrow and later to Bill Black.

Morrow had been working for Permaglass for more than a decade when Guardian acquired the company in 1969. Davidson made him plant manager of the Fort Lauderdale glass fabrication facility in 1970, and Morrow immediately found himself in a situation that severely tested his leadership. When he arrived on the scene, Morrow found a plant with sales and profits that were approaching all-time lows. In setting out to reverse the trend, he ran into opposition from the Glass and Ceramic Workers Union, which represented the employees at the time. After weeks of negotiations, plant management and the union were unable to come to terms on a new labor contract. On February 19, 1971, the hourly employees went on strike and set up their picket lines.[44]

For the next 12 months, Morrow and a handful of his people ran the plant in spite of the strike. They managed to produce and ship in excess of $1 million in product and generated the greatest profit contribution in the facility's history.[45]

During 1971, the union attempted to increase the pressure by filing a series of unfair labor charges with the National Labor Relations Board, but all of these were vigorously opposed by management and ultimately dismissed in the investigatory stage. In 1971, the union acknowledged defeat by disclaiming any further interest in representing the plant's employees. As Morrow noted, "Once the union had withdrawn, morale at the plant was great, and the employees had a new interest in improving efficiency and making the plant a smooth, cooperative, and profitable operation."[46] The plant very quickly set monthly sales records in February and March 1972 and was poised for continued improvement.[47]

Morrow became known for his "in-the-plant, shirt-sleeve management" style, his ability to build teams, and his perseverance. He was the smallest and youngest guard the Colgate University football team ever had, but what he "lacked in weight he made up for in determination."[48]

Davidson acknowledged Morrow's extraordinary contribution and leadership qualities when he named him 1972 "Employee of the Year" in recognition of his "outstanding performance in the management of the Fort Lauderdale plant, including the leadership throughout the year-long strike despite threats of physical violence to the plant and to himself. He successfully maintained the right of the company to operate its plant efficiently, and as a result, turned the operation from a deteriorating one to a winner."[49] Throughout the 1970s, Morrow was put in charge of additional areas, such as the Torrance, California, tempering plant and OEM automotive glass sales. In 1981, he was appointed group vice president with yet more facilities placed under his supervision. As Davidson recalled:

Bill Morrow was one of the key people in Guardian's history after 1969. He made a big mark on our operations and our culture, and set a great example for people to follow.[50]

After a brief period as a production foreman and engineer at GM's Fisher Body plant, Bill Black joined Guardian in 1972 as a Carleton plant superintendent. He did not see himself as "fitting into

Murray Yudin, top, and Alton Brown, center, in 1971. Yudin was named vice president and sales manager of the eastern region, and Brown was named vice president and sales manager of the western region. Yudin and Brown also had been "Employees of the Year" in 1964 and 1967, respectively.

Right: In 1970, Bill Morrow and his team ran the Fort Lauderdale plant in spite of a strike. He was named 1972 "Employee of the Year."

GLASS SAVES ENERGY

EVER SINCE THE LEVER HOUSE BUILD-
ing opened in New York City in 1952,
glass-walled buildings have dominated
the skylines of metropolitan areas. Lever House
was faced with 1,400 tinted windows, or one
square acre of glass. Shortly after, the 39-story
United Nations headquarters opened. It had
5,000 windows.[1]

Curtain Wall Construction

By the early 1960s,
architects were speci-
fying curtain wall
construction more
and more fre-
quently, largely
because glass
costs less than
other building
materials. In
1960, 94 million
square feet of
curtain wall was
erected. The volume
more than doubled
in two years. In
1963, it reached 237
million square feet,

representing 25 percent of the wall areas in
nonresidential buildings (except manufacturing), apartments, hotels, and dormitories.[2]

In 1968, the World Trade Center, compris-
ing twin towers that were the tallest buildings
in the world at the time, contained more than
half-million square feet of floor-to-ceiling
tinted windows.[3]

Curtain wall construction presented a
number of challenges to glassmakers. The
windows had to be attractive from the outside
and could not distort colors for people
looking out from inside the building.
The glass also had to be cut in large
sizes but maintain the strength to
meet building codes and with-
stand weather and the stress of
construction. The glass had to
allow natural light into buildings
but reduce glare. Most importantly, the glass had to help
maintain comfortable building
temperatures by preventing buildup
of heat from the sun and by retaining heating and air-conditioning.
Tinted glass was initially used in curtain wall con-
struction. It
absorbed heat

and looked attractive. But the glass itself became warm and did not reduce air-conditioning costs as much as future technology would.[4]

Insulating Glass

During the late 1950s, window manufacturers developed insulating glass, in which two panes of glass were hermetically sealed, leaving a layer of air in between. Insulating units reduced interior heat loss by 50 percent.[5] Double-glazed windows also prevented condensation and fogging during the winter.[6] They became the standard glazing product in cold climates.

Glass's insulating properties took on new importance during the 1970s, when the United States endured the oil embargo. Energy conservation became critical in building construction, and some people feared windows would get smaller. But the glass industry had developed a new, energy-efficient product during the 1960s—reflective glass.

Reflective glass proved to have energy-saving advantages over tinted glass. Tinted glass absorbed solar energy, but reflective glass stopped 50 to 85 percent of the sun's heat from entering a building,[7] which reduced air-conditioning costs. A February 1968 article in *Glass Industry* noted that the Tulsa Home Federal Savings & Loan building, built with reflective glass, required 28 tons less air-conditioning than if regular tinted glass had been used.[8]

When combined with double glazing, reflective glass significantly reduced heating costs as well. Reflective glass became the preferred glazing material in the southern and western United States, while reflective-insulated units were preferred in colder climates.[9] Building owners liked reflective glass not only for its environmental qualities but also for its appearance. It was available in a variety of colors, and it changed hue throughout the day, depending on weather conditions and the position of the sun.

The first reflective glass suffered from quality problems. The reflective coating was uneven, and sometimes it crazed or cracked.[10] In 1977, Guardian Industries teamed up with Airco to produce an improved reflective glass. The technology, used exclusively by Guardian for five years and purchased by the company in 1982, helped Guardian become one of the leading suppliers of architectural glass worldwide.

The industry continued to develop energy-saving glass products through the 1980s and 1990s. Cost savings were not the only motivation behind the new technology. Scientists warned that greenhouse gas emissions, especially carbon dioxide, were contributing to global warming. Carbon dioxide emissions are a by-product of many types of energy consumption, including natural gas and electricity usage for heating and air-conditioning. U.S. residential and commercial buildings account for more than one-third of all U.S. energy consumption.[11]

Carbon dioxide levels have been rising since the Industrial Revolution. Between 1973 and 1990, when fuel costs were high, fuel consumption slowed. But when prices declined in the 1990s, consumption soared again. The U.S. government has set goals for reducing greenhouse gas emissions by reducing energy use in buildings. The United Nations has attempted to set limits for greenhouse gas emissions worldwide.[12]

Low-E Glass

During the late 1970s, low-emissivity, or low-E, glass was developed. Low-E coated windows reflect heat back into buildings, preventing it from escaping.[13] In an insulating window, low-E glass retains 32 percent more heat than a conventional insulating unit.[14] It can be used both in residential and commercial construction.

Low-E glass is produced by coating one side of the glass with a transparent metallic coating. Guardian was one of the first companies to market low-E glass in the United States.

Glass products that control building temperatures and reduce energy consumption are collectively referred to as high-performance glass. Different products are used in different climates. In new construction and in replacement windows, they contribute to energy savings and a reduction of greenhouse gases worldwide.

the General Motors mold" and wanted a more challenging opportunity. He found it at Guardian.[51] In 1974, he was appointed plant manager of the newly acquired Webster, Masssachusettes, fabrication plant. After achieving a significant improvement in the plant's productivity, he returned to Carleton as plant manager in 1977, after Bob

Cobie left the company. He retained overall responsibility for Webster. That same year, Black was also given responsibility for the newly constructed Tillsonburg fabrication plant in Ontario, Canada. In later years he would continue to take on added responsibilities until his departure from the company toward the end of the next decade.[52] His early contributions were recognized by his selection as 1976 "Employee of the Year."[53]

Several new faces appeared as well and rose rapidly to key senior leadership positions during the 1970s. In 1975, Tom Gaffney joined Guardian as assistant to the president. Gaffney was a CPA with a master's degree in business administration from the University of Chicago and had impressive finance and business skills that were quickly recognized and utilized by Davidson. In 1976, Gaffney was appointed controller and, just a few months later, vice president of finance. In 1979, at age 33, he was appointed to a newly created position at Guardian—executive vice president—where he would be responsible for all financial, accounting, and information services and be heavily involved in corporate development and acquisitions.

"Tom was a very astute guy financially," said Jeff Knight, one of his hires in 1977 and the future CFO of Guardian Industries. "Bill Davidson had hired him at a time when Guardian was small but needed to get more sophisticated. So Gaffney brought that first wave of sophistication to the company. He started a new era of competency that was very important."[54]

His influence on Guardian over the next decade would be profound. Gaffney would lead many of the

Above: Tom Gaffney, executive vice president, helped build the foundation of Guardian's professional management team and led the company's acquisition efforts in the 1980s.

Left: Guardian responded to the energy crisis of the decade by developing a new energy-efficient product. Guardian also manufactured solar energy products.

initiatives of the 1980s, champion diversification, push Guardian to professionalize its management structure, and, of equal importance, recruit a new generation of key future leaders in the next decade.

Richard Alonzo, who had joined Guardian from Ford in 1968 as part of Sczesny's team, rapidly assumed increasing responsibilities for the construction and launch of both Carleton lines, the repair and expansion of line one in 1975, and numerous other projects. Like Gaffney, he hired and began to mentor others who would play major roles in engineering and operations during the following two decades.

The influx of new leaders at Guardian during the 1970s reflected Davidson's distinctive approach to management and people. As Alonzo later recalled, "In contrast to many entrepreneurs, Bill Davidson understood that for Guardian to be successful, he could not tightly control everything himself. As Guardian grew, he recognized the need for strong people who could bring skills and strengths that he did not possess. He also recognized that these lead-

ers needed to have both responsibility and authority for managing their areas. He hated micromanaging and came down hard on people who engaged in it. Of course, he also looked to his managers for results and expected them to be held accountable for their failures."[55] This approach of empowering people with responsibility, authority, and accountability became a hallmark of the Guardian Way.

Exploring Other Opportunities

During the 1970s, Guardian pursued limited opportunities in fields that would become far more important in later decades. Its first ventures into the international glass market, only of modest importance at this time, will be the subject of several chapters that follow. As to other business opportunities in new areas, however, Davidson had already stated in his 1974 President's Message to shareholders that "we believe your company has now reached a point where it should take a serious look at entering a third industry—in addition to glass and photo processing."[56]

In 1978, Sczesny saw a new opportunity that was worth pursuing. He had struck up a relationship with Ren Nebel, an employee of Johns-Manville based in Richmond, Indiana. At the time, Manville was a maker of insulation, which had definite market potential because of a developing building boom.

Working together, Nebel and Sczesny put together a plan to buy a 120,000-square-foot mineral wool insulation factory in Huntington, Indiana. The 30-year-old plant had sat idle for two years due to Environmental Protection Agency restrictions. Guardian renovated it and began production in April 1978.[57]

Mineral wool was a fibrous insulation used extensively in residential and commercial buildings. Because it had a high temperature tolerance, mineral wool was appropriate for use in areas where fire and heat resistance were desired.[58] The product was made by mixing and melting the raw materials, then passing the fluid onto a series of rotating wheels that spun it into fibers not unlike making cotton candy. Mineral wool was sold in blankets or cut and bagged for use as blown-in insulation. Initially, Guardian produced the blown-in product, which was sold to insulation contractors, wholesalers, national lumber, and home improvement retailers.[59]

The 1973 officers and directors are, from left, clockwise: Murray Yudin, Alton Brown, William Wetsman (standing), Warren Coville, Barney Hertzberg (standing), Charles Owen (standing), Bill Davidson, Bert Koski (standing), David Best (standing), Ed Sczesny, Mandell Berman (standing), Ross Steggles, Bryon Gerson (standing), Oscar Feldman, and Reymont Paul.

The Huntington plant had a difficult start-up. Although the company hoped the Insulation Group would show a profit by the end of 1978, it reached its break-even point only in October 1979.[60] By that time, Guardian had undertaken a project to manufacture a more sophisticated and commercially viable product—fiberglass insulation, at a new location in Albion, Michigan. Although Guardian sold the Huntington plant in 1980, the company had learned it could enter new markets successfully, and with an experienced cadre of insulation industry executives—in particular Duane Faulkner who had joined the Insulation Group in 1977 as director of research and development and would later become president of the Building Products Group—laid ambitious plans for the future.[61]

The Move to Kingsburg

The decade of the 1970s closed with an event that, while not presenting the same degree of risk for the company, in some respects nearly rivals the construction of Carleton in its importance to Guardian.

While confined to Michigan and the Midwest, Guardian was a regional player with limited opportunities to grow. The construction and immediately successful operation of the Kingsburg, California, plant in 1978, followed in 1980 by yet another float plant in Corsicana, Texas, demonstrated that Guardian was a force to be reckoned with on the national stage. More significant than the quantitative increase in production capacity and geographic scope brought by the new plants, however, was the flowering there of Guardian's unique operating principles and culture. These had been created and had gestated in Carleton, but Kingsburg, California, would witness the emergence of the Guardian Way in its essentially mature form. Kingsburg would also be the training ground—and proving ground—for a significant number of managers who would lead Guardian's expansion around the globe.

From its Carleton plant, Guardian shipped glass throughout the Midwest and to the eastern seaboard. In 1977, more than two-thirds of the company's raw glass production was sold to outside customers. Guardian sales increased 14 percent in 1977 and 29 percent in 1978.[62] Carleton had proven itself beyond the shadow of a doubt as a low-cost, dependable supplier to the automotive and architectural markets.

At Carleton, Guardian had proved it had a flair for the business, and it was eager to see if its model was transportable. Moreover, there were solid economic reasons for expansion. While it was economical to ship glass from Carleton throughout the eastern United States, it was costly to send it westward.

"You could ship glass from Michigan to California, but the cost was exorbitant," said Ron

Above: Mineral wool was a fibrous insulation used in residential and commercial buildings. Because of its high temperature tolerance, it also was used in areas where fire and heat resistance were desired. Guardian entered the insulation market in 1978.

Opposite: The groundbreaking ceremony for the Kingsburg, California, plant was attended by Guardian executives and local dignitaries. Seated in front are Ed Sczesny, wearing sunglasses, and Bill Davidson, right. Back row, from left, wearing sunglasses, are Oscar Feldman and Murray Yudin.

Nadolski, who started in western sales at Guardian in 1979 and was one of the foundations of Guardian's later success in that region.[63]

Thus, Guardian began to look west for an opportunity to build its second float glass plant and its third line. In 1976, after inspection and evaluation by Guardian's engineering group of some two dozen locations in California, Guardian selected on 80-acre site at Kingsburg, in the San Joachim Valley. In June 1977, Guardian broke ground on a new plant that was some 2,200 miles away from its Michigan base. The project construction was under the overall supervision of Richard Alonzo, while Dennis Arnold was appointed on-site project manager. Leading the group that would run the plant after launch was Russ Ebeid, then production manager of the Carleton plant and soon-to-be named plant manager of the new Kingsburg plant.

Ebeid is universally recognized as one of the principal contributors to Guardian's phenomenal

success following its entry into glass manufacturing in 1970. As he recalled it, his father was a "knapsack immigrant, who came to this country unable to speak the language, with a note pinned to his lapel which said 'Get me to Detroit.' "[64] Ebeid had earned a master's degree in industrial engineering from Wayne State University and was working for General Motors in 1969 when Sczesny "lured him away" (at the age of 29) for the challenge and opportunity of Guardian.[65] He started as the maintenance superintendent at Carleton but was soon named plant engineer and then promoted to production manager.

While at Carleton, Ebeid learned first-hand about Davidson's style and philosophy of leadership. "You learn from Bill by observing and absorbing, not from verbal lessons. In the early years at Carleton we did not have that much personal contact, but I did see him during his visits to the plant. It was very clear that he was driven to succeed and that excuses

were not acceptable. He would let you know this with a voice that carried to the furthest reaches of the plant. One early lesson that has stayed with me is his emphasis on a person's character. 'Find someone who has integrity, work ethic, and a practical business mind and set him free to work.' "[66]

Ebeid later described his time at Carleton as his "seven-year management training program" and thanked the people at that plant who "bore the trials and tribulations of that period."[67] Even with his schooling at Carleton, selecting and leading a team to open the frontier for Guardian in California was still a daunting task. That was a major leap, remembered Ebeid, who relocated to Kingsburg to organize the effort while the plant was being built by Guardian's team of engineers. "It was like the mother kicked the kid out saying,

In 1978, in the heart of California's grape country, Guardian launched its second float glass plant. The Kingsburg facility provided glass to the construction industry in the western United States.

'You're going to college. And don't come home till you graduate,' " Ebeid said.[68]

The challenges facing this group were both familiar and unknown. Building a major float glass plant is never easy, and Kingsburg presented a unique set of complexities. The project leadership—Dennis Arnold, David Rose, and Frank Wilhelm—had to relocate to California some 2,200 miles from Guardian's home base and its established vendors and contractors. They needed to find and select new sources of equipment, materials, and construction capability and to create an infrastructure for the plant. The regulatory and governmental issues involved in building a manufacturing facility in the heart of California's agricultural and wine growing region were also immense. As Alonzo recalled, "Our construction of the Kingsburg plant was of real concern to the community. This was prosperous farm country and they did not want a big smokestack belching pollution into the air. We had to appear at hearings to persuade the people that Guardian was going to be a good neighbor. We offered to put the most advanced anti-pollution equipment on the smokestack, which allowed us to

make the stack much smaller and to dramatically reduce emissions. In the end, they believed us, and things worked out well for Guardian and the community. We have had an outstanding environmental record at the Kingsburg plant ever since."[69]

As Sczesny recalled, "The Kingsburg plant construction and launch was like a relay race. While Alonzo and his engineering staff were building the plant, Russ was putting together and training his team to run it. When the launch came, Russ and his people took over without a hitch. The 'pass' was

---

The first glass comes off the new float line at the Kingsburg, California, plant in 1978. Because the weight of glass made it expensive to ship, Guardian was unable to economically supply the western states before this plant was built.

perfect."[70] Kingsburg was "the most orderly start-up to date."[71] When the Kingsburg plant was finally finished, Ebeid experienced a sense of pride and accomplishment that overshadowed even the Carleton experience. At Carleton, he had been so engrossed in making sure the mechanics of the float line were in place that he missed the first ribbon of glass. By contrast, at Kingsburg, when the first ribbon of glass rolled down the line, he and the team cheered and nearly wept with pride. "We were like proud papas," Ebeid recalled.[72]

Moreover, Ebeid and his crew could benefit from the lessons learned at Carleton. As he would later recall:

Many of the key strands of the Guardian Way were created at Carleton during the early years, but we made our share of mistakes there as well. We had

With the opening of its Kingsburg facility, Guardian expanded its North American glass business and became more accessible to West Coast customers. Shown here is a law office in Wichita, Kansas.

proceeded on a trial and error basis. There was no "how to" handbook with magical formulas for success. Now we were experienced, and had in Kingsburg a brand-new plant to try a second generation of ideas.[73]

At the same time, California was culturally unfamiliar to the Midwesterners. Not only did California operate in a different legislative environment, but the labor force in the San Joachim Valley was also much more culturally diverse than Guardian's typical labor force. Indeed, it was the perfect opportunity for Guardian to see whether the Guardian Way was a product of the Midwest or whether it was exportable.

"Not only was it a new process; it was, in effect, a brand-new business," Ebeid remembered. "And that was exciting."[74]

Guardian was confident it could prevail in the new circumstances. During the construction and launch of the plant, the company drew heavily on the experienced cadre of managers that traveled with Ebeid to California, including Chuck Croskey as production manager. Croskey was a graduate of the General Motors Institute in industrial engineering and had a law degree from the University of Detroit. He started at Carleton as maintenance engineer in 1971 and was promoted to superintendent of fabrication in 1976.[75] He later became plant manager at Kingsburg after Ebeid had assumed additional responsibilities within the Glass Group.

In Kingsburg, the group of employees invented as they went. They lived in one big apartment building that operated like a barracks, forcing a closeness that few experience in their working lives. Perhaps because of this, the Kingsburg group was extraordinarily effective and, in turn, extremely influential. Many in this first generation of Kingsburg leadership, such as Croskey, Jim Moore, Dave Ford, Dave Rose, Tom Wunderlich, Bill Valk, and Mike Gluckstein, went on to play significant roles in the 1980s and 1990s at plants and facilities across the globe, while five from this group and the next generation behind it went on to become a Guardian global "Employee of the Year," an enormous accomplishment. And Ebeid himself would eventually run Guardian's Glass Group and be a director of the company.[76] All of these individuals, and many others, were living examples of Guardian's enduring belief in providing opportunity for personal and professional growth to those who have the initiative, drive, and courage to reach for it.

Ebeid's style, carried over from Carleton, had a powerful impact on establishing the culture at Kingsburg. As fellow executive Bill Black described him in *Guardian World*:

Russ is a shirtsleeve, hands-on manager, a team developer and delegator. He is very practical, spends a lot of time on the floor. He communicates well with the entire staff and is respected for his leadership.[77]

To say that Kingsburg was a success would be an understatement. The plant's float line boasted a capacity of 500 tons of glass a day, boosting Guardian's total glassmaking capacity to 1,450 tons daily.[78] After just one full month of production, the plant was profitable." What was even more astonishing, the plant was paid for in less than two years. "It was like printing money," said Alonzo.[79]

"Customers loved us," Ebeid said. "We had great quality. The success of the Kingsburg plant was, in effect, the shot heard round the world. Guardian, a small company, had built a plant 2,200 miles away [from its headquarters], and the thing was gangbusters. It broke the myth of centralization. Bill [Davidson] said it was the best plant in the world, and it probably was. We were making all the products. The quality was superb. Pricing was fantastic. Profitability was great. All this gave Guardian tremendous confidence."[80]

Onward to Corsicana

Just as the Kingsburg plant was beginning production, Guardian announced plans to build its third float plant (and fourth line), in Corsicana, Texas, 50 miles south of Dallas. The plant, which would be completed in 1980, was designed to serve the Sun Belt states of the South and Southwest. Construction was booming in the region, making it the fastest-growing market for glass.[81]

Wally Palma was named manager of the Corsicana plant at the age of 36. He was later joined by Jay Waite, who headed up sales for the region. Palma had begun working at the Carleton plant in 1970 as a maintenance engineer and later became plant engineer and fabrication manager.[82]

When he moved to Corsicana, he selected a team that would include several people who eventually became plant managers of future Guardian facilities, including George Longo (plant engineer), Bob Edwards (production manager), Steve Hare (personnel director), and Tim Morrow (sales manager). Construction of the plant was under the direction of Alonzo and a team of his engineers, including Howard Benedict and Ajit Vashi, both of whom had been hired by Palma when he was Carleton's plant engineer. Guardian often trained its employees in established plants, then cut them loose in

The Corsicana, Texas, plant, completed in 1980, was the third float plant for Guardian Industries. The Sun Belt area was booming, making the region the fastest-growing market for glass.

new plants, where they had the authority and responsibility to develop as managers.

For some new employees, like Vashi, a recent expatriate of India, Guardian was initially a shock. "Wally Palma was the manager, and he offered me a job," Vashi remembered in 2001.

He got up, shook hands with me, and said, "All right. We'll see you in a few days." But I was sitting there telling myself I didn't have an appointment letter. Nothing was in writing. Without being impolite, I said, "You know, I recently migrated to the United States, and if you would be kind enough to give me an appointment letter, it would serve as a memento for me for years." He just stared at me, then had his secretary do one.

When I told this story to my relatives, they were astonished. They said, "Are you sure you joined the right company?" I just answered that we'll find out. That was my first taste of no bureaucracy, mutual trust, and concluding things with a handshake.[83]

Like most new manufacturing operations, the opening of Corsicana presented some surprises, as Lu Rimar, a former engineer with PPG who joined Guardian in 1980 as hot end superintendent at Corsicana, remembered:

We had a lot of challenges, including one where we lost the whole tin bath in about four hours. It was something that not too many people have seen. The problem, as we found out, is you cannot just take that leaked tin and cut it with a torch. We're talking 180 tons of tin in the basement. So you can't cut it with a torch because it just melts and heals up, like in one of those science fiction movies. We had to do it with jackhammers, but in nine days, we were back in operation. In nine days, we managed to get all the tin out and put it back in the tin bath and heat it up, and we pulled a ribbon of glass.[84]

Start-up challenges wouldn't stop Corsicana from becoming another hugely successful operation. Shortly after its start-up, the plant was producing approximately 550 tons of glass per day, boosting Guardian's glass production by 33 percent.[85] Much of the plant's glass was sold to mirror manufacturers, which required the highest-quality glass.[86]

Three years after the Coriscana plant opened, Guardian added a coating line there.[87] The new line expanded the company's coated glass products to include low-emissivity, or low-E, glass. This type of glass had a transparent metal coating that reflected long-wave radiation, helping buildings retain heat. It was used primarily in northern climates

Opposite: The Corsicana, Texas, plant opened in November 1980 to supply flat glass to the Sun Belt states from Arizona to Florida.

Above: Wally Palma was manager of the Corsicana, Texas, plant. The plant was Guardian's third float glass plant and fourth float line. With its construction, Guardian became one of the leading glassmakers in the United States.

Right: By the early 1980s, Guardian had become a major force in the U.S. commercial glass industry, providing coated glass for many large-scale projects such as the Emery Chemicals building, shown here, in Cincinnati, Ohio.

to conserve heat in cold weather and had been sold in Europe for several years. Guardian was one of the first companies to market it in the United States.[88]

Besides adding new tempering furnaces at Kingsburg and Corsicana, Guardian added new furnaces at Carleton in 1978 and at Fort Lauderdale in 1980. The newest furnaces gave Guardian the ability to temper glass for residential applications as well as for boat and recreational windows, thus opening up new markets.[89]

The Next Frontier Beckons

With major float plants in Carleton, Kingsburg, and Corsicana, Guardian had proved its mettle in the glass industry. It was a much more powerful company than it had been 10 years earlier. During the 1970s, sales increased at a compound rate of 22 percent and earnings at a compound rate of 26 percent.[90] By 1979, sales had grown to $280 million, some seven times the amount at the start of the decade.[91] The company had decreased its reliance on the auto industry and expanded into the architectural market as a supplier of raw glass and value-added products. By 1979, 75 percent of Guardian's glass sales were in the architectural market.

Guardian had established itself as the low-cost producer within each of its major businesses. It achieved this goal by building and maintaining modern plants and equipment. In 1980, 70 percent of the company's plants and equipment were less than five years old. Its lean and flat management structure allowed plant managers to respond to marketing and production needs quickly, without seeking approval from upper management. Giving plant managers the authority to run the day-to-day operations of their facilities left senior management with the time to engage in developing new opportunities for expansion.[92]

In fact, the company's intense focus on pushing decision making to people closest to the business and the customer had created a model that Guardian senior executives thought would succeed anywhere. History was on their side. In Carleton, the company had shouldered its way into the cloistered world of float glass manufacturers. Opening in Kingsburg, all the way across the country from Carleton, had been like moving into a new world

These shipping containers were filled with Guardian glass for sale overseas. Although Guardian was shipping glass overseas, the company remained convinced it could also export its glassmaking expertise, thus opening huge new markets.

with a different culture and different environment. By the time Corsicana opened, Guardian felt it had mastered the challenge of entering domestic markets. The company had proved that it could and would be a major player in the U.S. glass market.

This track record raised the obvious question of whether Guardian could be a major global glassmaker. The challenges were enormous. Everything that had worked for Guardian had been tested only in North America, and the company was a distinctly American enterprise with distinctly American leaders and ideas. The paradigm of self-empowered managers making their own business decisions and being held accountable for them was not widespread in the 1970s, although it was already deeply embedded in the Guardian culture. Then there were the obvious challenges of customs, traditions, labor relations, regulatory environments and tax structures, purchasing of necessary materials, and a myriad of other concerns.

Yet Davidson was confident of both Guardian's business model and its capabilities, and the search began for an overseas location. The company wanted to build its first plant in Europe. It hoped to find a location central to European manufacturing and with favorable export/import and taxation structures. After much consideration, Guardian made its choice and in 1979 launched an ambitious project to build a float glass plant in Luxembourg to supply the European glass industry. The plan was full of risk but also held the promise of great rewards. As Alonzo recalled, "We could see this gold mine over there, and we wanted to go over and get it."[93]

The interior of the Villosa plant in Spain. Throughout the 1980s, Guardian moved aggressively overseas, adding this giant complex to its string of new float plants.

CHAPTER FIVE

GROWING GUARDIAN

We really broke the sales paradigms over there.

—Russ Ebeid, on Guardian's entry into Europe

THE 1980s FOR GUARDIAN BEGAN with what Bill Davidson considers the "second most momentous event in the company's history after the construction of Carleton—the building of its first overseas float glass plant in Europe, located in the Grand Duchy of Luxembourg."[1]

Using its success in Luxembourg as a springboard, Guardian next acquired and modernized a major established glassmaker in northern Spain—a transaction that confronted Guardian with many challenges but also resulted in significant new capabilities. During this period, Guardian began to develop a cadre of administrative and operational talent with the sophistication and ability to direct and staff expansion into new regions and businesses. The company was thus positioned from an organizational and staffing point of view to diversify and expand in the 1980s on several fronts simultaneously.

Some of these efforts were experiments with only short-term importance, while others—expansion geographically into new float glass and downstream operations, continued growth in the North American glass business, new emphasis on the OEM automotive business, and the beginning of focused growth in the company's fiberglass insulation business—would have permanent significance. It is no coincidence that Davidson decided at this time to take the company private, a step that corresponded perfectly with the Guardian entrepreneurial culture that had developed over the many years of his leadership. As the company's success and confidence surged toward the end of the 1980s, Guardian would begin to venture into markets where even its far more established competitors had not yet dared to enter.

Becoming a European Glassmaker

Guardian's invasion of Europe was led by people who had limited international experience. They were, however, possessed of great energy, an eagerness to learn and succeed, and deep confidence in the Guardian business philosophy that had been developed and tested in the United States. Looking with hindsight at the company's seemingly effortless march through Europe, one can easily underestimate the unique challenges faced and overcome by Guardian. As Russ Ebeid later commented, "We didn't know enough to realize the scope and extent of the hurdles we would have to jump over."[2]

The most obvious one was the competitive situation. The glass industry in Europe on the eve of

With a strong foothold established in the United States, Bill Davidson turned his focus to global markets.

Guardian's entry was dominated by a very small number of well-known, financially strong, and deeply entrenched manufacturers. France's Saint-Gobain, in business continuously for some 300 years, was Europe's largest glassmaker. It had been established to make glass for the Palace of Versailles. Pilkington, the creator of the float glass process, was formed as Saint Helens Crown Glass Company in 1826.[3] It dominated the production and sale of glass in the United Kingdom and exerted significant influence over the industry as a whole through its intellectual property licensing system. Pilkington would spare no effort and expense to try to keep Guardian out of Europe.

In 1979, BSN-Gervais Danone, the other long-established glass company, abandoned the flat glass industry, putting a third of the continent's glassmaking capacity up for sale. Pilkington, joined by the U.S. giant PPG Industries and Japan's dominant manufacturer, Asahi Glass, purchased and divided up BSN's European operations.[4] While the entry of PPG and Asahi did shake up the established European order to some extent, these two companies were major licensees of Pilkington and had shown no inclination anywhere else to challenge the status quo. It took Guardian's appearance in the European market to precipitate "the collapse of the cozy arrangements of the past."[5]

The established glassmakers dominated the European market by selling almost exclusively through a limited number of powerful wholesalers. Fabricators and end users of float glass had virtually no access to the manufacturers and had relatively limited options among wholesalers. This stratification of the channels of distribution, combined with the tendency of the glass manufacturers to keep out of the "backyards" of their competitors, limited price competition and allowed the manufacturers and their favored wholesalers to control the market.[6] Guardian would ultimately have to devise ways to bypass the established network of wholesalers and create its own means of access to European customers.

There were innumerable challenges aside from the power and hostility of entrenched competitors and the closed structure of the market. In coming to Europe, Guardian also would be faced with the difficulties of managing a construction project some 4,000 miles from its home base and established suppliers, assimilating expatriates during the construction phase and actual operation of the new European plant, learning about product requirements and customer needs that differed sharply from those prevailing in the United States, and adjusting to the markedly different labor situation in Europe.

A New Home in Luxembourg

Guardian's selection of the Grand Duchy of Luxembourg as the site of its first European float plant was a carefully considered and, as it turned out, extremely farsighted decision. Luxembourg's central location between Belgium, France, and Germany gave it ready access to Europe's most important glass markets. Because Luxembourg itself had a population at the time of only some 340,000 people and was the size of a typical county in the United States, Guardian immediately focused on being a European supplier as opposed to being dependent on the market of any one country. As Russ Ebeid later remarked, Guardian was "not in Luxembourg to service the domestic market. Even before the economic borders actually disappeared in Western Europe, Guardian was already learning how to operate in a borderless environment and to view Europe as a single region."[7]

Luxembourg also was attractive because of its inviting business climate. While primarily an agricultural country, Luxembourg had once been a leading producer of steel and iron. When those industries declined, Luxembourg was eager to replace them with new manufacturing capability, and the government welcomed overseas investment.[8]

"The Luxembourg government was, if I may say so, intelligent enough to offer its help," commented Robert Goebbels, who later became Luxembourg minister of the economy and a member of the European Parliament. "We provided Guardian with appropriate industrial and state aid. In addition, we have a small government, a small state, and can be responsive to the legitimate needs of business."[9]

Davidson agreed with this assessment. "One reason we picked Luxembourg is that in a smaller country we knew we could get the attention of government decision-makers to get things done," he said. "We have never had to suffer with the kinds of bureaucracy you find in other countries."[10]

Guardian entered Luxembourg (and Europe) as the majority owner of Luxguard, as the new

Left: Bill Davidson laid the cornerstone for Guardian's new facility, Luxguard, on June 25, 1980. Luxguard was a joint venture, with Guardian owning a controlling interest.

Right: In the staging area, trucks are loaded for shipping to western European glass markets such as Germany and the Netherlands.

Below: The Luxembourg float glass plant was Guardian's first in Europe, setting the stage for worldwide expansion. The plant was a near exact replica of Guardian's Kingsburg and Corsicana plants, producing 500 tons of glass a day.

At the Luxembourg float glass plant in Bascharage, sophisticated computer controls require monitoring by only a few highly trained operators. Cultural differences, from dress and work hours to customer relations, initially made the expansion into Europe challenging.

company was then called. Its partner in the venture was Ferdinand Kohn, a prominent Luxembourg businessman and a major distributor and fabricator of glass throughout Europe. The new float plant, located in Bascharage, Luxembourg, was announced during the summer of 1979, and construction began the following year.

With majority ownership in the new company, Guardian was free to build the way it saw fit, and in true Guardian style, it turned to Howard Benedict as project manager. Benedict was young (only 29 years old) and had never directed a construction job of this magnitude before. While working at the Carleton plant and as a project engineer for the

Kingsburg and Corsicana construction projects, however, Benedict had earned the trust of senior management, including Dick Alonzo and Bill Davidson. "I believe I was the first expatriate employee from Guardian," Benedict said. "I was given the responsibility to set up all the engineering using the metric dimensioning system, with new contractors and many new equipment suppliers, different construction codes, the complication of working with a joint venture partner—and all this in a different language. It was incredible, and I'm sure they took a flying leap on that one and had their fingers crossed the whole time, as I did."[11]

Fortunately, the construction came together as planned, and Guardian moved on to the next step: staffing the plant and creating a new culture. The culture question, in fact, was one of the most important aspects of the new plant. Would Luxguard operate like a European glassmaker? Or would it operate like Guardian Industries? Davidson remembered the struggle:

When we went to Europe, we had a Luxembourg partner, and we had long discussions about what our operating philosophy should be. Was the business going to be run along traditional European lines or were we going to export the operating system that had served us so well in the United States? For the first six months or so, the issue kind of hung in the balance. I finally made up my mind: we were going to bring the Guardian system to Europe, but do it in a way that allowed for local culture and local capabilities to make us even stronger.[12]

The launch of Luxguard took place in November 1981. As had become the custom at Guardian, the start-up was accomplished through the combined efforts of the local workforce and experienced float operators from Carleton, Kingsburg, and Corsicana. In addition to the temporary staffing of the start-up, a small number of U.S. trained managers and technicians moved to Luxembourg at this time as expatriates to assume leadership roles within the plant. These individuals included the first plant manager, Dean Wiley, who was quickly succeeded by Jim Moore; David Ford in sales; Mike Gluckstein in finance; and Lu Rimar on the technical side. This team was instrumental in bringing the Guardian Way to a plant that had only a handful of people familiar

with glass manufacturing and even fewer familiar with Guardian's unique operating system.

Leading the charge was Moore, just 30 years old in 1981 when he arrived in Luxembourg. He had been a shift superintendent at the Kingsburg plant for three years when he was asked to take a "temporary" assignment in Luxembourg as production manager. Not long after arriving, Moore became plant manager and later managing director for Europe. He would end up living in Europe for some 11 years. Ford joined Guardian in 1971 at the age of 18 as an inventory control clerk with the Washington, D.C., distribution center. He possessed a natural affinity with customers and quickly moved into sales. He worked at a number of Guardian locations in the 1970s, including the Carleton, Kingsburg, and Corsicana float glass plants, until Russ Ebeid asked him to work on sales opportunities in Europe.[13]

In bringing the Guardian Way to the new Luxembourg plant, Moore's team had to be sensitive to the differences in relations between management and labor that generally prevailed in Europe. He was confronted with a workforce that would inevitably be organized into unions, protected by strict laws governing layoffs, firing, retirement, healthcare, and other aspects of the employment contract, and that was accustomed to a more distant relationship between managers and the workers on the factory floor.

The Guardian operating system as it had developed in Carleton and Kingsburg stressed the elimination of barriers between management and the shop floor, direct communication, and individual responsibility and accountability. As it turned out, these features would be embraced in Luxembourg and the rest of Europe, but they could only be introduced with care and with due recognition of the need to adapt to local cultural and social conditions.

Moore and his team were aware that they could not

Jim Moore was a shift superintendent at the Kingsburg plant before becoming Luxguard's production manager. He soon became managing director for Europe.

bludgeon the company's new employees with their distinctly North American Guardian Way. Guardian wanted to show its European employees the possibilities of working in a new and exciting environment, for a company that intended to break the rules in Europe as it had in America. In a careful process of give-and-take, Guardian learned how to function as a European company while a European workforce learned how to function as Guardian employees. Moore remembered some of the challenges:

> *If an American walked in and said, "This is the way we do it in America," the European workers and even managers would just shut down. What I realized over time was that the fundamentals of the Guardian system were inherently attractive and that people would come to recognize this on their own. Rather than have us ram things down workers' throats, which would always be counterproductive, we needed to give the workers the opportunity to see for themselves that our approach was valid. We explained why we did things, and they were much more ready to listen. And we also adjusted to how things needed to be done in Luxembourg, even if somewhat different from Carleton or Kingsburg. What I also learned from experience was that you've got to fight the big battles and not worry about the little ones. In the end the Guardian system of operation was adopted without a big battle because we demonstrated why this had been successful. Of course, some things, such as our fanatical stress on safety, are perfectly well understood in any cultural setting, and required no special explanation or persuasion.[14]*

During its first year of operation, Luxguard achieved its production goals while its workforce struggled to learn how to make high-quality glass. Early technical problems were addressed quickly with the help of Guardian's experienced operators, including Lu Rimar. Born in Czechoslovakia, he had worked for a time in Guardian's Corsicana plant but left Guardian to work at PPG. He readily accepted Ebeid's offer to return to Europe and help the effort in Luxembourg.

"When I got there, it seemed that the people didn't have enough training," Rimar remembered. "They were sent for training to Kingsburg. Of all the places Guardian had, Kingsburg was perhaps not the best place to train people because Kingsburg was, quite honestly, nearly perfect. People could not learn troubleshooting because there was nothing to troubleshoot."[15]

At Luxguard, Rimar made some changes in the basic setup of the tin bath, which immediately solved a recurring problem of broken ribbons. From there, the plant made other incremental improvements, moving machinery and tweaking the line. Before long, Luxguard had achieved stability.

From the outset of production, the plant had to adjust to the demands of the European market for so-called jumbo-sized glass lites, which required special cutting and transportation equipment. Within a year of the launch, under the leadership of Moore and sales manager Ford, Luxguard glass was being exported to some 10 countries, including France, Germany, England, Belgium, and Italy. Its workforce was equally multinational, with representation by 10 different nationalities and numerous languages.[16]

A principal reason for Guardian's rapid penetration of the European market was its "high-touch" customer service—something new to many European customers.[17] Traditionally more class conscious, European corporations often maintained strict walls between labor and management and between insiders and outsiders. It was very uncommon, for example, for a European company president or plant manager to meet with a customer. For Guardian, however, it was second nature. "We really broke the sales paradigms over there," said Ebeid. "We'd visit potential customers, and they'd tell us, 'You know, the boss of your competitor is three blocks away from here. I've never met him, and you're coming to visit me from America?' They were just incredulous."[18]

Right: David Ford joined Guardian in 1971 at the age of 18. He worked at a number of Guardian locations until he was asked to work on sales opportunities in Europe. He worked in Europe for 15 years until his untimely death in 1996.

Opposite: The Messe Tower in Frankfurt, Germany, used Guardian's architectural glass products.

Many customers saw Guardian as liberating them from reliance on a tightly knit group of float glass suppliers such as Glaverbel and Saint-Gobain, which also competed with them in downstream fabrication. Guardian provided wide-open competition that benefitted rather than threatened or stifled its customers. Franky Simoens, owner of a glass fabrication business in Belgium, recalled Guardian's management "followed the same philosophy as most independent companies. They knew the industry well and they knew the needs of their customers. So Guardian and its customers actually strengthened one another."[19]

The Guardian operating system which focused on direct and mutually supportive contact between the plant and downstream customers had arrived and was beginning to take hold.

Problems with Pilkington

European customers may have welcomed Guardian, but its competitors weren't so enthusiastic. In 1980, as Luxguard was under construction, Pilkington sued Guardian, alleging that Luxguard's use of float glass technology constituted patent and trade secret infringement.[20] Pilkington claimed that Guardian's entry into Europe—its home turf—required a new licensing agreement. "They were really stretching things in their effort to keep us out of Europe," said Alonzo:

They claimed that Guardian was infringing on their float glass patents and simultaneously violating trade secrets that supposedly taught how to use the patents. This was quite a reach; ordinarily a company asserts one or the other, not both. Patentable technology is supposed to teach everyone else how to use the invention, once the patent expires. That's why you're handed a patent. But they were saying they also had trade secrets.[21]

This case was the first of a series of lawsuits brought by Pilkington against Guardian in Europe and the United States.

Some possible insight into Pilkington's reaction to Guardian was provided many years later by Paolo Scaroni, who became CEO of Pilkington in 1997. During an interview Scaroni gave with the trade journal, *U.S. Glass*, the reporter mentioned Guardian,

remarking, "Many people tell me that the European manufacturers had no clue how to respond to Guardian when it began growing outside the United States... that they were in shock." Scaroni's answer was complimentary to Guardian but also highlighted the uneven nature of the European "club" members' response:

Saint-Gobain reacted to the Guardian shock much more quickly than Pilkington did. Saint-Gobain started benchmarking itself against Guardian earlier. They learned their lesson in the 1980s and 1990s. Pilkington watched the Guardian revolution and thought they could find other ways around it.[22]

Litigation was evidently one of the "other ways" of coping with the competitive challenges that Guardian posed to the old methods of doing business.

Guardian and Pilkington finally achieved a worldwide out of court settlement in 1986, on terms that never affected Guardian's rapid growth in Europe. In fact, while the litigation was ongoing, Guardian was ready to expand its Luxguard plant. In 1983, the plant grew by 120,000 square feet, adding a coating machine and tempering furnace for the production of value-added glass products. The state-of-the-art coating machine had a capacity of 18 million square feet of glass annually.[23]

Investing in Spain

In Luxguard, Guardian had proven that the Guardian Way was indeed exportable, that the company could take its operating system, its technology, and its business philosophy into even the toughest markets and succeed. It was a defining moment for the U.S.-based glassmaker. From the early 1980s on, Guardian would keep one eye glued to the world market, looking for new opportunities.

Indeed, even before the Luxguard launch in November 1981, Guardian was already investigating business opportunities in Spain. At that time, Spain was not an obvious choice for investment and expansion. The dictatorship of Gen. Francisco Franco had just recently ended with his death in 1975, and Spain was still in the early stages of embracing democratic values and practices. It was not yet enjoying the economic boom times or political stability that would come later. Many observers regarded Spain as a backwater of Europe; its entry into the European Community (later called the European Union) would not occur for five years.

Despite this, Guardian's leaders, in particular Executive Vice President Tom Gaffney, saw great potential on the Iberian Peninsula. Gaffney had spent years as a student in Spain, was conversant in Spanish, and had cultivated business contacts in that country.[24] In 1982, Guardian hoped to establish a foothold in Spain by buying two subsidiaries of Spanish glassmaker S.A. Financiera Alavesa ("Safina"), but talks between Guardian and the Spanish principals—Carlos and Alvaro Delclaux—broke off. While Gaffney continued to believe in post-Franco Spain as a great opportunity for Guardian, "he insisted on doing a deal that would be financially advantageous for us and that would allow Guardian

to be in control," said Jeff Knight, corporate controller and chief accounting officer.[25] With Spain momentarily on the back burner, Guardian aggressively pursued possible expansion elsewhere in Europe, coming very close to initiating float plant projects in Switzerland and Austria.

Ultimately, Safina invited Guardian back to the bargaining table in 1983 because of its deteriorating financial situation and need for technical help to reorganize its facilities and convert to modern float technology. Gaffney and the Delclaux brothers reached an agreement the following year under

On the Villosa, Spain, patterned line, molten glass is pulled through a metal roller, creating a desired pattern. In Guardian's unique glassmaking process, the flame is located over the product rather than under it.

which Guardian made an investment of $15 million in Vidierias de Llodio (translated as Glassmaker of Llodio, or Villosa for short), a subsidiary of Safina, which resulted in Guardian acquiring 48 percent of the stock of Villosa, along with an option to purchase the remaining shares. As part of this transaction, Delclaux Y Cia, the distribution arm of the Delclaux glass business with a network of warehouses throughout Spain, was reorganized as a wholly owned subsidiary of Villosa. The structuring of Guardian's investment allowed it to take advantage of what it saw as tremendous long-term potential for Spain while reducing its risk in the short term. Only after it had the opportunity to see if Villosa would be successful under its direction would Guardian be faced with the decision of whether or not to make a larger investment.

Located near the industrial city of Bilbao in the Spanish Basque region, Villosa had a long and proud history as a glassmaker. The company had originally been founded as a glass wholesaler in 1891 by members of the Delclaux family. In 1934, it began manufacturing sheet glass using the Fourcault process and in later decades expanded into the production of patterned glass, architectural and automotive tempered glass, mirrors, insulating units, non-glare glass, and silkscreened glass. By the time Guardian purchased its interest in 1984, the Villosa complex occupied over a million square feet and employed about 1,600 people, many with great experience in virtually every aspect of glassmaking.[26]

While Villosa was Spain's second-largest glass manufacturer[27] and had highly experienced and talented glassmakers within its ranks, by 1984 it was in serious need of capital, organizational improvements, and a technical makeover if it was to survive in the increasingly open Spanish economy. A disastrous flood in the Llodio area had caused considerable damage, although the workforce responded with magnificent energy and dedication to avert a potential catastrophe. After the joint venture was signed, Villosa used Guardian's $15 million investment to begin the immediate conversion of the sheet

Above: Guardian invested in Spanish glassmaker Villosa in 1984, purchasing it outright in 1986. Guardian added a new 500-ton float line in August 1985. The investment in Spain turned out to be enormously successful for Guardian.

Right: Plant Manager Alberto Subinas christens the new float line at Guardian's Villosa facility on August 7, 1985. Located in northern Spain, the facility also produced patterned, laminated, tempered, and nonglare picture frame glass as well as mirrors and automotive products.

Guardian recognized that Europe was a huge market for its architectural glass and looked to produce glass for local markets and projects. The glass used in the Guggenheim Museum in Bilbao, Spain, for example, was produced by Guardian.

plant to the float process.[28] The rest of the funds at this stage came from loans and grants, including some flood-relief incentives. Conversion to the float process was essential if Villosa was to compete successfully with French glassmaker Saint-Gobain, which dominated the Spanish market. The conversion took about 14 months and required Guardian's engineers, including Gary Cook and Fred Hartway, assisted by Villosa personnel, to overcome serious difficulties presented by the complexity and topography of the existing facility, including the need to accommodate the line to differing elevations within the plant.[29]

The new 500-ton float line began production in August 1985. While Guardian veterans David Rose and Mike Gluckstein provided on-site operational and financial expertise for a time, the plant was soon run entirely by local managers under the leadership of Alberto Subinas and Jesus Abrisqueta. In 1986, assured that the float conversion was successful

and comfortable with its business prospects, Guardian exercised its option and purchased the remaining 52 percent of Villosa, although Carlos and Alvaro Delclaux continued to provide service to the company.[30] Within a year of the float line's launch, Villosa started a major expansion of its fabricating operations, especially its OEM and replacement automotive glass business.

Guardian's investment in Spain would turn out to be enormously successful. The combination of Villosa's skilled and experienced glassmakers with Guardian's capital resources and operating philosophy created a formidable presence on the

Iberian Peninsula. The new company was perfectly positioned to take advantage of Spain's booming economy as it entered the European Union. This success would lead to significant additional investments in Spain by Guardian in later years.

Foundation for European Expansion

With the acquisition and conversion of Villosa to the float process, Guardian was now the world's sixth-largest glassmaker.[31] Looking forward to future expansion in Europe, Guardian established a European headquarters in Luxembourg in 1986. Moore, Luxguard's plant manager, was designated to lead the company's European operations as managing director; Ford was named director of sales; and Mike Gluckstein became financial director.[32] At around the same time, Guardian Europe established a separate engineering company based in Luxembourg, called CRVC, which would have primary responsibility for future construction projects in Europe and eventually the Middle East. Howard Benedict was named the first managing director of CRVC and Lu Rimar was appointed technical director.

Staffing a World-Class Organization

As Guardian expanded both within the United States and internationally, it became necessary to further elevate the scope and capabilities of the staff functions performed at its headquarters. While Guardian's culture continued to emphasize that business decisions should be driven down as close to the factory floor and customer as possible, it was becoming increasingly apparent that certain functions and capabilities needed to be introduced and coordinated by people with a high level of technical sophistication and a more global perspective. During the early 1980s, a number of new people were recruited while other company veterans were given additional responsibilities.

Tom Gaffney was especially committed to building a highly professional administrative operation at Guardian. In 1981, he promoted Jeff Knight to the position of corporate controller and chief accounting officer. During the 1970s, Knight had worked as a CPA on the Guardian account for the company's independent auditor, Coopers & Lybrand. He then joined Guardian in 1977 and became assistant con-

Right: Jeff Knight joined Guardian as an accountant and modernized the company's management information systems and financial reporting. He later became chief financial officer.

Below: Paul Rappaport joined Guardian in 1983 as tax counsel and manager of the company's tax department. He is credited for building a world-class organization.

troller in 1979. As Knight recalled his decision to leave Coopers and cast his lot with Guardian: "People wanted to be associated with Guardian because it was a winner and a fun place to be. It was aggressive, hard charging, and treated people well."[33]

During the early 1980s, Knight assumed responsibility for modernizing the company's management information systems and financial reporting. He also became heavily involved in the acquisition and diversification efforts initiated by Gaffney. In 1984, at the age of 33, Knight was appointed Guardian's chief financial officer.

Another key hire was made during this period when Paul Rappaport was recruited in 1983 as tax counsel and manager of Guardian's tax department. It was becoming increasingly clear that the company's tax department was basically geared to performing domestic compliance duties and that going forward, Guardian would need a tax staff that could handle more diverse and sophisticated tasks. As Rappaport recalled, "I was hired to introduce a new level of capability and experience to Guardian. We needed a department filled with people who could deliver comprehensive planning, compliance, audit, and litigation management for the kind of multistate, multi-national, multiindustry company that Guardian intended to become and was, in fact, in the process of becoming."[34]

Rappaport immediately took charge and in a remarkably short time built a world-class organization noted for its sophisticated and creative inter-

national planning and its aggressiveness in protecting Guardian's interests.[35]

One of his first steps was to recruit Gary Greene from Cincinnati Milicron as international tax manager. Years later, Greene would serve as an assistant vice president and head up the day-to-day functioning of the tax group.

During Gaffney's tenure, other individuals were recruited to Guardian to introduce new competencies and enhance existing ones. Richard Griffin was appointed corporate treasurer and held the position until he became chief operating officer of Continental Mortgage Investors, a Guardian affiliate. His successor was Wallace Rueckel, who came to Guardian in 1984 from the Sunstrand Corporation, where he had been assistant treasurer. While Griffin and Rueckel would both leave Guardian by the early 1990s, they built the foundation for a well-respected global treasury function. Similarly, Alan Schlang joined Guardian from Burroughs Corporation in 1983 to drive the formation of an inhouse legal function. As Knight recalled, "All these people came to positions of responsibility at a time when Guardian sorely needed

high caliber, professional expertise to support our domestic and international growth."[36]

While Guardian was bringing new people and expertise into the organization to prepare for future growth, Ken Battjes, its director of personnel, continued to launch innovative programs that enhanced the well-being of all Guardian employees. In addition to his prior emphasis on safety and benefits, Battjes at this time became the company's most outspoken advocate for physical fitness and health maintenance.

"HealthGuard" began as a formal program in 1983, with employees from all facilities competing for recognition as leaders in exercise and healthy living. The "President's Award" and "Winners Circle" became ways to recognize employees who excelled

Demonstrating its commitment to employees, Guardian created HealthGuard, through which employees from all facilities competed for recognition as leaders in exercise and healthy living. A full-time health promotion manager was hired, and each plant was encouraged to institute its own internal program.

in competition and in sound health practices. This inhouse health program was an extension of Davidson's longtime belief both in the virtues of competition and in the proposition that Guardian should support its employees in every way possible. Company health programs would become more common in the coming years, and Guardian was a recognized leader in the area.

Continued North American Glass Expansion

By the close of 1981, Guardian had five float lines worldwide supplying its own fabrication facilities as well as some 1,000 customers in the architectural and automotive markets. Its revenues for 1981 were about $365 million—with glass manufacturing and architectural glass accounting for about 75 percent of the total.[37] While Guardian was exporting its glass manufacturing expertise and business philosophy across the Atlantic, the company also remained focused on domestic growth.

To bolster its North American glass operations, Guardian made several acquisitions in the early 1980s. The first came in 1982 when it purchased the Airco coating facility located across from its plant at Carleton. Reflective glass was becoming an increasingly important market as companies realized how much energy it saved. Guardian's reflective glass sales skyrocketed to close to $30 million by 1982.[38] Davidson described Guardian's coating strategy:

Our plans are to expand in the reflective glass area to solidify our leadership position in this burgeoning market. The purchase of the Airco facility is an important first step toward this objective.

Guardian purchased the Airco coating facility in 1982. Researchers used a vacuum sputtering process to apply coatings to samples of glass. These coatings were then tested for spectral and physical properties.

We now will be supplying the architectural market with an exclusively Guardian line of reflective products which will immediately provide for improved service capabilities to our customers. Looking further ahead, we are now in a much better position to develop improved coating products and to enter new areas of coating technology.[39]

To help execute the company's strategy, a laboratory was opened at the Carleton plant in 1983 to research new kinds of glass. The laboratory was equipped primarily for development of glass coating technology and had a lab-size Airco coating machine and instruments to measure light reflectivity and transmittance, abrasion resistance, and the effects of temperature and other elements. The state-of-the-art equipment allowed the company's research team to develop new products and processes. Ray Nalepka, a 10-year veteran of Guardian's product development, headed the lab, while Karl Straky, one of the original group that had come to Guardian from Ford for the Carleton plant start-up, continued as manager of reflective glass sales.

Further downstream expansion took place in 1982 and 1983 with the acquisitions of Double Seal Glass and C&T Glass. Double Seal, with plants located in Flint, Michigan; Rogers, Arkansas; and Millbury, Ohio, brought Guardian additional capacity in tempered and insulating glass windows and doors for the residential and commercial construction, boating, and recreational vehicle markets.[40]

The Rogers plant made insulated glass units for the window market and tempered glass for recreational vehicles. The facility was put under the direction of Wally Palma, manager of the Corsicana float plant, whose team helped lead Rogers to record sales in 1983.[41]

The reacquired Millbury plant had previously been owned by Guardian in the 1970s, but it had subsequently been sold. C&T had a facility located in Walled Lake, Michigan, which fabricated painted and unpainted tempered parts for the appliance and furniture industries.[42]

In 1985, Guardian acquired Buchmin Industries, located in Reedley, California, not far from the Kingsburg float glass plant. Buchmin (later known as Guardian Reedley) produced mirrors for commercial buildings, hotels, and furniture and also produced laminated safety glass for windows, skylights, and other architectural applications. Bob Edwards, former Corsicana production manager, was named plant manager of the Reedley plant.[43] He was succeeded by Gary Werner, who achieved outstanding operating results at the plant.

The downstream acquisition of the Buchmin mirror operation required existing Guardian employees to extend themselves. Ron Nadolski was designated by Ebeid to head sales for the new business.[44] "We're sitting there and Russ said to me, 'Ron, how would you like to be in the mirror business?'" Nadolski remembered. "Because we're going to buy [Buchmin]. I think we can get into the mirror business, but this is going to mean a change for you. Right now you don't have to tap into all your abilities because you've found an easy way to sell. When I put you in the mirror business, you're going to have to dig real deep to bring out all those other talents you have and show your customers that you're the right kind of guy and we're the right kind of company to be in the mirror business.'"[45]

In the 1980s, Guardian made several acquisitions, allowing the company to offer a growing array of commercial glass products, including reflective glass, mirrors, laminated safety glass, and other architectural applications.

Top: Some of Guardian's products in the 1980s included the patterned glass in shower stalls. This glass was produced by Guardian's plant in Fullerton, California.

Inset: Guardian also developed its capabilities in mirror production beginning with the acquisition of Buchmin Industries in Reedley, California.

Right: One of the 30 Peterbilt trucks that helped launch Guardian Transportation.

The acquisition of additional glass manufacturing capacity completed the picture of glass division expansion in North America during the first half of the 1980s. In 1983, Guardian acquired from Hordis Brothers a controlling interest in Pennsylvania Float Glass, located in Floreffe, Pennsylvania. While the float line was relatively new, having been built in the 1970s, the Floreffe plant had been in continuous operation as a glassmaking facility for some 100

years. Guardian purchased the remaining interest in 1984 and decided to dedicate the plant to tinted glass production. Floreffe required a substantial rebuild and modernization in 1989 in order to produce high-quality auto glass. Tinted (green) glass was used in automotive and architectural applications to reduce glare and solar heat.[46] The plant could produce 350 tons of glass daily, which was enough to supply all of Guardian's automotive glass fabrication plants and to support any expansion in that business. The remaining tinted glass would be sold to outside customers.[47]

In a related transaction with Hordis Brothers, Guardian also acquired a patterned glass plant located in Fullerton, California. The Fullerton plant produced patterned glass for use in shower doors, patio furniture, and other privacy and decorative applications. In later years the Guardian Fullerton plant showed significant improvements in production and quality and became a steady contributor to Guardian's sales and earnings. Interestingly, it also became a training ground for many future Guardian leaders. Every person who served as Fullerton plant manager between the 1983 acquisition and 2003—Dave Rose, Gary Cochran, Tom Wunderlich, Mark Mette, Jim Pettis, and Firas Sakkijha—went on to become a plant manager at one of Guardian's growing number of float glass plants around the world.

Finally, in 1983, Guardian established a subsidiary called Guardian Transportation to ship materials between plants. Conceived by Vice President Bill Black, Guardian Transportation was headquartered in Millbury, Ohio, and used 30 Peterbilt trucks to

haul raw materials and finished goods between plants and customers.[48]

Expansion of Guardian Automotive

Although the Glass Group was Guardian's largest and most financially significant, the Automotive Group was also near the company's core. After all, Guardian had been born as a supplier of windshields in 1932. Guardian remained a major provider of windshields and side windows to the automobile industry, and, as an added benefit, Guardian's auto glass fabrication facilities were among the largest customers for the glass being manufactured by Guardian's float lines.

However, Guardian's emphasis in its automotive business was changing in the early 1980s from reliance on the replacement market to establishing itself as an original equipment supplier. Until then, some 75 percent of Guardian's windshield production went to the replacement market, and most of the OEM business was for trucks and buses. In

1982, Upper Sandusky received a huge order to provide windshields and rear windows for General Motors pickups and vans. This was a signal that Guardian was now being recognized as a major player in the original equipment market.

When it took this order, Guardian committed to delivering the parts "just in time," meaning it would deliver only what General Motors needed for short production runs. This way, the automotive giant wouldn't have to warehouse glass, which resulted in significant manufacturing savings. Just-in-time manufacturing and other like-minded philosophies were beginning to gain serious traction in American plants. Imported from Japan, where automobile companies were producing

The Automotive Group was a major supplier of windshields and side windows to the auto industry. In the 1980s Guardian established itself as a significant original equipment supplier in the industry.

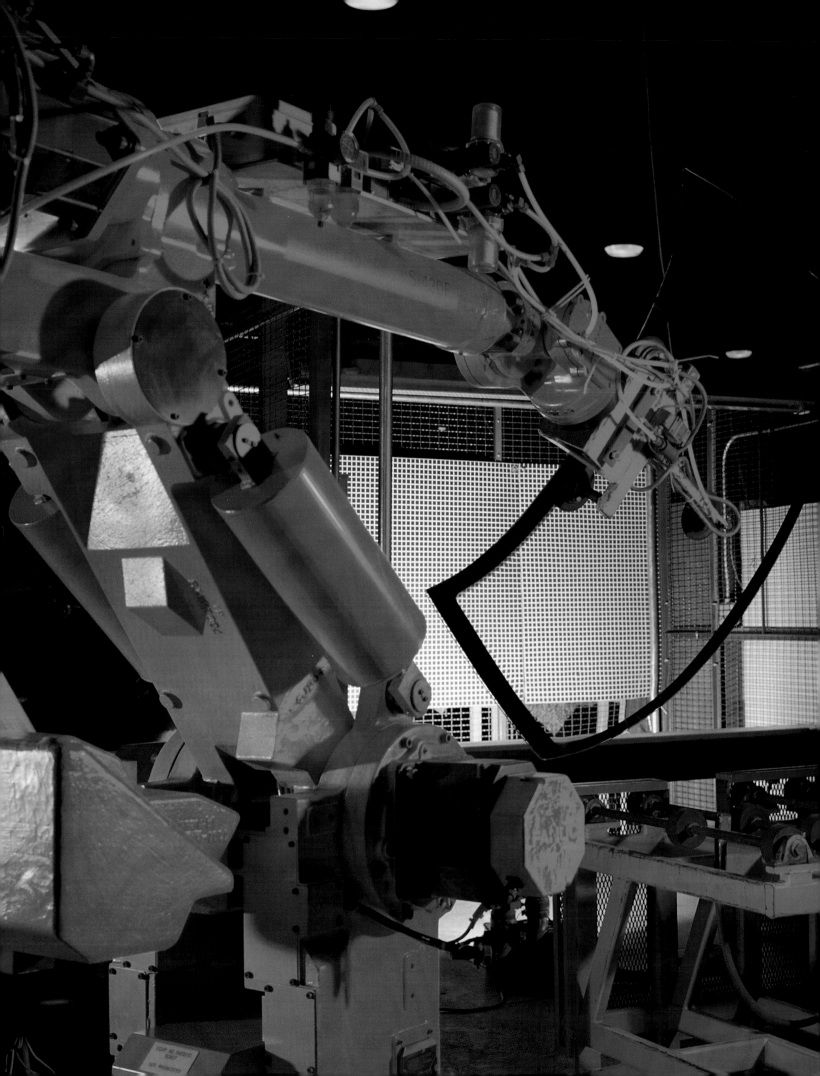

higher-quality cars from more efficient manufacturing operations, these new techniques promised a revolution in American manufacturing—one that would ultimately restore the American automobile industry to competitiveness.

The movement, however, would take many forms and require great change throughout the industry. In the mid-1980s, automobile companies began a gradual evolution away from systems engineering. Instead of designing discrete parts and outsourcing their manufacture, the big carmakers began to offload some of the engineering onto suppliers. The suppliers, in turn, were expected to develop complete systems, such as brakes or windshields, for delivery. Although this trend would take years to gain real momentum, the first seeds can be found in the mid-1980s, a time of great upheaval in the automobile manufacturing business.

Naturally, Guardian would be affected. The company had long supplied glass for windshields and side and back windows. Other suppliers, meanwhile, had produced trim, sealants, and mounting hardware. But auto companies now wanted window systems: complete windshields and windows that were ready to install. Guardian developed the technology to encapsulate windows, which involved molding a frame around the glass so the window could be installed easily.[49] Under the leadership of Ray Landes and his team of automotive glass engineers, Guardian also began to develop a revolutionary capability to bend windshields into dramatic shapes that would in later years be highly desirable to the auto industry.

In 1985, reflecting its commitment to expanding the automotive glass business, Guardian started up a new automotive glass fabrication plant in Auburn, Indiana. The 270,000-square-foot plant increased the company's auto glass fabrication capacity by 50 percent.[50] This plant specialized in original equipment manufacturing of General Motors windshields and side windows. Its first plant manager was Tom Havey, recruited from Upper Sandusky, although Auburn did not begin to reach its potential until Mike Panther took over as plant manager in 1987. Now with two plants, Upper Sandusky and Auburn, devoted to the automobile industry, Guardian was poised to become a major OEM player and had laid the foundation for future growth.

Guardian Aviation

To keep up with its rapidly growing geographical reach, Guardian took steps to develop its own transportation capabilities. In 1975, the company formed an internal aviation department with the purchase of a Bell Jet Ranger helicopter. The helicopter was used to fly management, engineers, and sales people between the company's offices, various plant locations, and customers in southeastern Michigan, Ohio, and Indiana. It was also a valuable tool for looking at possible locations for future plant sites.

"I thought it was far more productive to develop an efficient way of moving the same people from place to place rather than having to duplicate functions in different places," said Bill Davidson.

In 1976, with the site selection and construction of the Kingsburg facility, it became necessary to provide transportation on a nationwide scale. Guardian purchased a Learjet 24 and based both it and the helicopter at the Detroit Metropolitan Airport. Guardian now had the capability to reach the West Coast in five hours with the flexibility of leaving and returning on a moment's notice.

In 1978, Guardian Aviation added an Aerospatiele helicopter to the fleet for use in the Midwest and sent the Jet Ranger first to Kingsburg, later to Corsicana, and ultimately, to Canada to aid the sales teams of those plants in calling on customers. Also in 1978, the Learjet was replaced by a Sabre 60A, which provided a larger cabin and allowed greater range, flying non-stop from California to Detroit. In 1982, as Guardian launched

Opposite: A robot moves a windshield at one of the plants in Guardian's Automotive Group. Guardian relied on advanced tooling to create the complicated window shapes that automakers were demanding for their new models.

Right: Chief Pilot Chuck Shipp, who joined Guardian in 1978, was instrumental in expanding the company's travel capabilities as Guardian's business eventually covered the globe.

its expansion into Europe, the Sabre 60A was replaced by a Sabre 65, an aircraft able to cross the Atlantic Ocean.

Under the long-term leadership of department manager and chief pilot Chuck Shipp, who joined Guardian in 1978, Dewey Norton, who took charge of maintenance in 1977, and Dusty Kozloff, who came to Guardian as office manager and chief flight attendant in 1987, the aviation department continued to expand as Guardian's business covered the globe. Sophisticated Gulfstream aircraft—housed and maintained at Guardian's own hangar at Detroit Metropolitan Airport and capable of reaching any location in the world—became the cornerstones of Guardian's fleet. Guardian's managers, engineers, business development, and other personnel have logged millions of miles and have flown to more than 50 countries through Guardian Aviation in pursuit of new opportunities and in the fulfillment of Bill Davidson's vision.

Diversification into the Fiberglass Business

The first half of the 1980s witnessed not just continued growth in the traditional core business but an emphasis on diversification into other areas as well. Some of the non-glass businesses acquired by Guardian in the 1980s would turn into profitable, important parts of the company. Others would be only brief and relatively inconsequential episodes in the Guardian story.

Perhaps the most important of these new ventures was launched in 1980. By that time, Ed Sczesny, whose focus had shifted to business development, was looking for investment opportunities in businesses where Guardian already possessed competencies. The search led him to the fiberglass industry, which used a batch process similar to glassmaking and had some synergy in terms of raw materials and barriers to entry. Back in the late 1970s, Sczesny and Ren Nebel had put together a deal to buy a mineral wool insulation factory in Huntington, Indiana. A group of former Johns-

Manville employees, including Duane Faulkner, ran the plant for a couple of years. Then in 1980, Sczesny and Guardian were given the opportunity to start a fiberglass insulation business at the site of an empty television-tube manufacturing plant in Albion, Michigan, formerly owned by Corning Glass Works. Guardian bought the vacant plant, and the mineral wool group from Huntington relocated to Michigan, planning to build a $10 million fiberglass insulation operation from the ground up.

In many ways, this effort was similar to the opening of float glass plants, even beyond the technological similarities shared between the two industries. In Albion, Guardian was building the first completely new fiberglass plant in the United States in about 40 years. Similarly, it was entering a hotly contested industry with high barriers to entry and specialized technology. Furthermore, the fiberglass industry was dominated by relatively few players, including Johns-Manville, from which the Albion team had come.[51]

Unfortunately, the similarities to Guardian's experience in glassmaking didn't end there. In February 1981, less than a year after the fiberglass plant was up and running, Johns-Manville filed suit against Guardian and its former employees, claiming that the new plant was infringing on certain patents and using other trade secrets that its employees had taken from Johns-Manville when they left the company. Specifically, Johns-Manville contested the use of a process known as HERM, in which a centrifuge spins molten glass into thin fibers. Duane Faulkner had been the head of Johns-Manville's HERM development team and was named as the inventor of the process.

Johns-Manville asked the court to stop Guardian from using the technology and sought compensatory and punitive damages. Guardian management countered that the processes in its plant were either independently developed or already known to the trade.[52] Unfortunately, in 1983, District Court Judge Philip J. Pratt ruled that Guardian had indeed infringed upon Johns-Manville's patent for fiberization and had appropriated four trade secrets. Pratt also ruled that six former Johns-Manville employees had violated employment agreements. He awarded nearly $15 million to Johns-Manville and stopped Guardian from using the technology.

Guardian, however, did not agree with the ruling and requested a stay while it appealed. The stay

---

Opposite: A worker watches as fiberglass spins during the production of fiberglass insulation. This remains a core product in the Building Products Group.

was granted, and the case would drag into the next decade and result in Guardian having to pay the award plus accumulated interest to Johns-Manville. In the meantime, Guardian continued to develop a robust fiberglass business using its own technology and opened a second plant in Mineral Wells, Mississippi, in 1986. While Albion and Mineral Wells entered the Guardian family under extremely difficult circumstances, they formed the foundation of what eventually turned into Guardian's Building Products Group.

Investing in Noncore Businesses

The company's diversification efforts did not stop with fiberglass. Gaffney also led an effort to diversify into areas outside the traditional glass business with the objective of cushioning Guardian's earnings against the vagaries of the glass industry. He believed that Guardian's growth had reached the stage where cash flow exceeded the opportunities to invest in its core business. Gaffney reasoned that attractive returns could be achieved through investments or acquisitions outside the core, typically in transactions that could leverage the company's growing financial and tax sophistication.[53]

During the early 1980s, an unlikely group of new companies with no connection to the glass industry joined Guardian. In 1981, Guardian started GIC Financial Services Corporation, which was involved in leveraged leasing. "We had an interest, in the spirit of diversification, in getting into financial services," remembered Knight, who handled the acquisition. "We viewed financial services as having attributes quite different from our manufacturing business. We studied a lot of different financial services–type businesses and became intrigued with the economics of leveraged leasing."[54] GIC, based in Chicago, purchased capital equipment such as trucks, aircraft, railroad cars, and machinery and leased it on a contract basis. During its first four years of operation, GIC Financial Services purchased and leased more than $300 million of equipment. Walter Crowley, former president of Gould Financial, in Chicago, was president of GIC.[55]

In 1982, Guardian acquired control of Windsor Plastics, an Evansville, Indiana-based manufacturer of decorative thermoplastics for business machines, household appliances, automobiles, and plumbing.

Control of Windsor was accomplished through Guardian's investment in CUE Industries, which simultaneously acquired Windsor. CUE was a publicly traded company that had prospered for many years as a fast food chicken franchiser known as Chicken Unlimited but had gone into bankruptcy prior to the transaction with Guardian. CUE did, however, have attractive tax attributes that would enhance the future profitability of Windsor Plastics. At the time, Windsor was viewed as a stand-alone business opportunity, with no connection to Guardian's core business. No one could have predicted that some 14 years later, it would serve as the basis for the Guardian Automotive Group's dramatic expansion into the exterior trim business. In 1988, Guardian acquired Windsor Plastics from CUE and owned it outright after that.[56]

Guardian's investment in CUE was followed in 1983 by its acquisition of Continental Mortgage Investors (CMI), a bankrupt Boston-based real estate investment trust. At the time of Guardian's acquisition, all of CMI's assets had been liquidated for the benefit of creditors with the exception of Hawaii Loa Ridge, an undeveloped parcel of residential real estate outside of Honolulu representing 550 single-family home lots.[57] In addition, CMI had substantial carry forward tax losses. As Jeff Knight recalled:

CMI had been one of the largest, if not the largest, real estate investment trusts in the United States, but it over invested and got into financial trouble in the 1970s. The property in Hawaii had not been previously developed because it was costly to do so, and CMI simply did not have the resources. We developed and sold the parcels throughout the 1980s, a period of unprecedented strength in the Hawaiian real estate market, and the property turned out to be worth far more than we had ever imagined.[58]

CMI in turn acquired American International Manufacturing Company (AIMCO) in 1984. AIMCO, based in Fort Worth, Texas, made hydraulic oil field pumping units.[59] Unfortunately for AIMCO, oil prices collapsed in the mid-1980s, resulting in a substantial

Opposite: Guardian employees examine windshields in Guardian's increasingly sophisticated laminating technology.

curtailment of domestic drilling. AIMCO struggled for years to recover but was never able to do so and eventually was forced to shut down.

Labor Problems

Guardian's growth and diversification in the late 1970s and early 1980s did not come without some negative consequences. A hallmark of the Guardian Way was a direct and constructive relationship between management and labor—one that did not lend itself to unions becoming an intermediary in the factory. Over the years, in otherwise heavily unionized industries, Guardian managed to maintain congenial and constructive relations with its labor force.

In the early 1970s, for instance, the United Glass and Ceramic Workers were decertified in two Guardian plants—the Fort Lauderdale and Millbury facilities. In 1973, the same union was rejected in the Carleton facility after an organizing drive.

By the early 1980s, however, the situation was changing, and Guardian's leadership, focused as it was on growth and finding itself becoming stretched too thin, was not taking adequate notice of a looming problem. During the summer of 1981, Guardian announced that its Detroit fabrication plant was no longer profitable and attempted to reach a new agreement with the United Auto Workers, which had represented workers in the plant for 40 years. Guardian hoped to keep cost-of-living increases to a minimum while better controlling healthcare premiums. The company offered to increase other insurance benefits, pensions, and shift premiums.[60]

Guardian warned the union that without the requested changes, the plant's future was questionable. The union did not believe Guardian would close the plant. On September 13 it began a strike, and after it twice rejected Guardian's contract offer and seemed unwilling to accept the plant's economic reality, Guardian did in fact close the Detroit plant.[61]

Unfortunately, the labor issues were not confined to Guardian's small Detroit plant. They were also beginning to gain legs at the company's flagship Carleton plant, a fact all the more troubling because Carleton was the birthplace of the Guardian Way. The plant had been founded on the

premise that treating workers as professionals and having them participate in plant decisions would eliminate the need for union representation. "[Bill Davidson] said, 'We want a very hands-on workforce. We want everybody to realize we're in this together,'" recalled Richard Alonzo. "[Davidson said,] 'I want them to see how they're doing every day when they come into work. I want to tie them to the bottom line. I want every employee to feel like an entrepreneur.'"[62]

The workers would, in essence, represent themselves to management, and everyone would work together as a team.

For the plant's first several years, this approach worked. Carleton workers rejected union representation six times between 1970 and 1979.[63] This was an exceptional record considering the plant was located 30 miles south of Detroit, where the United Auto Workers had been very successful in union organizing efforts.

But by the early 1980s, conditions were deteriorating at the Carleton plant. When the Kingsburg, Corsicana, and Luxguard plants opened during the 1970s and early 1980s, they needed experienced managers, and Carleton lost some of its best people to the new facilities. "We kept mining people from Carleton," said Don Tullman, a plant manager of Kingsburg and later of Carleton.[64] As a result, Carleton did not measure up to Guardian's other plants in terms of leaders who understood Guardian's operating philosophy and who could command the confidence and trust of the workers on the shop floor. Production and profitability also began to suffer during those years. Looking back on the management crisis, Bill Davidson acknowledged that Guardian caused its Carleton plant problems "ourselves."[65]

While it was a long time in coming, the crisis was precipitated by proposed shift changes and other unpopular actions in 1985. In August 1985 the workers voted to become part of the United Auto Workers Union, and in November 1985, UAW representatives opened contract negotiations. Six months later, no agreement had been reached. Workers threatened to strike and expected that if they did, the plant would shut down, but Guardian warned that the plant would continue to operate despite a walkout. "It's not that we're anti-union," explained Ebeid. "It's only when you try to make us uncompetitive that we tend to fight back."[66]

On May 15, 1986, about 360 Carleton workers went on strike. Guardian management and supervisory workers continued to operate the Carleton plant and advertised for permanent replacement workers. By the first week, some 100 workers had been hired,[67] and with the help of management staff and non-striking workers, production continued.[68] By the third week, nearly a third of the jobs had been filled.[69]

The strike, however, proved to be very acrimonious. The replacement workers bore the brunt of the strikers' anger. Picketers shouted obscenities and other abusive language at replacement workers. Rocks, clubs, and boards were thrown at cars and buildings. Some protesters even used slingshots to shoot one-inch ball bearings at office windows.[70] One struck a security guard, who had to be taken to the hospital.[71]

Karl Straky, director of commercial glass products, was working out of the Carleton plant during the strike. Coming to work then was "like going through a gauntlet," he said. "You'd drive up to the gate and find police and security to keep the people clear. There were court orders that prevented [strikers] from keeping people from coming or going."[72] Workers parked their cars in the warehouse or in a protected area behind the building to avoid damage.

Tensions erupted on the night of August 7, when 500 striking workers and UAW sympathizers demonstrated outside the plant. The *Monroe Evening News* reported that around 9:00 p.m., replacement workers driving onto the plant property "were met by groups of demonstrators wielding clubs, slingshots, paint bombs, and other projectiles."[73] A WJBK television news reporter also reported that nail pads, intended to puncture car tires, were found at the scene.[74]

Bill Valk, a veteran Guardian human resources manager, who had been interviewing new employees "12 hours a day," vividly remembered the scene that night. Tired after a long day, he and other personnel looked toward the front gate as they were preparing to leave and saw hundreds of cars lined up there and back onto the highway.[75]

Around 9:00 p.m., Valk recalled, a woman who had come to interview that day and brought along her baby was allowed to return to her car only after police pleaded with the demonstrators. "This poor woman," said Valk. "I remember her car was parked outside the gate. She had to get to her car,

and you could just see the crowd open up as she walked through the gate with her baby, and you knew they were yelling and calling her names. When she finally got to her car, they were rocking it. Finally she took off."[76]

With this backdrop, in September Guardian workers filed a petition with the National Labor Relations Board to decertify the United Auto Workers. Strikers and replacement workers were eligible to vote in a dual election, which let workers choose the United Auto Workers, the United Steel Workers, or no union representation. Between October 16 and 17, Carleton workers and strikers voted to decertify the UAW and remain independent.[77]

The experience had been traumatic for everyone involved, not least of all Guardian's leaders. Until this episode, Guardian's record of employee relations had been stellar, and now the company was forced to reexamine much of its basic philosophy toward employee relations. Ultimately, Guardian realized that its operating philosophy was sound but that the company had not paid sufficient attention to the specifics of the deteriorating situation at Carleton. Many of the leaders who had created the harmonious conditions in the 1970s had moved to other locations, and the company had merely assumed, but not assured, that the initial employee relations would go on as before. Guardian had become complacent about a key component of its success. The Carleton strike was a "wake-up call" that made Guardian's management refocus on "people" issues as a critical component of Guardian's culture and future success.

Taking the Company Private

In 1983, Guardian boasted sales of $469 million and earned a place in the vaunted *Fortune* 500. It was Guardian's first and last year on the list. In July 1984, Davidson, the primary shareholder in Guardian, announced a plan to repurchase the 57.3 percent of the stock he didn't already own. By early 1985, Guardian would once again be a private company.

Guardian had enjoyed enormous success as a public company. Its sales had grown an average of 19 percent per year for the 17 years of public ownership (1968 through 1984). Its earnings growth was 21 percent per year for the same period. In fact, Guardian had enjoyed year over year earnings

growth in all years except 1974–75, when the U.S. economy was in the throes of an energy crisis and "stagflation." Guardian's financial performance successes continued in the early 1980s despite escalating interest rates, a precipitous drop in housing starts, and a lengthy recession that hit the construction and automobile industries particularly hard.

During its time as a public company, Guardian's sales had grown from $34.2 million in 1968 to $543 million in 1984. According to the *Detroit News*, a Guardian stockholder who purchased 100 shares at $10 a share in 1968 would now own 1,896 shares, reflecting six stock splits. At $21.75 a share (the price of Guardian stock when Davidson announced his plan to take the company private), the stockholder's $1,000 investment would have been worth $41,238.[78]

Davidson did not make the decision to take the company private lightly. While Davidson himself never took advantage of the public market for Guardian stock and never sold even one share while the company was public, he was fully aware that many employees valued ownership of shares in their company. As he said at the time in his "Letter to Employees":

I am aware of your pride in this ownership of the company and the financial rewards you have enjoyed in your investment in Guardian. However, I am confident that your long-term interests will be served through the private ownership I am proposing.[79]

As he recalled later, "I was always very pleased by the level of employee ownership of Guardian stock during the public years. This gave employees a stake in the company and made them feel that their individual and collective performance had a real effect on their lives and prosperity. I was truly sorry to lose this connection when we went private."[80]

The reasons for taking the company private were practical and philosophical. During the years preceding his decision, Guardian's share price failed to fully reflect the company's excellent financial performance. As Davidson explained in 1986:

For the past several years the stock market has not been in an investment mode. Rather than investing in companies that were doing well, investors were more interested in companies that were potential takeovers. In this kind of market Guardian stock would not do as well in the future as it had in the past. The time was right to get out of the market.[81]

In Davidson's estimation, going into 1984, the stock was undervalued and was likely to remain that way for some time. This was a compelling reason to go private.

Another reason was Davidson's commitment to Guardian's identity and continuity. While a hostile takeover of Guardian was not likely considering his substantial ownership of the company, he did not want to expose Guardian to the possibility of such an outcome. As he explained:

Being private prevents us from ever being a takeover target by some other company. Hundreds were taken over in the last several years and for most, their identity was lost. The continuity of Guardian ownership is now assured.[82]

In a message to Guardian's employees, Davidson emphasized that "the move secures the continued ownership of the company in a way that could never be assured while publicly owned."[83]

Finally, going private was a logical outgrowth of Davidson's business philosophy as it had evolved over the years. He and his management team epitomized the entrepreneurial spirit. He believed in taking prudent risks for the long-term success and growth of Guardian and did not want good decisions thwarted by short-term expectations of market analysts. He had come to believe that being a public company was not the best structure for carrying out the Guardian Way. As Davidson explained at the time:

To expand successfully into other markets will require bold and creative management in the future. Decisions by management are sometimes constrained by the conditions under which a public company must operate. Having now operated Guardian as a private and a public company, I am convinced that Guardian's ability to meet its goals will be enhanced by being privately owned at this time.[84]

Opposite: The exterior of the JK Financial Center in Saõ Paolo, Brazil, was built with Guardian's Sun-Guard product.

Davidson strongly believed that going private made Guardian "free to manage our business in our best interest, not that of the market."[85]

In 1984, Davidson felt that the time was right to initiate the transaction to private ownership. While the low stock price presented itself as an opportunity, it was not without risk. Upon completion of the transaction in February 1985, Guardian had debt totaling about $450 million, including some $300 million incurred in the buyback. For a company with 1984 sales of about $535 million and net income of $39 million, this was a heavy debt load, particularly considering the interest rates at the time that ranged between 13 percent and 16 percent for bank financing. As a result of going private, the national rating agencies—Moodys and Standard & Poors—dropped Guardian's debt rating to "junk" status.

The transaction had significant short- and long-term consequences. As Jeff Knight recalled, "We needed to tighten our belts, drastically curb all but absolutely necessary capital expenditures, and focus on our core businesses. This definitely marked the end of the stream of noncore investments we had made beginning in the early 1980s."[86]

Shortly after completing the buyback, Davidson reorganized Guardian into four relatively autonomous groups. John P. Ory was named president of the Automotive Group, which included the manufacturing plants, distribution centers, and retail operations,[87] Frank Abissi was named president of Guardian Photo, and Bill Morrow headed the Insulation Group.

Bill Davidson believed that going private made Guardian free to manage its business in its best interest, not that of the market. These certificates recognized the completion of the "going private" transaction.

Staff gathered at the 1987 world staff meeting. The annual meeting gave the company's far-flung but tight-knit management group an opportunity to gather and discuss new growth opportunities.

Not surprisingly, the most significant of the management changes took place in the Glass Group, which included the float glass operations at Carleton, Kingsburg, Corsicana, Luxguard, and the new Spanish plant. Russ Ebeid, whose areas of responsibility had steadily been increasing throughout the 1980s, became president, responsible for the glass manufacturing and fabricating plants worldwide.

Both the decision to go private and its timing turned out to be highly beneficial to Guardian. By the time the transaction was closed, interest rates were falling dramatically, the housing market was recovering, and the economy was beginning a period of expansion that would last for many years. As the sole shareholder, Davidson was now completely free to lead Guardian without many of the limitations that prevailed among publicly held companies. The culture that he had nurtured among Guardian's management and employees could now take off and lead to even greater future growth and success.

Growth of the Glass Group Resumes

After only two and a half years of focusing on internal reorganization and debt reduction following the return to private ownership, Guardian's strong financial position had been regained. In mid-1987, the company's debt rating was restored to "investment grade" status, a remarkable achievement in such a short period. At the same time, Guardian sent a message to its employees and the rest of the glass industry that the company's unprecedented growth was about to resume. In the middle of 1987, Guardian announced plans to build two new 600 ton-per-day float glass lines, one in Luxembourg (Luxguard II) and one in the United States (Richburg, South Carolina).[88] Later that year, the company announced an ambitious $250 million capital improvement campaign that, in addition to the new float plants, contemplated additions and improvements at the Auburn automotive glass plant and Millbury fabrication plant, tank repairs at Carleton, Floreffe, Kingsburg, and Fullerton, and a new coater in Luxembourg.[89]

The cornerstone for the second float plant in Luxembourg was laid in February 1988 in the city of Dudelange, some 12 miles from Guardian's first Luxguard plant. As Ebeid recalled, "Luxembourg was chosen for this plant partly because of its central location but, more importantly, because of the excellent business climate and motivated workforce we had there."[90]

Once again, Howard Benedict was called upon to manage the construction project from his position at CRVC. This time around, Benedict said, Guardian had the benefit of experience and the presence of talented European engineers. "We had some of the staff from the first facility, and it was a lot easier," he said. "In the first project, we were, as any American company would be, a little hesitant about using European contractors, European specifications,

European equipment. The second facility offered the chance to improve and fix all the mistakes we made, whatever they were, on the first facility, and take it a step further and really Europeanize that plant. That was really the challenge."[91] When Luxguard II opened in December 1988, it was Guardian's largest float line in Europe.[92]

Construction of the Richburg plant was under the direction of project manager Gary Cook. It was located 40 miles south of Charlotte, North Carolina, and served customers in the southeastern United States. Richburg also had a furnace capable of tempering 40 million square feet of glass annually.[93] When the Richburg plant opened, on November 11, 1988, plant manager Dick Pagenkopf said that "during the whole launch process I was as anxious as an expectant father. When the first glass came down the line, I was just downright proud."[94] This plant, together with Luxguard II, brought Guardian's glass manufacturing capacity to more than 5,000 tons a day.[95]

Inset left: Bill Davidson starts the heat-up process in the Richburg, South Carolina, plant furnace prior to the plant's 1988 launch. Plant Manager Dick Pagenkopf (inset right) used a bottle of red wine to christen the new line in Richburg, South Carolina (below).

Right: Dick Pagenkopf sent a bottle of red wine to Luxguard II Plant Manager Leo Schneider to christen the new line in Guardian's traditional fashion.

Below: Luxguard II, located in Dudelange, 12 miles from Guardian's original Luxembourg plant, launched in December 1988. With this addition and the new plant in Richburg, South Carolina, the company's glass manufacturing capacity increased to more than 5,000 tons per day.

The 1980s were monumental years for Guardian. It bulled its way into the closed European market, rapidly expanded glass manufacturing and fabricating both in the United States and Europe, demonstrated a new commitment and capability in making parts for the automobile industry, entered the insulation business and diversified in other areas as well, underwent internal reorganization, added people with new competencies, developed existing Guardian personnel, and made the transition from a public to a private company.

In 1986, Davidson was honored for his contributions to the glass industry with the Phoenix Award, designed to recognize those who have achieved great things in their industry. But neither he nor Guardian was finished. In the summer of 1988, Guardian announced plans to build new float glass plants in the emerging market of Venezuela and then-communist Hungary—projects that would prove to be every bit as challenging as Guardian's prior ventures.[96] Guardian was now positioned to exploit and build on its core competencies in flat glass, automotive glass, and fiberglass insulation.

During the 1990s, Guardian initiated a major glass fabrication strategy that included this laminating line in Luxembourg.

CHAPTER SIX

WHERE ANGELS FEAR TO TREAD

It was a very complicated negotiation. In some respects we had to make up the rules as we went along.

—Ralph Gerson, executive vice president,
on Guardian's expansion behind the Iron Curtain

IN MANY WAYS, GUARDIAN'S history in the 1990s is a microcosm of the globalization of the world economy that became the decade's hallmark. Globalization later came to mean many different things to different people—some with positive and some with negative connotations. At its root, however, globalization involved the creation of a more interdependent world, with all the regions of the planet connected by instant communications, a web of financial relationships that transcended national borders, the explosive increase in access to information, and a common language and practice of free market economies.

Globalization promoted the dismantling of trade barriers and the transition of planned economies to free market systems. It has brought unprecedented economic opportunities around the globe—and Guardian during the 1990s was a part of that process. Guardian's expansion into Hungary on the eve of the collapse of the Soviet Empire; its effort to break down trade barriers in Japan and other parts of the world; its visionary construction of world-class manufacturing, housing, and educational facilities in India; and its creation of economic opportunities in Latin America and the Middle East all represent the most positive aspects of the phenomenon of globalization.

The 1990s for Guardian also was a period of major consolidation and growth in its existing businesses. The Automotive Group expanded through internal investment and acquisitions into new product lines and geographical areas, as it became a significant OEM supplier to the worldwide automotive industry. The Insulation Group was transformed into a multifaceted building products business through the construction of additional fiberglass manufacturing facilities and the acquisition of extensive downstream distribution capabilities. The Flat Glass Group continued to grow and deepen within its now established market areas of North America and Europe. All in all, the 1990s saw Guardian transform itself from a regional glass company with relatively minor automotive and insulation capabilities into a global player in three major industries—flat glass, automotive, and building products.

A New Generation of Leadership

While many of the leaders who oversaw the groundwork and astonishing growth of Guardian's glass manufacturing in the 1970s and 1980s remained at the helm during the 1990s, their ranks

The European flag is the symbol of the European Union and Europe's unity and identity. The circle of gold stars represents solidarity and harmony among the people of Europe.

were reinforced by others who seized the opportunities Guardian offered for personal growth. Ralph Gerson joined Guardian in 1985 in a part-time capacity as vice president for government and corporate affairs, while still maintaining his law practice in Washington, D.C. He had previously been director of commerce for the state of Michigan. In 1988, Gerson was appointed executive vice president of Guardian with globalization as one of his principal mandates.

Peter Walters first came to Guardian in 1985 as assistant to the president. He had previously been deputy director of Michigan's Department of Commerce where he was responsible for attracting new businesses to the state. In 1987 Walters became Guardian's vice president of purchasing and in July 1989, as a new group vice president, he was given responsibility for Guardian's international business development and government relations. In 1989, Bob Gorlin left a partnership at Michigan's largest law firm to become general counsel in charge of worldwide legal matters. Joe Bruce joined Guardian's information technology department in 1985 before transferring to the purchasing area where he would ultimately head up global purchasing. Don Trofholz transferred from an affiliated company to take charge of the accounting function. David Clark and Ann Waichunas developed a global treasury function, while Paul Halpern joined the tax department to work on planning, significant corporate transactions, and energy matters. A short time later, Bruce Cummings joined Guardian as head of human resources, charged with the development of leadership at all levels of the organization.

Meanwhile, in Europe and around the globe, both veteran and new leaders in glass operations such as Lajos Sapi, Luc Theis, Mark Lacasse, David Rose, Mark Mette, and George Longo, would begin to meld Guardian's business philosophy and operating principles with diverse local cultures. While somewhat overshadowed during the successes and global sweep of the glass business, Guardian's Automotive and Fiberglass Groups also continued to grow and prosper and to develop their own teams of leaders, including Jack Sights, Ray Landes, Mike Panther, Steve Markevich, and Tim Morrow from Automotive, and and Bill Jacoby from Fiberglass. In the 1990s, these leaders would once again change the way the world viewed Guardian.

When the company announced its first float glass plant in Carleton, it was dismissed as too small, too provincial, and lacking the wherewithal to challenge the glass industry. Less than 20 years later, Guardian had swept aside those arguments, revitalizing an industry that had been encrusted with layers of tradition, bureaucracy, and oligarchy, and was ready to conquer new worlds. The explanation for Guardian's initial success and the dynamic role it would play around the world lay in its culture and people. As Bob Gorlin recalled:

Below from left to right: Ralph Gerson came on board with Guardian Industries in 1985 in a part-time capacity. In 1988, he was appointed executive vice president of Guardian, with globalization one of his principal mandates. Peter Walters joined Guardian in 1985. He was appointed group vice president in 1989 and named "Employee of the Year" that same year. Don Trofholz, Guardian's chief accounting officer, joined the company in 1979. Ann Waichunas joined Guardian in 1984 and spent several years as treasurer of Guardian Europe before becoming treasurer of Guardian Industries.

Above: Members of Guardian's legal team included, from left, Craig Baldwin, David Jaffe, and Tom Pastore.

Right: Guardian shook up the establishment when it entered Europe, as indicated by this article in the *Financial Times*.

When I first met Guardian people in 1988 and actually joined the company in 1989, I was struck by the common mission that virtually everyone understood and expressed. Guardian was going to bring its unique business philosophy and operating culture to the world. The energy, enthusiasm, confidence, and excitement were powerful and irresistible.[1]

Latin America: Venezuela Revisited

In 1988, Guardian announced that it would construct a float glass plant in Maturin, Venezuela. This was Guardian's newest and simultaneously one of its oldest projects. Back in the early 1970s, a consortium of primarily governmental entities in Venezuela had negotiated with Guardian to provide technology for a proposed float glass plant in that country. For many

FINANCIAL TIMES Thursday June 7 1990

US raging bull charges at European glass

William Dawkins on how Guardian has shaken up a traditional industry

Twenty years and one day after Guardian launched its first float line, number 10 was christened in Maturin, Venezuela. The VIMOSA plant was unique at the time in that it featured on-site hydrogen and nitrogen generation facilities and a larger-than-usual 30-day inventory of raw materials.

years the project made little progress, and Guardian's attention was focused elsewhere.[2]

In 1978, the Venezuela float project came under the control of Flotados Venezolanos S.A. (shortened to "Floven"), a company comprised of private and governmental entities and interests in Venezuela. In 1980, Guardian agreed to provide technical and project management assistance to Floven, without taking an equity interest. Guardian's sole responsibility was to design and engineer the plant, supervise construction and procure U.S.-made components and equipment, for which it would be paid a fee.[3] Construction of the Maturin plant began in late 1980 but was not

completed due to financial difficulties experienced by Floven. At the time construction was suspended, the plant was about 45 percent complete.[4]

As Jeff Knight recalled, "The complicated history of our Venezuela project" next saw ownership of the Floven float project assets transferred in 1986 to a company called Corporacion Venezolana de Guayana (or "CVG" for short), with a mandate to implement the project. CVG wanted Guardian to take over the project, but Guardian believed a private sector partner should also be involved.[5] In 1988, Guardian agreed that the time was finally right for the project to be injected with new life and completed. Guardian entered into a joint venture with CVG and Dezider Weisz, a prominent Venezuelan industrialist, to form CVG-Vidrios Monagas S.A. (VIMOSA for short). CVG soon sold its interest in VIMOSA and ownership was left to Guardian and Weisz, with Guardian having management control of the construction and operation of the new float glass plant. Eventually, Guardian acquired 100 percent

ownership of VIMOSA, which changed its name to Guardian de Venezuela in 1995.

Venezuela would be one of Guardian's most difficult projects for many reasons. Much of the equipment for construction and outfitting of the plant had to be imported, which created complications due to the regime of currency regulations periodically in effect in Venezuela. Unlike other Guardian plants at the time, Venezuela's weak utilities infrastructure required that Guardian maintain its own hydrogen and nitrogen generation facilities. For the same reason, VIMOSA's stand-by emergency power system also had to be much larger than that normally installed in a Guardian facility.[6]

Further, Venezuela itself, while rich in oil and natural gas, is a small and relatively undeveloped country, and it was clear before Guardian made its investment that a significant percentage of the plant's production could not be consumed domestically and would have to be exported. It was anticipated that Guardian would sell about 35 percent of the plant's output in Venezuela and that the rest would be exported throughout Latin America. This marketing plan presented logistical, cost, and currency control complications for the plant's operation. These difficulties were accentuated by the fact that the location and size of the Maturin plant were not what Guardian would have selected if it were starting from scratch. Finally, while Venezuela was in form a democratic republic, political and social instability had been a fact of life throughout the country's history and would not magically disappear after Guardian's arrival. The people operating the Maturin plant would have to become masters at navigating through extremely difficult governmental regulations over the years that were some-

times purposefully designed to discourage rather than promote business activity.[7]

Construction of the Maturin plant took place under the direction of project manager Dave Younker. He was assisted by other representatives of corporate engineering and engineers from Llodio in Spain.[8] The plant started up in August 1989. The first plant manager was Randy Parker, although there was considerable instability in this position and in Guardian de Venezuela's financial performance until Juan Roestel became plant manager in 1999. Mark Lacasse noted, "Since Juan took charge of operations, there has been a tremendous turnaround in the performance and stability of the plant, which is particularly impressive considering the anti-business climate that sometimes pervades Venezuela."[9]

Behind the Iron Curtain

While Venezuela was an extremely challenging new frontier for Guardian as the decade of the 1980s came to a close, an equally intriguing opportunity presented itself in Europe, behind the "Iron Curtain." In

Above: Mark Lacasse, director of Guardian Latin America, helped meld Guardian's business philosophy and operating principles with diverse local cultures.

Right: Times Square in Moema, Saõ Paolo, Brazil, used Guardian's Sun-Guard Silver-20 coated glass. The structure was completed in 1999.

1985, Mikhail Gorbachev became general secretary of the Communist Party and president of the Soviet Union. After 40 years of the Cold War and suspicion between the West and the U.S.S.R., and an expensive military buildup, the Soviet Union was exhausted and broke. Hoping to retain but modernize the communist system, Gorbachev announced new policies of *perestroika* (restructuring) and *glasnost* (openness) for the Soviet Union. The significance of these actions was hard to overstate: Gorbachev had put in motion forces that would soon end the Cold War, unleash a liberal and democratic spirit that had long been suppressed in much of Eastern Europe, tear down the Berlin Wall, and ultimately remove the Communist Party flag from the Kremlin.

Political and economic liberalism came to Hungary before it spread to its neighbors within the Soviet Bloc. In 1945, Hungary was overrun by the Red Army and was ruled by a communist regime beginning in 1950. Hungary remained, however, a western-oriented country by culture and inclination, notwithstanding the imposition of an economic system dominated by state planning and hostile to market capitalism. In the late 1960s, Hungary began to

experiment with reforms that relied increasingly on market mechanisms. By the 1980s, while some 85 percent to 90 percent of Hungary's enterprises were state owned, the private sector was the most dynamic element of the Hungarian economy.[10] Hungary would be the country most prepared to take immediate advantage of the liberalization that Gorbachev initiated within the Soviet Bloc upon his ascension to power. As Peter Walters recalled, "By the mid-1980s you still couldn't enter into a joint venture in the Czech Republic, Poland, or Russia. In contrast, Hungary had the most liberal investment

The agreement establishing Hunguard, the largest post–World War II foreign joint venture in Hungary at the time, was signed and sealed in 1988. From left, front row, are Guardian Executive Vice President Ralph Gerson; Bill Davidson; Dr. Lajos Schmidt, senior partner of Baker & McKenzie (standing next to Davidson); and Hungarian Glass Works General Manager Sandor Czina. Hungarian Prime Minister Karoly Grosz stands in the back row, over Schmidt's right shoulder. Grosz is flanked by other Guardian officials and members of the Hungarian delegation.

laws and was interested in attracting capital and technology from the West."[11]

In fact, the start of Guardian's involvement in Hungary actually preceded Gorbachev. In August 1983, representatives of the state-owned Hungarian Glass Works (HGW) requested permission to tour Guardian's new Luxguard plant and expressed their interest in exploring a joint venture to convert HGW's sheet glass process to a float plant.[12] This type of conversion, of course, was precisely what Guardian undertook at the Villosa facility in Llodio a year later. While Guardian was not yet prepared to focus on Hungary, the Hungarian officials continued to show interest. In the fall of 1985, a group from HGW suggested to Guardian executives during the Glasstec glass show in Dusseldorf, Germany, that a joint venture arrangement would be mutually beneficial. In January 1986, Russ Ebeid visited the Hungarian Glass Works facility in Orashaza and agreed to continue discussions. While fully aware that many problems would have to be overcome before a joint venture company could be created and the conversion of Orashaza to a modern float process accomplished, Bill Davidson and Sandor Czina of HGW negotiated and signed a letter of intent in October 1986 agreeing to the project in principle.[13] As Ebeid recalled, "This was only the first step in what turned out to be an incredibly difficult and complicated process of turning the talk into reality."[14]

As it turned out, the formal joint venture agreement between Guardian and Hungarian Glass Works, negotiated on Guardian's side by Ralph Gerson and company attorney Alan Schlang, was not signed until July 1988. Ground for the new construction project at Orashaza would not be broken until June 1989, almost three years after the letter of intent was signed but still five months before the Berlin Wall fell.

After execution of the letter of intent, it was necessary to undertake an extraordinary amount of study and analysis to determine the feasibility of a joint venture project. In every one of its aspects—determining the legalities of ownership, organizing construction, assuring adequate infrastructure, obtaining acceptable financing, navigating through the maze of governmental requirements, establishing a marketing plan, and launching production—this project would be uniquely difficult under the best of circumstances. As Gerson recalled:

Arpad Goncz, left, president of the Republic of Hungary, visited Guardian's Hunguard plant on July 19, 1993. Janos Egyud, operations manager, center, gave hands-on glassmaking tips to the president and a member of his security team.

The complexity was compounded by the fact that the project started while Hungary was still a heavily regulated, planned economy operating in the Soviet orbit. All of our initial assumptions, for example, regarding ownership, availability of energy and markets for the converted plant's output of float glass, were premised on continuation of the old system, even though it was already liberalizing. Then midstream we had to deal with the rapid breakup of the Soviet Bloc and an extremely abrupt disintegration of the planned economy in Hungary and the rest of the East. We and our counterparts at Hungarian Glass Works and the quickly changing Hungarian government sometimes had to make up the rules as we went along in order to keep the project moving forward.[15]

The ownership structure of the new joint venture company—to be named Hunguard Float Glass Co.—evolved as the legal and regulatory regime changed. Because of Hungarian legal requirements, the project at the outset was to have 49 percent ownership by Guardian and 51 percent by HGW.[16] Within a relatively short time, however, Guardian was permitted to have 80 percent ownership and eventually, in 1992, it acquired 100 percent ownership.

The initial project investment was estimated to be $115 million, $30 million of which was to be equity investment by the two partners (when the ownership division was 51/49) and the balance to be provided as debt. Hungarian Glass Works' equity contribution would be in the form of the existing sheet glass facility and associated assets while Guardian's contribution would be cash. For the balance of the project's needs, Hunguard would borrow both Hungarian forints from local banks and convertible currency from Western sources.[17] At $115 million, the project was the largest post–World War II foreign joint venture in Hungary and received considerable public attention.[18]

"The financing was very complicated. One initial problem was that the Hungarian side had very few people who knew much about Western finance. In addition, with the changing political, legal and economic landscape, the project looked risky and obtaining favorable financing was made particularly difficult," said Gerson.[19]

In addition to a complicated legal and financial picture, conversion of the Orashaza sheet plant into a modern float operation also posed significant technical challenges. Many of the buildings and facilities at the sheet plant needed to be upgraded and in many cases completely rebuilt.[20] For example, while

Guardian entered into a joint venture with Hungarian Glass Works to create a modern float glass plant. The venture became a reality as Hungary was making the difficult transition from a command to a free market economy.

Many of the buildings and facilities at Hungarian Glass Works needed to be upgraded, and in some instances completely rebuilt, for the conversion to the modern float glass process.

the new float line would use the existing furnace of HGW, the furnace had been built above ground, which required that the new tin bath and annealing lehr be elevated some 22 feet above grade level and that an inclined conveyor bring the glass from the annealing lehr to the cutting line.[21]

Overall responsibility for project management was in the hands of CRVC, Guardian's European engineering affiliate. It was led by Albert Franck, who was joined by 10 experienced and highly capable engineers and management personnel from HGW.[22] Howard Benedict, who provided general supervision over the project, specifically recalled the challenges created by starting construction in June 1989 before the Berlin Wall fell (in November) and concluding it during a chaotic transition from state planning to a market economy. "At the first part of the project, we were dealing with central planners," he remembered. "And then in the second part of the project, we were dealing with individuals who had embraced free market principles. In some cases, it was actually easier to deal with people from the old

regime because they had experience operating within their system. One time, I asked a contractor to give us a price before he did the work. He said, 'No, I'll give you the price after I'm done.' I said, 'You don't understand. We need the price.' He said he didn't know how to provide one in advance. So we had to teach many of our suppliers and vendors how to estimate cost because previously everything had been a government-to-government transfer. They had never cared about cost before."[23]

Financial management of the Hunguard project was led by Mike Morrison, who moved to Budapest from Luxembourg where he had been treasurer of Bascharage and project finance manager for the Dudelange float glass plant. He later performed a variety of functions in Guardian's Thai operation and ultimately returned to the United States with significant responsibility for Guardian's glass fabrication plants. In going to Hungary in 1989, Morrison was faced with completely novel financial and governmental issues that required ingenuity and a willingness to depart from any established script. As he recalled, this is precisely what he liked about the company. "At Guardian, there are certain base requirements, but you're going to be given different challenges in different areas you might not have handled before," said Morrison. "Part of the challenge is to grow within your job. When I arrived at

Above: The staff of Hunguard celebrated 1 million injury-free hours. Regardless of its global location, Guardian always maintained high safety standards.

Below right: Lajos Sapi was the first managing director of the Hunguard facility.

Opposite: In Rotterdam, Holland, these two glass towers used Guardian-supplied glass.

Guardian from Comerica Bank, this was the biggest difference I saw right away."[24]

Hunguard was launched in February 1991 and from the start showed that it was up to Guardian's worldwide operating standards. Within three days of the launch, glass quality was high enough to permit packaging for shipment and production yields soon approached 80 percent.[25] The disparity between many of the assumptions governing the original feasibility studies and the realities of post-communist Eastern Europe, however, did have an impact on the business for some time. As Jim Moore recalled, "The original marketing plan called for more than half the plant's output to be sold to the communist countries of Eastern Europe, where there was more or less a captive market. However, by the time the plant was

completed, those countries were in turmoil and it was necessary to ship far more of Hunguard's glass to more distant markets in the West. This situation lasted for several years. In addition, some of the original pricing assumptions for energy were not realized and we ended up paying higher rates for natural gas from the newly capitalistic Russia."[26]

The Hunguard management team was led by Managing Director Lajos Sapi and included Production Manager Janos Egyud and numerous experienced glass operators from HGW. Sapi's career presented a vivid example of a success story in the globalizing world economy. He received his engineering degree from the University of Miskolc in Hungary in 1971 during the height of the Cold War. He immediately entered the Hungarian state-owned glass industry and rose through the ranks to become technical-production deputy general manager of the Hungarian Glass Works in 1982, on the eve of HGW's overtures to Guardian. As Jim Moore later recalled his introduction to Sapi:

When I first met Lajos, he was on the other side with HGW. As the number two guy at HGW,

he did most of the negotiating. When I saw the way he handled himself—in a very professional, tough manner, with an unprecedented level of confidence—I knew I wanted him on our side.[27]

Sapi became the first managing director of Hunguard where, as he recalled, "I basically took a crash course both in Guardian's operating philosophy and free market business practices."[28] The success of Hunguard led to increased responsibility within Guardian. Sapi was instrumental in the construction and launch of a new float glass plant in the former East Germany, which started operation in 1997, and became the first Hungarian to receive a resident permit to work as managing director in Germany of a company (Guardian Flachglas) that was not Hungarian-owned.[29] As Sapi observed, " I guess you can say that as a representative of Guardian I personally broke down some barriers, and I appreciate the opportunity Guardian gave me to do that."[30] Sapi was Guardian's "Employee of the Year" in 1998 and was responsible for its operations in Central and Eastern Europe.

Because Guardian was one of the first American manufacturers to create a joint venture with a local company and make a significant investment behind the Iron Curtain, the Hunguard project received a great deal of recognition. Guardian and Hunguard were featured in a CBS *Nightly News* television report on joint ventures in Eastern Bloc countries.[31] Later, the project would become the subject of a case study at Harvard Business School. For Guardian, Hunguard was significant not for its symbolism or the publicity it received but rather for its demonstration that the blending of Guardian's operating system with local talent and expertise could breed success anywhere, even in the most turbulent environment imaginable. No challenge was now beyond the range of Guardian's vision and capability.

Thailand and the Pacific Rim

Although it was too soon for financial results from Venezuela and Hungary to be assessed, the experience of creating these joint ventures helped Guardian realize that Asia, the region with the world's fastest economic growth, had to be next on the horizon. Ralph Gerson led an evaluation of investment opportunities that extended from India across Southeast Asia and into China. The develop-

ing countries throughout that part of the world had enjoyed enough economic growth during the 1970s and 1980s that a burgeoning middle class was beginning to demand apartments, homes, automobiles, and other consumer goods. These economies had reached the take-off point for an increase in the per capita use of float glass products. As a result of Guardian's market analysis and investigation, during 1988–1990 Gerson and Peter Walters conducted joint venture negotiations simultaneously in India, Thailand, and Indonesia.

While Guardian was exploring many potential opportunities in Asia, its first project in the region was done in Thailand, a country with a population of some 55 million people and a booming economy. In 1989, Gerson and Walters negotiated a 50/50 joint venture with the Siam Cement Company Limited to build a float glass plant in Nong Khae, some 60 miles northeast of Bangkok. Siam Cement was a 100-year-old Thai industrial conglomerate with a major market position in cement, refractories, and a wide variety of building products.[32] It was partially owned by Crown Properties, the investment company of the royal family.

As Walters recalled, "Siam Cement was different from any of our previous joint venture partners. It was not a family business but rather a prestigious and diversified public Thai company run by professional managers. Siam Cement's annual revenues were comparable to Guardian's and its history went back to the late 19th century. While they didn't know anything about glassmaking and had less international experience than Guardian's managers, the people at Siam Cement were extremely confident about their abilities and their company's accomplishments. There definitely was a Siam Cement way of doing things."[33]

From Siam Cement's perspective, the joint venture with Guardian added a totally new manufacturing capability and product line to its expanding group of companies. "We figured that glass was probably one of the areas we should invest in considering our strong presence in the construction industry," said Dusit Nontanakorn, an executive with Siam Cement who was appointed the joint venture's first managing director. "Further, Thailand had only one glass manufacturer [Asahi Glass] at the time. So we thought that introducing a second manufacturer, apart from being good for our operations, would probably be good for the country

Above and inset: Construction of Siam Guardian, the company's first float glass plant in Thailand, began in April 1991.

because it would create more competition in an important industrial sector."[34]

The effort to break the local glass monopoly would not, however, go unopposed. Shortly after the Guardian-Siam Cement joint venture was announced and after a new investment by Japanese glassmaker Asahi had been officially approved, the Thai government banned the construction of additional float glass plants.[35] Asahi reportedly controlled 90 percent of the Thai glass market.[36] As Gerson recalled, "The ban was an obvious effort on the part of Asahi, which had a monopoly in Thailand, to preserve the status quo and keep Guardian and other competitors out of the country. If Asahi expected us just to accept this outcome without a fight, they were sadly mistaken."[37]

Guardian immediately sought help from the United States government. As it turned out, Guardian's dilemma was met with great sympathy by a U.S. administration that was intent on encouraging U.S. overseas exports and investment. Shutting Guardian out of the Thai glass market to preserve a domestic monopoly was precisely the kind of issue that would stimulate action at high levels. William Davidson and Ralph Gerson met with U.S. Secretary of Commerce Robert Mosbacher to seek his active assistance in 1990, and soon thereafter, Mosbacher raised the U.S. concern with this ban in a meeting with Thai Prime Minister Chatichai Choonhavan.[38]

Guardian's case also received a boost when Vice President Dan Quayle protested the ban in his meetings with Thailand's leadership while on an official visit to Thailand. "We spent a year battling with our competitor to be allowed to build a float glass plant in Thailand," recalled Gerson.[39]

The persistence paid off. With tireless help from the U.S. ambassador to Thailand, Dan O'Donahue, the Thais finally lifted the ban, and construction of Guardian's 600-ton per day float glass plant began in Nong Khae in April 1991.[40] The launch took place in September 1992 in what Chuck Croskey, Guardian's managing director for Asia and the Pacific Rim, called a "symphony in team-work" among Guardian personnel from many of its worldwide plants.[41]

One of the challenges facing the leadership of the plant was the difference in corporate cultures between Guardian and Siam Cement. "Siam Cement was the IBM of Thailand," remembered Croskey:

They had a complicated organizational structure, and here comes Guardian with the "Guardian Way" and its principles of flexibility and responsibility. Our initial discussions with Siam Cement on the engineering level were very difficult because of the different cultures, and we were struggling to combine them. All of the Guardian principles—of decentral-

ization, of giving somebody the opportunity to succeed, of empowering people to make decisions—were really difficult concepts for them to grasp, but as we worked with them, you could see that they liked it. It's human nature to want to be empowered.[42]

As with other overseas operations, Guardian was careful to adapt to the local cultural and religious context. Consequently, the Thai plant contained shrines and prayer stations for Buddhist workers.[43]

The challenge of blending diverse corporate and national cultures and seeing people of different backgrounds work together is one of the things that attracts quality people to Guardian.

"That's what really has kept me fired up for all these years," said Mark Mette, initially the production manager of Guardian Thailand. "When you think of Hungary and Thailand and South America, the different cultural and social aspects, I really do enjoy the diversity. It's such a great learning experience because you have to deal not only with the cultures and the language, but the different ways of doing things as well. In Thailand, for example, instead of building scaffolding in steel, they do it in bamboo, and they work in bare feet. It's incredible. It's eye opening."[44]

Although the Americans and their Thai colleagues had to work through some cultural issues in the early years, productivity, sales, and profitability

Below left and right: Exterior and interior views of Siam Guardian. Guardian entered into a 50/50 joint venture with Siam Cement Company Limited to build a float glass plant in Nong Khae, Thailand. The plant opened in September 1992.

Above: Chuck Croskey, center, with Krij Kulanet, Siam Guardian's marketing manager, left, and Dusit Nontanakorn, Siam Guardian's managing director, right. In 1997, Guardian opened a second float glass plant in Thailand, also a joint venture with Siam Cement.

Left: Siam Guardian employees gathered in front of the Thailand I plant on its first anniversary, forming the traditional "G" of Guardian's logo.

Right: Ralph Gerson accepts a token of appreciation on behalf of Guardian from the King of Thailand, His Majesty King Bhumibol Adulyadej Rama IX. By the late 1990s, Guardian was operating two major float plants in Thailand.

coastal province of Rayong. "The plant is about 150 kilometers southeast of Bangkok," said Dusit Nontanakorn. "It is almost adjacent to the sand supply and very close to the port. We deliberately put it in that location to be closer to raw materials and to have more of an export orientation."[46]

The plant's general manager was Somyod Tangmeelarp, former plant engineer at Nong Khae (Thailand I).[47] The new facility made tinted glass, which was widely used in Thailand, Asia, and the Middle East, while Thailand I continued to produce clear glass.[48]

The timing of the second Thai plant proved less than ideal, however. Just a few months after its February 1997 launch, Asia tumbled into a financial crisis, and the effects reverberated through the business world. Guardian, like many other companies doing business in Asia, had to regroup quickly or face substantial losses. Because Guardian was so diversified geographically, it was in a better position to ride out the storm than most other companies, many of which were forced to close facilities or go out of business altogether. "I had some pretty sleepless nights and spent a lot of time on the road that year, but things were very solid in the United States and Europe," remembered Chuck Croskey.[49]

As Guardian had demonstrated many times over the years, adversity often creates opportunities for those who are willing to take risks. Such was the case again in Thailand. The two Thai plants lost significant money in 1998 and 1999 as a consequence

flourished. The plant successfully penetrated the domestic Thai market that had been virtually locked up by Asahi and also exported throughout Asia, Australia, and New Zealand. It was embraced by customers such as John Bedogni of Metropolitan Glass in New Zealand, who had previously relied on Pilkington for his glass supply.

"The Thailand operation is superb," Bedogni said. "It's run by superb people, and the service and documentation are great."[45]

After some three years of operation at Nong Khae, in November 1995, the joint venture company started construction of a second float plant in the

of the Asian crisis. At this time, Siam Cement decided to refocus on traditional core operations and concluded that its glass investments were expendable. Its top management indicated a willingness to sell the company's shares in the joint venture, and Guardian, confident in the long-term attractiveness of the Asian market and sensing an opportunity to acquire 100 percent ownership on attractive financial terms, agreed to buy out Siam Cement. The transaction closed in December 1999.[50] The timing would prove to be very fortuitous for Guardian. The worst of the crash in the Pacific Rim passed fairly quickly, and

although real growth in the region would remain elusive for several years, Guardian Thailand returned to substantial profitability in 2000.

It was during these events that George Longo became managing director of Guardian's Thai operations. Longo had experienced a classic Guardian career. He worked as a plant engineer at Corsicana, Texas, and then moved to the Richburg, South Carolina, plant before beginning overseas assignments in the Middle East. He became plant manager of the DeWitt, Iowa, float plant before moving back overseas to Bangkok, Thailand.

Above: Nearly three years after opening Thailand II, Guardian purchased Siam Cement's equity in both Thailand float glass plants, making Guardian the full owner of the two facilities. From left to right are Montri Chumnarm, Somyod Tangmeelarp, Dusit Nontanakorn, Peter Walters, George Longo, and Sanjiv Gupta.

Left: After three years of operation at Nong Khae, the joint venture company started construction on a second float plant in Rayong. The plant opened in February 1997, but months after the opening, Asia faced a financial crisis.

Opposite: Guardian glass in Shanghai's Jin Mao Tower—at the time the world's second-tallest building.

Breaking into the Japanese Market

In Thailand, Guardian found itself in direct competition with a local subsidiary of Asahi Glass, Japan's largest glass manufacturer. Japan, Asahi's home base and the second-largest economy in the world, boasted a $4 billion glass market. In that home market, Asahi and the smaller Japanese manufacturers—Nippon Sheet Glass and Central Glass—benefited from extremely high domestic glass prices. *Forbes* magazine reported that float glass for use in windows sold for $700 a ton in Japan versus $350 a ton in the United States.[51] Like much of Japanese industry, however, this sector fended off imports and foreign investment with a combination of tradition, complex business structures, and overtly restrictive trade barriers. Despite the disparity in glass prices, only about four of the 400 Japanese glass distributors handled imported products.[52] And those that did risked retaliation.

Gerson, who had significant experience with Japan from his years at the office of United States Trade Representative and doing international trade

Guardian's Thailand operation provided glass to regional markets where it was used in projects like the Tokyo International Forum in Japan.

work at a major Washington, D.C., law firm, recalled the issues Guardian faced:

Breaking down trade barriers in Japan was important to us for two principal reasons. First, it was a huge market and our freedom to sell there became increasingly important as we expanded our manufacturing capacity in nearby Southeast Asia and offered new value-added products made in the United States. Second, Asahi was a global competitor that was expanding its reach and impact in every market where Guardian had a presence. We would be at a competitive disadvantage if Asahi were permitted to rake in huge profits in its protected home market and use those profits to buy up marketshare and other companies elsewhere. To keep Asahi and its fellow Japanese manufacturers honest, we needed to take the fight to their home market."[53]

The fight would prove very difficult. "Nobody played in their sandbox but them," said Walters. "If you want the definition of a closed market, the Japanese customers that we visited didn't even care about a price quote. They were not going to buy based on price. In fact, in the beginning they wouldn't even meet with us because they were scared of retaliation."[54]

Guardian's efforts focused on increasing its commercial presence in Japan through the establishment of a subsidiary in that country and seeking assistance from the U.S. government on market access.

In 1991, Guardian was one of 20 companies selected to participate in the U.S. Commerce Department's Japan Corporate Program. The initiative offered support to U.S. companies seeking to export to Japan.[55]

When President George H. W. Bush visited Japan in January 1992, glass was one of the industries he asked to be opened for more U.S. imports. During the visit, the Japanese government agreed that it would attempt to open the Japanese glass distribution system, eliminate exclusionary business practices, and ensure that construction codes did not serve as barriers to market entry. In anticipation of enhanced trade opportunities in Japan, Guardian formed a distribution subsidiary, Guardian Japan, in 1992.[56]

Some two years later, however, the market barriers remained. Japanese domestic manufacturers Asahi Glass, Nippon Sheet Glass, and Central Glass continued to have the same market shares they had enjoyed in the 1960s. Foreign glassmakers' share of the Japanese market stood at just 5 percent. Flat glass sales by U.S. companies to Japan had actually declined; their market share was less than half of 1 percent. Long-time Guardian veteran Karl Straky, director of commercial glass products, believed that Japan was the toughest market Guardian had ever encountered.

"Historically, Guardian can go into a marketplace and in a very short period of time establish a very strong position for its products and for the company. On a scale of one to 10 with Japan being a 10, the next closest would be a five," Straky said.[57]

Despite all the promises and commitments, Guardian still encountered "cartelistic behavior, exclusionary business practices, an exclusive distribution system, and two-tier pricing," according to Gerson, and Japanese glass distributors and glaziers were still being pressured to buy and use only domestic glass.[58] As Walters wrote in a *Journal of Commerce* article. "Japanese negotiators will agree, at least privately, that the market is closed. But there is [no progress] on how the change should occur."[59]

The effort to break into the Japanese market would continue, both for Guardian and for a succession of administrations of the U.S. government. Progress was to be painfully slow.[60] By the mid-1990s, however, the Japanese economy finally began to pay for its encrusted layers of bureaucracy and

Guardian supplied the glass for the NTT Shinjuku building in Tokyo, Japan.

protectionism. It slipped into a downward spiral of bad debts, unemployment, and contraction that would continue into the next decade. In the meantime, Guardian kept the pressure on to create a level playing field.

The Challenge of India

While the Japanese economy continued to maintain trade barriers and began its slide into a long recession, Guardian was busy with opportunities elsewhere. As early as 1988, Guardian had reached an agreement in principle with Modi Rubber Limited,

---

In early 1988, Guardian reached an agreement with Modi Rubber Limited to form a joint venture—called Gujarat Guardian Ltd.—for the construction and operation of a float glass plant in India. Seated are Vinay Modi, center, white suit; Peter Walters, center, dark suit; Alan Schlang, Guardian corporate secretary, second from right; Alok Modi, seated far left. Standing in the back in blue suit with glasses is Wally Rueckel, Guardian treasurer; Ajit Vashi, in middle with white shirt; N. G. Rau, standing with white shirt on right side, looking down; and Ajit Surana, standing behind Walters in suit.

an Indian company, to form a joint venture—called Gujarat Guardian Ltd.—for the construction and operation of a float glass plant in the Indian state of Gujarat. In 1990, definitive agreements were reached under which Guardian and Modi Rubber would each have 40 percent ownership and the remainder would be sold to the public (later changed to certain governmental entities in Gujarat and ultimately converted essentially into a 50/50 venture). Vinay Kumar Modi was the individual at Modi Rubber who represented that company in all its dealings with Guardian and the joint venture.

The risks and possible rewards surrounding an investment in India were enormous. India was a society of staggering contrasts. It was the world's second most populous country in 1990, with some 830 million people and an explosive birth rate. It suffered from endemic poverty and disease, its cities were bursting with people, and in many places its infrastructure was crumbling or nonexistent. In fact, much of India lacked even plumbing, electricity, and access to fresh water.

On the other hand, India under British rule had developed an advanced legal system and powerful national identity. India was a proud country with an active and growing middle class and a long

tradition of entrepreneurialism. Despite the pervasive poverty, it had actually achieved agricultural self-sufficiency, had a solid industrial base and possessed millions of well-educated and motivated workers and professionals.[61] As Guardian would learn, this environment of extremes and contrasts was unlike anywhere else the company had ventured. Joe Bruce, vice president of global purchasing, remarked, "It was pretty frontier-like but it had tremendous potential."[62]

Bringing the Gujarat plant from the agreement stage to reality required Guardian and Modi to overcome what seemed like an endless succession of obstacles.

"It was like running a high hurdles race. There was no time to cheer when you jumped over one barrier because the next one was immediately in front of you, waiting to trip you up," said Walters.[63]

One of the main challenges for Guardian and its Indian partner was dealing with the sprawling and bureaucratic regulatory process. Industrial licenses, including licenses authorizing construction and operation of a float plant, needed to be obtained from the Indian government and were available only in extremely limited numbers.

"We went through this incredible system where other groups had licenses, but they never actually built anything," said Gerson.

"To apply for a license, mountains of documents describing all the details of the project had to be submitted. The regulators not only reviewed all the paperwork but actually started to second-guess technical details such as the plant size and quality of technology. It was unbelievably cumbersome," he added.[64]

Above left and right: The joint venture with Modi Rubber created Gujarat Guardian. Construction at the site sometimes involved as many as 2,300 workers.

Below: Raw materials are supplied to the Gujarat Guardian plant from sand deposits like this in Bhavani, Gujarat, India, where the mining is done by hand. Many of the people shown here had never had their picture taken.

Vinay Modi also remembered the process of obtaining a license. "It took us one and a half years to get a license because the Indian government had already licensed a float glass plant in the eastern part of India to Pilkington," Modi said. "But that project was not making much progress, and therefore, we had to convince the Indian government that it should license another plant."[65] Guardian sent a team of engineers armed with documents, facts, and figures

to help make the case. Patience and perseverance finally were rewarded with the basic license, but this was only the first of the hurdles on the obstacle course. In India, the government also required a license to import foreign machinery. Such imports were necessary because the Indian economy did not manufacture many of the specialty items required for a float plant. Once again, Guardian and its partner had to appear before governmental agencies to explain "in endless detail" why the plant needed so much foreign machinery.[66]

Even success at this stage did not create a clear path to implementation of the project. The next obstacle was arranging financing. Guardian had

Left: Vinay Modi used a coconut to christen the new float line in Gujarat.

Below: Dave Rose, managing director, christened the new India float glass line in a more traditional Guardian way, using a bottle of wine. The Indian project was one of the more complex in Guardian's history.

accumulated substantial experience in financing new float projects around the world, but India would present very different challenges. Flexibility was severely constrained by government regulations that limited long term financing to only one source—Indian financial institutions that were government owned, highly regulated and intensely bureaucratic. Progress moved at a snail's pace, taking almost a year to receive a commitment letter and almost three years to complete the financing, something that would normally take six months. Ann Waichunas was Guardian's assistant treasurer at the time and led the financing efforts:

I personally found the experience one of the most difficult and challenging of my entire business career. This financing was the longest to put together of any Guardian project ever. It took an excruciating amount of time to reach even the smallest decisions. I personally visited India 15 times between July 1990 and December 1992 to work on the financing, which was made even more problematic due to inflation and currency devaluation during the period.[67]

While Guardian and Modi were arranging project financing, Gujarat Guardian proceeded to acquire the necessary land. The site the joint venture company selected was in a rural area near the village of Ankleswar located about 150 miles north of Mumbai (Bombay). The property at the

Above, left and right: The Indian project included housing, left, and a school, right, for Guardian's Indian employees and their families.

time was occupied by large numbers of subsistence farmers. Negotiating with each farmer would have taken years. Instead, the local government stepped in and purchased the land en masse under a notification procedure, then transferred the desired parcel to Gujarat Guardian.[68]

The selection of Gujarat involved tradeoffs for the new joint venture. "Among the reasons we went to the rural area of Gujarat were the availability of energy and certain raw materials needed for operating the plant, and favorable governmental incentives," remembered David Rose, the first managing director of the plant. But there were downsides as well: "The major disadvantage of such an undeveloped area was, of course, that the infrastructure of power, water, gas lines, and roads was nonexistent. It took a tremendous amount of work with different government agencies to bring power and water and gas. The power line had to come approximately 10 miles. The gas line was eight miles long, and the water line was about 14 miles in length."[69]

Every element presented a major challenge. The appropriate pipe for the gas line, for instance, was not available in India and had to be located in Houston and imported to Gujarat.[70]

Many aspects of the construction of the Gujarat Guardian float plant reflected unique Indian conditions. As project manager Ajit Vashi, a native of India and long-time Guardian engineer, recalled: "Because of the abundance of labor available, much of what

would be done elsewhere with mechanical equipment, such as digging and material handling, could be done manually in India. The number of workers on the plant site at times reached almost 2,300, six times the normal construction workforce."[71] Many of them lived right on the site with their families. Another unique feature of the Gujarat plant was the need for a company owned and operated sand processing facility to wash sand and improve quality. Normally, the sand supplier would carry out this activity, but suppliers in India at the time were not reliable enough to satisfy the plant's requirements for this crucial raw material. Due to the rural location, the plant also featured its own 14-unit guesthouse to accommodate those working on the project or visiting the site.[72]

When finally launched in January 1993, Gujarat Guardian was the first float glass plant in India. True to Guardian tradition, Gujarat Guardian represented a careful blending of local culture with Guardian's operating principles. Gujarat Guardian might, in fact, be both the purest expression of the Guardian Way and simultaneously the clearest showcase for the benefits of globalization. To house its employees, Guardian built a compound around the plant that included excellent housing and schools. Living standards within the compound were superior to those prevailing in the surrounding countryside, and Guardian could pick from the best workers, both locally and nationally.

"Guardian normally puts up plants, but does not build housing and schools," Modi said. "But considering the Indian conditions, I was able to show Guardian the desirability of going much further than usual. When I explained the situation to Mr. Davidson, he gladly agreed. I said that if we want to have good productivity and get talent from all over

India, we must set up housing. We have built a hundred houses near the plant, in addition to a guest house and school, because in those days, there was no school in that area that could teach in English."[73]

Enrollment at Gujarat Guardian's school ultimately reached more than 1,000 students.

The plant was launched under the leadership of Dave Rose. He had been a draftsman at General Motors in 1969 when Richard Alonzo offered him an engineering job at Guardian. After working in corporate engineering and at the Carleton plant, he helped build and launch the Kingsburg plant and later assisted Villosa in making the transition to a Guardian operation. As he recalled, however, "the toughest management assignment I ever had was bringing our Gujarat float plant on line and making it a profitable operation."[74] Rose was named "Employee of the Year" in 2001.

Unlike many of Guardian's float glass plants, Gujarat Guardian was not immediately profitable. The new company had to undertake the burden of transitioning customers from sheet glass to the higher quality but more expensive float glass. The sales team initially ran into problems because Indian buyers were not familiar with their product

and balked at the slightly higher prices. Customers also had to be educated on how to handle and use float glass.

"The glass industry was very primitive in parts of India," said Gerson. "I remember having to explain to some of the dealers that we would not be accepting oxcarts for transportation, that you had to have motor vehicles to pick up glass."[75]

While the production capability at the plant reached a very high level in a short time, it took longer to educate potential customers, put the sales team in place, and build a market in India for float glass.

Seriously compounding the challenges faced by Rose and his team was the problem of ongoing debt service costs. All of the unique circumstances in India had resulted in a plant that was very expensive to build, requiring a substantial amount of project financing. In addition, during the 1990s India

---

Gujarat Guardian, the first float glass plant in India, opened on January 23, 1993. Hundreds of coconuts were broken during its two years of construction, an Indian tradition symbolizing wishes for success.

From left: Vinay Modi, Ajit Vashi, Bill Davidson, and Dave Rose on a visit to Gujarat Guardian. While the production capability at the plant reached a high level in a short time, it took longer to educate customers, put the sales team in place, and build a market in India for float glass.

experienced very high interest rates, often exceeding 20 percent. This combination resulted in debt service costs that, for a period in the early and mid-1990s, threatened the financial viability of the venture. Often lost from view during these years was the fact that the plant's operations were continually improving, and by most measures would have been considered a success.

Guardian had known from the beginning that operating the first float glass plant in India would not be easy. Working with its partner, Guardian's leadership remained confident that India would ultimately prove to be a hospitable region for its business, and was prepared to deal with the short-term difficulties. Government reforms initiated by Prime Minister Rao began to improve the economic and regulatory environment within which Gujarat Guardian operated. Deregulation enhanced the general business climate and the Indian economy began to grow at rates more typical of other transitional economies. Of great significance, a restructuring of the debt was finally worked out with lenders in 1995, which, combined with additional equity from the partners, eased the immediate financial burden on the company. In the years that followed, operating profits continued to improve as the highly effective Gujarat team perfected its approach, interest rates eased and debt was rapidly reduced. Gujarat

Guardian had also become a spawning ground for Guardian's worldwide operations. Due to their education, work ethic, and mobility, many of the company's employees successfully took positions in other Guardian locations. By the end of the decade, Gujarat Guardian had turned the corner and positioned itself as financially strong and consistently profitable. Once again Guardian's patience, determination, and focus on the longterm had been rewarded.

Other Opportunities in the Pacific

Originally, Guardian planned to build a float glass plant in Indonesia. Considerable work was done to this end during the years 1989 through 1991. The project ended, however, when Guardian discovered an Indonesian company building a nearly identical float glass plant next door to the Guardian site, using engineering drawings Guardian believed were stolen from one of its U.S. facilities.[76] Throughout the 1990s, Guardian would continue to explore possible investments in Indonesia, which remained a potential area for Guardian expansion.

During the mid-1990s, Guardian also announced a joint venture with a local Chinese governmental entity to build a float glass plant in Wuxi, Jiangsu province. At the time, many American companies were moving into China seeking lower

labor costs and well-trained employees and hoping to become part of the world's largest market. For Guardian, however, while it reached definitive agreements on construction and operation of the plant and completed the permitting process, business conditions changed and were no longer favorable for the investment. A glut of float glass manufactured by the heavily subsidized domestic glass industry along with the Asian financial crisis caused Guardian to withdraw from the project, although China remained an important market for Guardian exports and potential investment.[77]

The Middle East

The Middle East was the last substantial market in the world that did not have indigenous float glass manufacturing. Throughout the 1980s, the Middle East had in fact become a high quality glass market and was consuming increasing volumes of glass imported from Europe and Asia. As Peter

Above: A group of Guardian employees in the Saudi Arabian desert. From left to right are Richard Alonzo, Russ Ebeid, Georges Franck, and Bruce Cummings.

Right: Groundbreaking at Gulfguard in Saudi Arabia. Seated in the center in a black suit is Russ Ebeid.

Walters recalled, "While we had never really sold much glass to the Middle East, our new global presence and economic trends in the region during the 1980s and early 1990s created an incentive for us to focus on possible investments there."[78]

After Ebeid and Walters made an exploratory visit to Iraq in 1989 to assess investment opportunities, the government of Saudi Arabia decided to entice a float glass producer to build a plant in that country. Guardian then learned that a Saudi quasi-governmental agency, "the National Industrialization Company (NIC)" had started negotiations with Guardian's European competitors. Guardian entered the fray and ultimately was chosen as the Western partner for the float glass project. As Walters recalled, "the first Gulf War interrupted negotiations with NIC but we were certainly pleased that we had decided to go forward in Saudi rather than Iraq."[79]

Negotiations were completed following the conclusion of the first Gulf War and a site was chosen in the Al-Jubail Industrial Estate located on the Persian Gulf in the shadow of the immense Aramco Petrochemical complex. Construction of the Saudi plant started in June 1995, with Georges Franck of CRVC as on-site project manager, and as usual, certain unique local challenges had to be overcome. From an engineering point of view, the plant represented the first time that Guardian added a separate line to produce patterned glass from the same furnace serving the float line. Other challenges were of a more local nature. As an example, due to the close

proximity of the plant to the Persian Gulf, the water table at the plant was just 3 feet below the surface. Before any building could be done, more than 500,000 tons of sand was brought in to raise the site grade an additional 10 feet.[80]

Further, in preparation for operating the plant, it was necessary to recruit workers from numerous countries and obtain visas for them, find reliable sources for raw materials in a market that did not have existing demand for many of the needed materials, obtain huge quantities of water in a desert environment, and procure a steady supply of wood for boxes in a country with no timber.[81]

The new plant—known as Gulfguard—was launched in October 1996. Its management team, headed by managing director Tom Wunderlich and sales manager Don Pettus, was among the

most international in Guardian's history, with representatives from the United States, Saudi Arabia, the Phillipines, India, and Luxembourg.[82]

In addition to the challenges of ramping up production of international quality glass at the first float glass plant in Saudi Arabia, Gulfguard faced huge hurdles on the marketing and sales side. As Chuck Croskey recalled:

Probably the biggest hurdle was transitioning the market. Saudi Arabia's entire glass supply had previously been supplied entirely by imports. Individuals who had earned a living by importing and trading glass were now faced with transitioning to fabrication and distribution of a domestic supply of float glass. Guardian's philosophy is to help customers develop their businesses and advance the local glass industry. We supported our customers, many of which had previously just traded in glass, by providing products manufactured to the most stringent standards at internationally competitive prices. We helped them develop fabrication capabilities and as a result the Kingdom's glass fabrication industry has flourished. Guardian's goal of giving customers freedom to expand their own businesses meshes well wherever the entrepreneurial spirit lives, and Saudi Arabia is no exception.[83]

As later events would show, Gulfguard was only the beginning of Guardian's expansion into the Middle East.

Above right: Abdul Rahman Abdo, chairman of the board of Gulfguard, breaks the glass ribbon, launching Guardian's plant in Al-Jubail, Saudi Arabia, on October 8, 1996. Abdul Rahman Bin Zarah, another board member, looks on. The plant's workforce consisted of employees from many nations, including the United States, the Philippines, India, and Luxembourg, as well as the host nation.

Below: The Gulfguard plant was the first full-scale float glass plant to open in the Middle East. It supplied the entire Persian Gulf and areas throughout the Middle East.

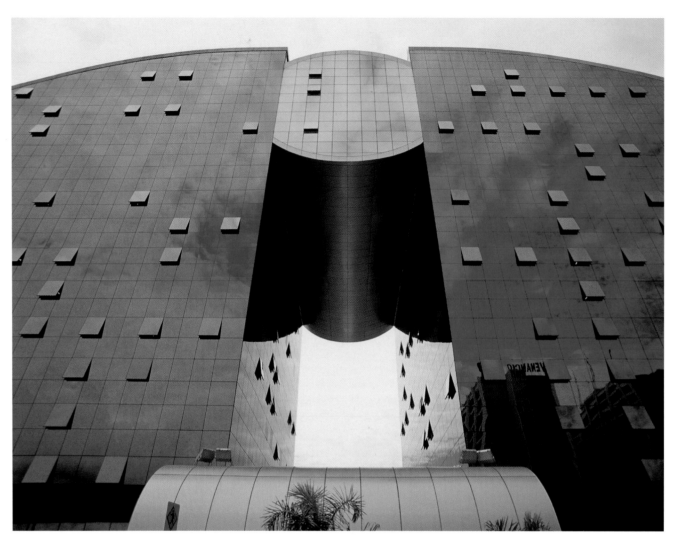

Guardian's Porto Real, Brazil, float glass facility supplemented Guardian's growing Brazilian presence as indicated by glass supplied to the Brasilia Shopping Center.

Brazil

Despite the challenges facing Guardian in Venezuela, the operation in Maturin did provide the immediate benefit of serving as a springboard for access to the rest of Latin America. When Mark Lacasse took charge of sales for the region in the early 1990s, he developed a strategic vision that facilitated eventual expansion. Venezuela's glass exports were turned toward seeding potential major markets to the South, especially Brazil, and learning about customer desires and conditions in those markets. In 1995, Guardian established a physical presence in Brazil by opening up a distribution operation in Sao Paolo (a city of more than 14 million inhabitants). The Venezuelan government named Guardian de Venezuela the 1995 Export Company of the Year, an award that reflected the growing connection between the operation in Maturin and upcoming expansion to the South.[84]

In June 1996, after preparing the Brazilian market for some time with exports from Venezuela, Guardian announced plans to build a new float glass plant in Porto Real, some 110 miles west of Rio de Janeiro. Brazil was the fifth largest country in the world and the sixth most populous. Its economy ranked as the 10th largest in the world, and for a number of years strong growth in the Brazilian construction and automotive industries coupled with deregulation had led to a substantial increase in demand for float glass.[85] The only available domestic sources of float glass, however, came from joint venture partners Pilkington and Saint-Gobain, who looked at the country as their exclusive domain. Brazil was now clearly ready for Guardian's entry as a glass manufacturer.

After a complicated construction project, under the direction of Juan Roestel, that included leveling the hill-top site and enduring Brazil's rainy season, Guardian's Brazil float plant was launched in the summer of 1998. Lacasse, named managing director, recalled the biggest issues he faced in his new operation:

Commercially, our biggest challenge was to sell out in a market where our plant had brought a 33 percent increase in production capacity, without creating a glut on that market. Our strategy was to take advantage of the fact that our competitor had operated as a monopoly and left much to be desired in terms of quality and service. We concentrated our efforts on the customer base that had been built up from our warehouse distribution system over the years and slowly added new customers who were interested in paying for quality and extraordinary service. We focused on how to help these customers grow their own busi-

nesses, which in turn of course helped us sell more of our glass at reasonable price levels.[86]

One of Guardian Brazil's principal innovations was the introduction of just-in-time delivery. "We knew that by improving customer service we would have an instant edge over the competition. When we opened the plant, we made a promise to our customers to load and ship trucks 24 hours a day, every day of the year, and that's exactly what we're doing today," said Lacasse.[87] Customers within a 200-mile radius of the Brazil plant can place orders by 4:00 p.m. for delivery by 7:00 a.m. the next morning, "which for Brazil is extraordinary."[88] This focus on service captured the attention and allegiance of customers. "Guardian broke the monopoly in the glass markets here in Brazil," said Wilson Farhat Jr., a coowner of Valeria Vidrios, a glass fabricator and customer of Guardian Brazil. "The glass market was closed here, and we were almost forbidden to import glass. After Guardian opened the plant, it took only a short time for Brazilian customers to realize how badly they had been treated."[89]

Guardian also faced unique issues in Brazil in blending its business philosophy with the local culture and capabilities. As Lacasse recalled:

Culturally, our biggest challenge was to marry the Guardian way of thinking for yourself, having very few rules and regulations and employing a flat organizational structure with the historical Brazilian approach of a more bureaucratic environment, huge class differences and considerable formality. Our strategy was simply to show by example how we could be different from the norm. We also had to hire the right people who could adopt a more Guardian approach to things. As it turned out, Brazilians are hungry for the opportunity to explore new things and prove what they are capable of doing. Today, from a Brazilian perspective, we are clearly one of the most dynamic, least bureaucratic, informal, flat, and low-cost operations to be found."[90]

These characteristics were quickly turned into outstanding financial performance by the Brazilian operation, and eventually led to record operating profits for a Guardian float glass plant.[91]

With the launching of plants in Thailand, India, Saudi Arabia, and Brazil, Guardian was now well

The Porto Real glass plant in the state of Rio de Janeiro, Brazil, opened in 1997. It produced 600 tons of glass daily and sold to both the automotive and architectural markets.

situated to participate in all of the world's major glass markets. This did not mean, however, that Guardian was ignoring its more established glass markets or its other businesses.

Further Growth in Europe

By the early-1990s, Guardian was on a worldwide mission, steadily opening new plants in entirely new regions. At the same time, however, Guardian continued to expand its presence in what were now the well-established regions of Western Europe and North America. While this form of expansion may seem more "routine" and may have been accomplished with somewhat less fanfare than its entry into exotic locations in emerging markets, the results were just as important for Guardian.

In the fall of 1992, Guardian announced that it would build a second float glass plant in the northeastern part of Spain, to be located in the city of Tudela, state of Navarra.[92] The plant was launched in 1993 under the direction of Luc Theis, its first plant manager. Theis, a native of Luxembourg, started at Guardian in 1990 as fabrication superintendent and then production manager of Luxguard I. In later years, Theis would go on to become responsible for Guardian's southern European operations and was named Employee of the Year in 2002.[93]

The challenges facing Theis and his management team in Spain were first to make Guardian Navarra a world-class float glass plant and then to blend and harmonize the new facility in Navarra with

the existing one in Llodio. Beginning virtually from the day of its launch, the plant in Navarra generated financial results that put it in the top tier among

---

Left: In 1993, Guardian opened a second float glass plant in the northern part of Spain. The plant was launched under the direction of Luc Theis, its first plant manager.

Left bottom: The king and queen of Spain were honored guests at the 1994 inauguration of Guardian's Navarra float plant. From left are Guardian Executive Vice President Ralph Gerson, Queen Sofia, Glass Group President Russ Ebeid, and King Juan Carlos.

Right: Executives planted a time capsule at a groundbreaking ceremony. From left: Ferd Kohn, Guardian Europe Managing Director Jim Moore, Guardian Executive Vice President Ralph Gerson, the mayor of Tudela, and the president of Navarra.

Right bottom: Guardian employees celebrated the running of the bulls in July 1995 in Pamplona, Spain. From left to right are Ken Lange, Bruce Cummings, Jim Moore, Antonio Girbau, Russ Ebeid, Luc Theis, Dave Ford, and Michael Hissette.

Guardian's worldwide operations.[94] In explaining Navarra's extraordinary success, even by Guardian's standards, Theis pointed to several factors:

We had a great deal of encouragement and cooperation from governmental authorities that welcomed investment and created a positive business climate. The plant was superbly designed and we staffed it with 200 outstanding people from among 9,500 job candidates. In that way, we were permitted to focus on attitudes and behaviors of our employees rather than overly emphasizing finding people with technical skills. In fact, we had the great advantage that the personnel from Llodio, who had decades of experience in glassmaking, could be our teachers in the technical side of things. We engaged in very intensive training of personnel and from day one set expectations very high. Our workforce responded superbly and demonstrated a sense of pride and ownership that translated into outstanding operating and financial performance.[95]

In 1994, Theis was given full responsibility for all of Guardian's operations in Spain. His next challenge was to blend Llodio and Navarra into a harmonious and integrated operation. As Theis recalled, "Llodio had a long and proud history of its own as a glassmaker, and some of its people had been doing things a certain way for decades. Navarra had no history and no indigenous expertise in glassmaking but it started with a clean slate and could adopt Guardian's values very quickly. The trick was to create harmonization and coordination while at the same time retain the particularities and autonomy of each where this was important."[96] Theis and his senior team worked hard to create organizational structures that linked the two Spanish centers together and then focused on establishing procedures and encouraging behaviors that supported cooperation and teamwork. While not achieved overnight, the exchange of ideas and personnel, and a cooperative focus on finding solutions to common Spanish problems eventually turned Llodio and Navarra into harmonious parts of one large operation.

"Breaking down barriers between Llodio and Navarra, even though the facilities were only about 100 miles apart and the people spoke a common language, was no easy task, and it is a credit to Luc and all the people in those plants that they

Below left: Tudela, the float glass plant in Navarra, Spain, opened in 1993. It was an extraordinary performer from the beginning of its operation.

Below right: In 1995, construction began on what would be Guardian's sixth European float glass plant in Wolfen-Thalheim, located in the state of Saxony-Anhalt in the former East Germany.

Above: Following the 1997 dedication of Guardian's float glass plant in Germany, Chancellor Helmut Kohl, right, congratulated Glass Group President Russ Ebeid.

Below: Guardian Flachglas supplied glass to Germany and central Europe. Its glass was used for the restoration of many buildings in Berlin, including the Reichstag, the German parliament building.

Opposite: Guardian Flachglas supplied the glass for the EU Central Bank in Europe.

embraced a bigger picture for the good of the company," said Jim Moore.[97]

Within a short time after Guardian Navarra was launched, Guardian began investigating other opportunities for expansion in Europe. In August 1995, construction, under the direction of Jean Braun of CRVC, was started on what would be Guardian's sixth European float glass plant (named Guardian Flachglas) in Wolfen-Thalheim, located in the state of Saxony-Anhalt in the former East Germany.[98] The area had been a site of chemical, rubber, paper, and machinery manufacturing but had suffered significant unemployment since German reunification.

The plant was launched in November 1996. It had a capacity of 600 tons per day and housed one of the world's largest coaters. Unlike Guardian's other coaters, the Flachglas coating machine was connected directly to the float line, thereby increasing efficiency. The coater was used to produce low-E glass, a product that is increasingly mandated by law in Germany for energy conservation.[99] Guardian Flachglas would supply glass to Germany and central Europe. Its glass would be used for the restoration of many buildings in Berlin, including the Reichstag, the German parliament building.[100]

Above: His Royal Highness Prince Henri of Luxembourg initiated the new laminating line at Luxguard II on October 8, 1997. On the left is Ferd Kohn, and on the right is Leo Schneider, Luxguard II plant manager.

Below right: In 1996, Guardian Europe's sales director and 1987 "Employee of the Year" David Ford was killed in the same plane crash that took the life of U.S. Secretary of Commerce Ron Brown and others. He is shown here several years earlier in Pamplona, Spain.

The ceremonial innauguration of Guardian Flachglas took place in October 1997. The significance of Guardian's investment in the former East Germany was underscored by the presence of Dr. Helmut Kohl, chancellor of the Federal Republic of Germany. During his remarks, Chancellor Kohl recognized Guardian's plant as a showcase for how economic investment can promote lasting peace by creating fulfilling jobs. Bill Davidson expressed Guardian's commitment to being in the forefront of technology and added that "doing so will ensure continued growth and prosperity both for this new facility and for the people of the Wolfen-Thalheim region."[101] Guardian was also expanding at its existing European locations. In 1997, Luxguard II opened an architectural glass laminating line, adding to the existing tempering and mirror lines.[102] Demand for architectural laminated glass was growing in Europe. Because laminated glass offered

safety, sound control, and solar heat control, it was used widely in residential and commercial buildings.[103] Before the opening of the laminated glass line at Luxguard II, the laminated glass Guardian sold in Europe was produced at the plant in Llodio, Spain.[104] Shortly afterward, Guardian opened a mirror line at its Hunguard plant. About half the mirrors produced at the plant were sold in Hungary, and the rest were exported to neighboring countries.[105]

A Bittersweet Anniversary in Europe

Within just a few days of the Wolfen launch, Guardian celebrated the 15th anniversary of the November 1981 Luxguard I launch that had established its presence in Europe. From its modest beginnings, Guardian's European operations now had six float lines, a patterned glass line, three coaters, three mirror lines, a modern OEM automotive glass fabrication plant (at Grevenmacher, Luxembourg) and tempering facilities at three plants.[106] The leadership team had evolved over the years both with continuity and the addition of new talent. Moore remained the managing director of Guardian Europe. Sapi was responsible for central and Eastern European operations, Theis was in charge of Spain and Southern Europe, Leo Schneider was plant manager of Luxguard II, and Rene Fiorese was plant manager of Luxguard I. A Guardian employee since 1981, Fiorese

Above: Jean Braun, left, managing director of CRVC; Alain Biver, project manager of CRVC; Lu Rimar, technical director of CRVC; and Ajit Vashi, director of float process engineering.

Left: Benoit Thiry, Jean Heyart, Renato Paladin, and Jean Harlange are part of Guardian Europe's research and engineering group, CRVC.

would soon be appointed sales manager for all of Guardian's European operations. His replacement at Luxguard I was Georges Bourscheid. Guardian Europe's research and engineering group—CRVC—was led by directors Albert Franck and Lu Rimar. This period also saw the maturation of senior Guardian Europe departmental leaders, including Michael Gluckstein, Jean-Luc Pitsch in finance, Jean-Pierre de Bonhome in tax, Ann Waichunas in treasury, Germain Hames in purchasing, David Jaffe in legal, and Jean Ries in business development.

Sadly and tragically missing from the anniversary celebration was David Ford, Guardian's long-time European sales director and one of the principal architects of the company's tremendous successes during those 15 years. In April 1996, Ford was on a humanitarian mission to Bosnia with U.S. Commerce Secretary Ron Brown and other business executives when their airplane went down in a storm. There were no survivors. Ford had joined the mission to donate 23 tons of glass for the reconstruction of a Sarajevo hospital. The glass eventually reached the war-ravaged city, and a plaque at the hospital commemorates Ford's efforts.

The Bay & Dundas office building on Bay and Edwards streets in Toronto, Ontario, Canada, used glass produced and coated at Guardian's Carleton plant.

In commenting at the time on Ford's tragic death, Davidson said:

This is a tremendous loss, both personally and professionally, for the entire Guardian family. David joined the Guardian team 25 years ago, and throughout his career, he made incalculable contributions to the company. He was one of Guardian's most dynamic, hard working, dedicated employees and a friend to all of us. He loved his job and worked to expand Guardian's presence throughout the world. His observations on business and life in general were always well thought out, frequently witty, and usually complemented by a smile and a chuckle. I know I speak for all of Guardian when I say that

it was an honor to have known and worked with David. And, although he will be greatly missed, he will never be forgotten.[107]

The colleagues he left behind to celebrate their company's 15 years in Europe all recognized the debt they owed to an individual who had become an integral part of the legend of Guardian Industries.

North American Expansion

Throughout the 1990s, Guardian continued to expand its North American fabrication business, mostly through acquisition. Unlike the burst of acquisitions in the 1980s, which diversified the company into new businesses, these acquisitions were relatively small and usually designed to bolster Guardian's core glass business.

Guardian began the decade by expanding in Canada. In 1977, it built a glass fabrication facility in Tilsonburg, Ontario, but had not significantly increased its presence in the region since then. In 1990, Guardian acquired control of Industries Cover, a Canadian glass fabricator and distributor that was one of the major producers of insulated glass units in Canada. Cover operated five plants in Quebec and Ontario under the leadership of James Boudreault and employed some 500 people.[108] A year later, Guardian purchased an interest in another Canadian firm, Trenline-Laramee Glass Products, which manufactured mirrors, laminated glass, and insulating units at its facility in Rexdale, Ontario.[109] Guardian next acquired Walker Atlantic Glass of Toronto. Walker Atlantic made mirrors and decorative doors for the Canadian architectural and furniture industries. It also made heavy glass products used in malls and commercial buildings, including the Toronto Skydome's corporate offices and private boxes.[110]

Ultimately all of Guardian's Canadian facilities were placed under the direction of Boudreault, whose operations at Cover were extremely successful throughout the period.

Around the same time, back in the United States, Falconer Glass Industries became part of the Guardian family. Falconer operated plants in Jamestown, New York, and Lewistown, Pennsylvania. Its Jamestown plant, which Guardian eventually closed down in order to move its production capacity to other locations, housed the largest mirror line in North America[111] with a capacity of 6,000 feet of mirror an hour.[112]

Finally, in 1992 Guardian acquired Consolidated Glass & Mirror, of Galax, Virginia, a supplier to the furniture industry and the largest of the recent string of acquisitions. Through these acquisitions, Guardian had acquired considerable mirror-making capacity. In 1993, Guardian announced the addition of mirror

Guardian produced glass for many recognizable facilities across the United States, including the USAir Terminal at New York's Laguardia Airport.

lines at Luxguard II and India, making the company the largest mirror manufacturer in the world.[113]

Guardian's downstream acquisitions and the natural growth of demand for glass in North America supported the construction of additional float plants in the United States. In late 1994, Guardian announced plans to build a new float glass plant in DeWitt, Iowa. Under the direction of onsite project manager David Younker, construction was completed in just 12 months, the quickest of any Guardian float plant to date, and the facility was

launched in May 1996.[114] The DeWitt plant had Guardian's largest furnace, with a capacity for producing approximately 700 tons of glass per day. The plant also had tempering facilities and added a mirror line in 1998. DeWitt's first plant manager was George Longo, a Guardian veteran who had started his career with the company in 1980 as Corsicana's plant engineer.

Shortly after DeWitt was successfully launched, Guardian announced plans to build another float glass plant to be located in Geneva, New York. In terms of jobs, this would be the largest new investment in the state by a non-New York–based company in two decades.[115] While the region around Geneva was economically depressed and new jobs were badly needed, the residents of the town were concerned about the impact of a new manufacturing facility on the community and environment. Rich Rising, city manager of Geneva, was director of city planning when Guardian came to the town of 14,000. He remembered its cautious approach to inviting a new manufacturing company. "We did our due diligence on Guardian," Rising said. "What kind of corporate citizens were they? What kind of incentive

Above and below right: The float glass plant in Geneva, New York, opened in 1998 and expanded shortly thereafter.

Below left: In late 1994, Guardian announced plans to build a new float glass plant in DeWitt, Iowa.

did other cities provide? What was the community impact? Our research basically concluded that they were very good corporate citizens. They got involved in the community, but at the same time, they sort of kept to themselves and just ran the business."[116]

After another 12-month construction period that matched DeWitt's record pace, the Geneva plant was launched in May 1998. Mark Mette, a veteran of the Fullerton patterned glass plant and the Kingsburg and Thailand float plants, was named the first plant manager. The plant would supply clear float glass to customers in the northeastern United States and southeastern Canada, including Guardian's own fabrication plants in Quebec, Ontario, Massachusetts,

In 1995, Guardian moved its headquarters to Auburn Hills, Michigan. The company built a 113,000-square-foot building in a wooded area within sight of Bill Davidson's sports arena, The Palace of Auburn Hills.

New York, and Pennsylvania.[117] The plan also called for later introduction of a high-speed coater for production of low-E glass.

Amidst all the growth of the 1990s, Guardian announced plans to move its world headquarters to Auburn Hills, Michigan, north of Detroit. The company had long outgrown the spartan offices

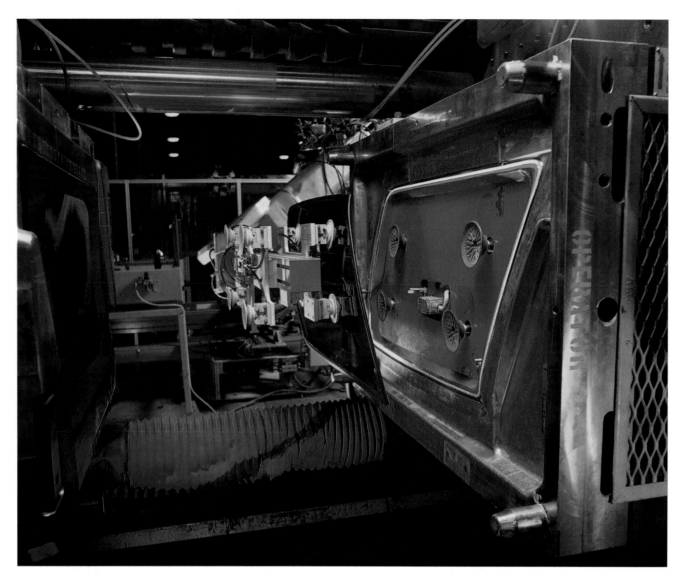

that it had occupied in Novi, Michigan, since 1972. Guardian planned to build on 55 acres adjacent to The Palace, the arena Bill Davidson's Detroit Pistons had occupied since 1988. The 113,000-square-foot building, opened in 1995, was nestled in a wooded area within sight of The Palace.[118]

Guardian developed technology to encapsulate automotive glass, which involved molding a frame around the glass so that it could be installed easily on an automobile.

Automotive Keeps Rolling Along

The steady drumbeat of expansion had an electrifying affect on Guardian Industries. In 1990, still at the beginning of its drive into non-traditional markets, Guardian's sales passed the $1 billion mark. Another significant milestone in 1990 was Guardian's receipt of an "A" credit rating for the first time in its history, a remarkable sign of the company's financial strength

only a few years after the going private transaction was completed. Although the company owed a great deal of its success to its glass manufacturing division, Guardian's traditional fabricating business, especially the automotive division, remained an important part of the company.

As the decade of the 1990s began, the automotive business was a vastly changed industry. Over the previous 15 years, Guardian had watched as automotive manufacturers steadily outsourced more and more of their design and fabrication. By 1990, the big car manufacturers were not only driving down the cost of their materials, they were demanding that their vendors supply complete systems. Thus, brake companies would provide entire braking systems, and window suppliers would develop not only the glass windows, but also the fittings (called "encapsulated glass") and technology to install them.

Underscoring Davidson's view that Guardian needed to expand its role as a major player in the automotive glass business, in 1988 Guardian hired Jack Sights to lead the group's sales and strategic planning efforts. He would be named president of the group in 1992. Before joining Guardian, Sights had spent his 25-year business career in the auto-

motive industry, which meant that he was a car expert first and a glass expert second.

"Guardian had invested fairly significantly in the auto glass business," Sights remembered. "And Bill Davidson had decided it was time to make a larger move into automotive glass but there was no one at Guardian who came from an automotive background."[119]

Guardian was already a major supplier of glass for General Motors Blazers, Suburbans, and Crew Cabs.[120] In fact, the Automotive Division's Upper Sandusky and Auburn plants had gone to seven-day schedules to meet the demand for OEM parts.[121]

"We had a pretty solid reputation as an encapsulator and a glass fabricator," Sights said of the General Motors business. "There weren't many people who were doing both, and we had the technological edge."[122]

Like many vehicles in the early 1990s, the GM products had complex windshield designs, which sometimes required curves in two different directions. Guardian had to develop the tooling to create the radical bends in the new windshields.[123] The Upper

In the sterile "white rooms" of Guardian's automotive glass plants, employees trim excess laminate from new windshields. The room must be kept entirely dust-free to ensure quality of the glass product.

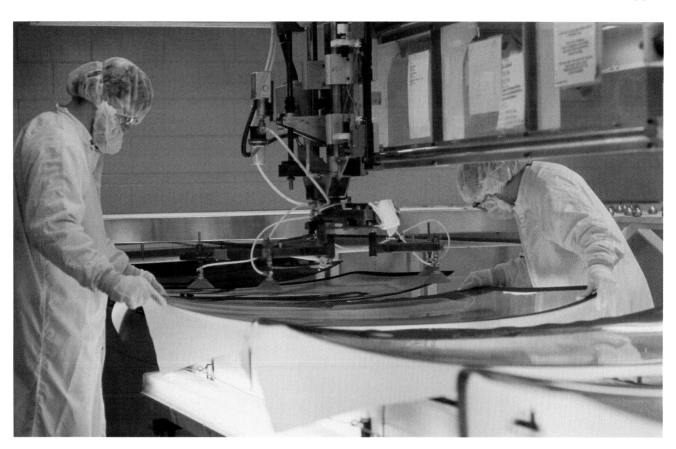

Sandusky technical staff, under the direction of Ray Landes, had developed a press bending process for making compound bends in windshields. The technology involved heating the glass to a softened state and bending it in a press to the desired shape.[124]

In 1991, as new business rolled in, Guardian Automotive opened a new automotive fabrication plant located in Ligonier, Indiana. The 375,000-square-foot facility was built to accommodate an order for Chrysler's new line of LH cars, introduced in 1992. The series included the Chrysler Concorde, Dodge Intrepid, and Eagle Vision. It featured an innovative cab-forward design that moved the vehicle's interior cabin forward, providing more space for passengers and cargo. The design resulted in a

15-square-foot windshield—the largest passenger car windshield in use. It was 25 percent larger than that of previous Chrysler cars and had the deepest side-to-side bend and steepest installation angle of any passenger car.[125]

Built at a cost of almost $50 million, Ligonier was Guardian's most automated fabrication plant. It had laminating, tempering, bending, encap-

Automotive Group engineers Bill Troutman, left, Robert Vandal, and Kevin Bano worked on the development of a robotics program for automated windshield inspections at the Ligonier, Indiana, plant.

Right: Ferdinand Kohn, on the left, and Bill Davidson, right, look on while Robert Goebbels, minister of the economy, cuts the ribbon at Grevenmacher.

Below: Employees inside the white room in the Grevenmacher plant. This plant was able to produce the same high-tech products for Europe that Guardian's Ligonier facility supplied to the U.S. automotive market.

sulation, and silk screening capabilities. It utilized 20 robots for materials handling and process operations.[126] Ligonier's first plant manager was Bernd Brockmueller. He was followed by Tim Morrow, a longtime Guardian employee who had started his Guardian career in Fort Lauderdale.

Guardian has had an extremely positive impact on the Ligonier community. "They are a very good corporate citizen," said Glen Longardner, the town's mayor. "When they had to cut back, rather than laying off people, they shut down their night shifts and made these people available to nonprofit organizations in Ligonier. They bought them shirts and hats to wear so they were all identified, and they've done everything from helping paint a day care center to helping park cars at our county fair."[127]

Guardian Automotive, however, would have few slowdowns in the 1990s as it increased in both sales volume and technological complexity. Although the number of windshields shipped rose steadily, the new automotive styling had a side effect that required a technical solution. The larger windows resulted in interior heat buildup and sun damage to upholstery and dashboards. Glassmakers were challenged to develop glass that could reduce the vehicle's air-conditioning requirements and prevent sun damage. In 1993, Guardian received a patent for its Solar Management Glass. The glass reflected sunlight, thereby reducing ultraviolet radiation by 40 percent and infrared radiation by 30 percent.[128] The glass looked like regular green-tint automotive glass and was produced at the Floreffe plant.[129]

Just after the Ligonier plant was completed, Guardian announced a new automotive glass fabrication plant in Grevenmacher, Luxembourg. The Grevenmacher plant was built under the supervision of Albert Franck, then in charge of CRVC, Guardian's European engineering group. Franck was appointed plant manager several years later, following John Crncich and Robert Martin. The plant took automation to a new level for Guardian and created the potential for extremely high output and

productivity. While Grevenmacher struggled to achieve profitability for several years, under Franck's leadership it became a consistent performer. As Franck explained:

While we were having difficulties a few years ago, we have now developed a diverse customer base that lends itself very well to our highly automated process and high technological capability. With our new tempering furnace, two laminating lines and sophisticated cutting and grinding capabilities, we have expanded the role of glass beyond a simple commodity product and this is enhancing the success of Grevenmacher.[130]

Between its new products, its new orders and plants, and its steady migration toward being a complete systems supplier, Guardian Automotive represented an increasing share of the company's business. By 1995, the Automotive Group's revenues reached $500 million and represented some 30 percent of the company's overall revenue. "I thought it was particularly important that our group recognize themselves as automotive suppliers, not just glass manufacturers," Sights later remarked.[131]

Guardian Automotive Transformed

As the decade of the 1990s unfolded, this vision would be realized and Guardian would be transformed into a full-service, top tier supplier to the automotive industry. Under Jack Sights, the company had gained increasing sophistication in its role as an automotive supplier.[132] By the mid-1990s, Guardian was recognized as a technology leader in encapsulated glass for windshields and side and rear windows, in press bending and in solar management glass. At the same time, it was about to take a significant strategic step in expanding its base as an automotive supplier.

Windsor Plastics had come into the Guardian family as part of the CUE acquisition in 1982. It was a manufacturer of high-quality decorative injection molded products. Over the years it had developed important automotive business, supplying interior and exterior trim parts. Windsor had, for the most part, operated outside the mainstream Guardian businesses.

By 1995, Guardian realized that it either needed to grow this segment of the business or exit from it. The capabilities required of an effective OEM supplier were substantial and demanded a certain amount of scale to be successful. Guardian made the decision to use Windsor as a base and grow from there. David Clark, who had joined Guardian in 1990 in corporate finance, led the expansion effort. In 1996, he negotiated the purchase of a 70 percent interest in Automotive Molding Company (AMC), a leading manufacturer of plastic and metal exterior body components. AMC was owned by Norm and Drew Peslar, brothers whose family had started the business in 1948. Headquartered in Warren, Michigan, AMC had four manufacturing plants located in Michigan and Georgia.[133] Its products included side moldings, back lite and windshield trim, rocker panels, and other body components. It had a reputation as a leader in its field and had earned many quality awards from major automakers.[134]

Opposite: Glass is prepped for tempering at the Grevenmacher, Luxembourg, glass plant. The plant received Guardian's first major contract to supply automotive glass to a European manufacturer.

Right: Design engineers in the Automotive Group review plastic molding specs. Throughout the 1990s, as it became a more sophisticated system supplier, the Automotive Group moved further up the design chain.

As Clark said of the acquisition: "We felt there was an opportunity to grow the business, and that over time there would be some areas that could potentially overlap between automotive plastics, metal trim, and glass."[135]

The acquisition of AMC, along with the full integration of Windsor Plastics, which was renamed Guardian Automotive Trim, transformed Guardian's capabilities. Guardian glass and trim products were used as original equipment on more than 80 different cars, trucks, vans, buses, and recreational vehicles. With both injection molding and glass fabrication expertise, Guardian was in a position to supply the entire exterior trim and molding system of cars and trucks, and was the only supplier in the automotive industry with this capability.

Exploiting this capability became part of Guardian's overall strategy. "I remember a conver-

Above: Guardian workers handle plastic for a car exterior. Guardian Automotive was recognized as a top-tier automotive supplier to the North American automotive industry in the 1990s.

Opposite: Chrome-plated plastic was produced at a Guardian Automotive Group facility.

sation I had with Tom Stallkamp, who was then vice president of purchasing for Chrysler," Jack Sights recalled.

We came up with this notion of chunks, or chunking a vehicle. You could divide a vehicle up into chunks, and you could source a chunk of the vehicle rather than individual components. It was very radical at that point in time, so we devised a

strategy that said we could provide the ability to supply everything on the exterior of the vehicle with the exception of the sheet metal.[136]

With the acquistion of AMC, Guardian's trim business skyrocketed. Interior and exterior trim panels, emblems, cowl panels, and front radiator grilles, like those shown, are just a few examples of the parts Guardian manufactured for the global automotive industry.

The acquisition of AMC brought Guardian Automotive Trim "real substance and took it on another path," said Sights. "That took the trim business from $50 million to well over $200 million in sales. It expanded product and manufacturing competencies, brought some really talented people into the Guardian family and enabled us to grow further at an accelerated pace."[137]

Guardian's new automotive strategy became an international one in 1998 when Guardian acquired trim manufacturer Lab. Radio of Valencia, Spain.[138] Guardian now had the ability to supply automotive trim in Europe as well as North America. Founded in 1977, Lab. Radio had a reputation for quality and engineering excellence. Its products included wheel covers, interior trim panels,

emblems, cowl panels, door belt moldings, front radiator grills, and air bag covers.

"That acquisition gave us a jumping-off point in Europe for the trim business just as the Grevenmacher plant had opened the way for us to be a European OEM automotive glass supplier," Sights recalled.[139]

These expanded competencies and synergies led to substantial new business opportunities, and Guardian embarked on a major capital expenditure program in the late 1990s to keep up. In December 1997, a new trim plant opened in Morehead, Kentucky. It had injection molding

Above: In December 1997, Guardian opened a new trim plant in Morehead, Kentucky. The plant's primary customer was Ford Motor Company, for which it manufactured parts for some of Ford's most important platforms, including the Econoline, F150, Expedition, Explorer, and Lincoln.

Below: The Morehead, Kentucky, plant, below left, and the Lab. Radio plant in Valencia, Spain, below right, expanded the capabilities of Guardian's Automotive Group.

presses as well as substantial painting and electroplating facilities.[140]

Initially, the plant's primary customer was Ford Motor Company, for which it manufactured parts for some of Ford's most important platforms, such as the Econoline, F150 Truck, Expedition, Explorer, and

Lincoln.[141] In the year 2000, Morehead underwent a major expansion that enabled it to make additional parts for Ford as well as for Daimler-Chrysler.[142] Even more changes would be in store for the automotive group as Guardian entered the next decade.

Evolution of Guardian Building Products

In 1990, Guardian's fiberglass sales were about $75 million.[143] The company's two fiberglass plants, in Albion, Michigan, and Mineral Wells, Mississippi, were operating at full capacity to keep pace with growing demand. In 1994, Guardian added a third fiberglass manufacturing facility in Erin, Ontario. The plant was formerly owned by Graham Fiber Glass and supplied the residential Canadian market. Erin was located near Toronto, and Guardian planned to service Ontario as well as the northeastern United States from the plant.[144] The group's growth continued in 1998 when it built another fiberglass plant in Inwood, West Virginia.[145]

Despite its steady growth, Guardian Fiberglass was only the fifth largest manufacturer of fiberglass in the United States and a very small player compared to industry giants such as Owens-Corning, John-Manville, and CertainTeed.[146] Guardian had prospered by seeking out specialized niches and distribution channels where it would not be overwhelmed by its competition and where it could earn an acceptable return. It had been very successful at private labeling products for resellers in the market. Another of its long-term strategies had been to sell to relatively small independent lumberyards and building products dealers. For a time in the 1990s, as part of this strategy, Guardian owned and operated a number of small-scale insulation contracting companies that

installed Guardian fiberglass into new homes. Eventually, Guardian elected to give up direct ownership of contracting companies and to support and work with independently owned insulation contracting companies that bought Guardian products. Ultimately, much of the insulation contracting business would be consolidated by building supply giant Masco although Guardian's customer base of small independent dealers would also remain in the market.

As the decade passed, Guardian Fiberglass was confronted by several market factors that compelled a significant response. First, certain of its fiberglass competitors were adding new product lines and were offering rebates to customers

A worker installs fiberglass insulation. Guardian grew steadily in the fiberglass industry, seeking out specialized niches and distribution channels where it would not be overwhelmed by its much larger competitors and where it could earn an acceptable return.

and other downstream buyers based on the number of different products they purchased.

"Since Guardian Fiberglass only made fiberglass insulation, we were at a serious competitive disadvantage," said Martin Powell, the division's head of marketing and sales.[147]

Second, Guardian's customers were being pressured by the emergence of the so-called "Big Boxes"—gigantic chains such as The Home Depot and Lowe's that had tremendous buying power and exerted powerful downward pressure on their profit margins. Guardian's independent dealers were moving from a general consumer to a professional contractor focus and Guardian needed to have the resources to support this transition. On the other hand, many of Guardian's distributor customers such as Ace and TruValue continued to focus on the general consumer market but also needed help in avoiding a fatal squeeze from the Big Boxes.[148]

In 1998 Guardian Fiberglass responded to the changing competitive conditions by making an investment in Builder Marts of America (BMA), a privately held building materials wholesaler to more than 1,000 lumber and building material retailers across the country. The Greenville, South Carolina, company had annual sales of $590 million.[149] It had been founded in 1966 by a group of 18 independent building supply dealers who formed a buying group to help them compete with large retail chains. BMA became a full-service organization offering financial control, inventory management, merchandising, customer service, and other value-added programs. BMA brokered a wide range of building products such as windows, doors, moldings, lumber, paneling, roofing, insulation, sheetrock, and more.[150]

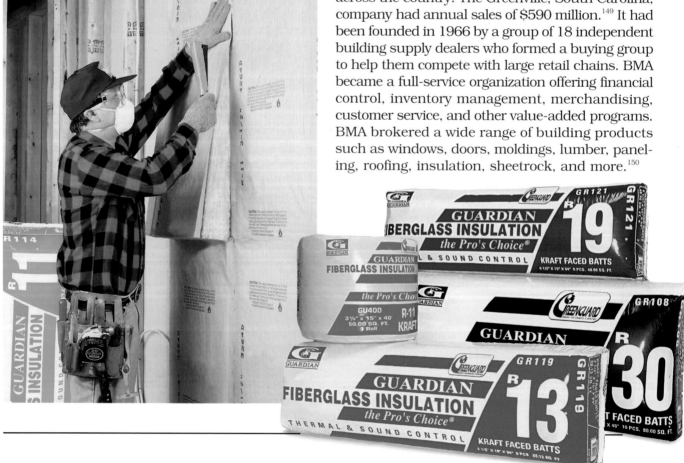

Faulkner recalled some of the benefits of purchasing a controlling interest in BMA:

We positioned ourselves to exploit developments in our industry. With the vast array of product offerings available through BMA, we were able to offer pricing efficiencies to our customers superior to those available from our fiberglass competitors. BMA also allowed us to offer better programs that would help our independent dealers sell to professional contractors. Guardian's investment in BMA and later similar acquisitions enabled us to create real purchasing power that would benefit our independent dealers. Finally, BMA became a reliable outlet for selling the increasing volumes of fiberglass we were making at our factories.[151]

Subsequently, BMA acquired the lumber and building materials divisions of Ace Hardware and TruServ, thereby acquiring more than 1,500 new dealers and becoming the largest wholesale buying and distribution group in the lumber, building materials, and millwork industry.[152] These acquisitions and

investments were followed by even more significant transactions as Guardian Fiberglass transformed itself into a multi-faceted building products company.

OIS – Optical Imaging Systems

Guardian's growth was explosive in this decade, but not everything went according to the script. In the early 1990s, the company ventured outside its core

Above: The Building Products Group headquarters. Through BMA, Guardian was one of the largest wholesale buying and distribution groups in the lumber and building materials industry.

Right: Duane Faulkner, president of the Guardian Building Products Group, joined Guardian in the early days of its insulation division. Faulkner was "Employee of the Year" in 1999.

Above: In 1998, Guardian Fiberglass responded to changing conditions by making an investment in Builder Marts of America (BMA), a privately held building materials wholesaler to more than 1,000 lumber and building material retailers across the country.

Below: BMA acquired the lumber and building materials division of Ace Hardware and TruServ. These investments allowed Guardian Fiberglass to transform itself into a multifaceted building products company.

businesses with an investment in a high technology company called OIS [Optical Imaging Systems]. OIS was a publicly traded company that had developed impressive know-how in active matrix liquid crystal displays, but was desperately in need of financial backing and management skills to convert from a small-scale research company to full-fledged manufacturing. Guardian felt it could help facilitate the move to full-scale production, although it clearly understood that this was a high-risk proposition. Japanese companies like Sharp had already spent billions on related technology and had large-scale production of similar, albeit less sophisticated, displays for laptop computers. OIS was initially targeting an emerging market for more complex flat panel displays to be used in military and commercial aircraft cockpit instrumentation systems.

Guardian made a modest investment in 1992 and followed that up the next year with further investments that allowed it to gain control of 80 percent of the outstanding shares, with the rest continuing to be traded on NASDAQ. Rex Tapp, Guardian's technical director, was named president of OIS and immediately began plans to build a state-of-the-art manufacturing facility in Northville, Michigan. The United States Department of Defense provided a grant of $50 million, roughly half the cost of the plant. The state of Michigan provided further assistance in the interest of bringing high technology capabilities to the state.

Unfortunately, the high-risk nature of the venture would eventually prove out. Once the plant was operational, the complexity of the process was overwhelming and the learning curve steep, which severely limited yields and drove costs high. Eventually, OIS was able to stabilize the production process, but by then it was becoming clear that the market for military and commercial avionics would not be sufficient to sustain profitability, and the company would not be competitive in laptop and other markets against the huge and expensive Asian plants. As things turned out, although OIS developed cutting-edge technology and produced world-class displays for U.S. military aircraft and the space shuttle, it was not viable as an ongoing business and in 1999, was shut down. For Guardian it was an expensive lesson learned in straying too far from its core business. Fortunately, in the overall context of

Executives pose at the world staff meeting in 1997. Bill Davidson is in the front, wearing a blue suit.

growth and success in the 1990s, it was viewed as a relatively minor abberation.

A Momentous Decade

The decade of the 1990s began with Guardian's construction of float glass plants in the emerging or transitional economies of Hungary, Venezuela, Thailand, and India. As the decade advanced, Guardian further extended its position in the glass industry by expanding into Brazil and Saudi Arabia. It had become a truly global company. During the same period, Guardian also deepened its presence in the more mature markets of Europe and North America with the construction of additional float glass plants and significant investments in downstream operations. Simultaneously, Guardian's automotive and building products divisions transformed themselves both through internal growth and by acquiring companies with new product lines and manufacturing capabilities. All of the divisions during this decade created new opportunities for long-term Guardian veterans and also attracted new people who possessed needed expertise and talents. Guardian as a whole was ready for the "new millenium."

"DAVIDSON'S FOLLY" BEGINS ENTERTAINMENT EMPIRE

SINCE GUARDIAN INDUSTRIES BUILT ITS first glass plant in 1970, the company has had a reputation as a maverick in the glass industry. Bill Davidson has also been called one of the "most powerful forces in sports."[1] He's built a sports empire that includes basketball, hockey, and arena football.

Davidson ventured into sports ownership in 1974, when he bought the Detroit Pistons basketball team. The team first played at Cobo Arena. In 1978 Davidson moved the team out of downtown Detroit to the Pontiac Silverdome, a football stadium in nearby Oakland County. Some Detroiters claimed Davidson was abandoning the city and catering to affluent suburbanites. Davidson, however, had his own vision. A decade later, in 1988, Davidson built The Palace of Auburn Hills with private financing. The arena is host to a handful of Davidson's professional sports teams, including the Detroit Pistons, the Detroit Shock, and the Detroit Fury. The Palace—owned and operated by affiliate Palace Sports & Entertainment—also plays host to numerous concerts and special events such as wrestling, boxing, sno-cross, ice shows, circuses, rodeos, seminars, clinics, graduations, and other family shows. It attracts more than 2 million people annually, making it one of the top drawing indoor arenas in the country.

The Palace was dubbed "Davidson's Folly" because critics believed the Detroit area could not support another entertainment venue.[2] It wasn't the first time Davidson had been second guessed for decisions he made about the Pistons.

Davidson Knows Entertainment

Davidson's critics needn't have been concerned about his decision to build a new arena. Davidson grew up in a family of theater owners, so he knew plenty about entertainment. And as owner of Guardian Industries, he was accustomed to going out on a limb. In 1970 he entered the float glass business by building a plant despite threats from entrenched rivals. The risky move began the company's ascent to leadership in the flat glass industry.

The Palace proved to be just as shrewd a business decision. The $70 million,

Above: Palace Sports & Entertainment owns and operates The Palace of Auburn Hills in Michigan, one of the nation's leading multipurpose entertainment centers. The Palace is home to the Detroit Pistons (NBA), the Shock (WNBA), and the Fury (AFL). *(Photo courtesy of David Roberts Photography)*

The Shock's Dominique Canty shoots (left). The Lightning's Martin St. Louis (top). *(Photos courtesy of Allen Einstein)*

22,000-seat multipurpose entertainment center was unlike any other arena. Its developers studied entertainment centers around the country and borrowed ideas from many of them, most notably the Disney parks, where visitors are well treated throughout their stay.[3]

The arena housed 180 private suites on three levels. The lower-level suites were closer to the action than any other arena's and brought in significant revenue. The arena also boasted amenities previously not available in large arenas, such as large, attractive merchandise stands, a variety of food services, and a banquet facility for parents accompanying children to rock concerts.[4]

No expense was spared when building The Palace. Its computer-designed seating arrangement guaranteed excellent views from every seat. A movable grid system in the ceiling made it easy for entertainment acts to set up their lighting and sound systems.[5] The Palace had the finest scoreboard; the best sound system; cushioned, cloth seats; a spacious locker room; and plush offices. It quickly became one of the most profitable facilities of its size in the country and was emulated by other arenas. It was voted "Arena of the Year" by *Performance* magazine eight times and by *Pollstar* magazine twice.[6] The Palace's launch was aided by two NBA championship titles for the Pistons—in 1989 and 1990.

An Eye for Talent

Much of the credit for The Palace's success goes to Tom Wilson, who joined the Pistons

Left: Tom Wilson, Palace CEO, joined the Pistons in 1978 at age 29. *(Photo courtesy of Allen Einstein)*

Above right: Joe Dumars, a retired player, later became president of basketball operations for the Detroit Pistons. *(Photo courtesy of Allen Einstein)*

in 1978 at the age of 29 and later became the CEO. At the time, most sports teams chose managers with abundant sports experience and little business acumen. But just as Davidson did at Guardian Industries, he hired a young, eager manager and gave him a lot of freedom.

"You give people you entrust with responsibility an equal amount of freedom to make their own decisions and then basically consult with them periodically," he said.[7]

The empire has grown to include other sports teams and entertainment venues, including DTE Energy Music Theatre (formerly Pine Knob), in Independence Township, Michigan, an outdoor concert facility. When purchased, the aging facility primarily hosted rock concerts for a younger crowd. With renovation and an expanded focus, the venue now includes entertainment for diverse audiences. It hosts 70 to 80 shows a year.[8]

In 1994, another outdoor concert venue, Meadow Brook Music Festival, on the campus of Oakland University in Rochester Hills, Michigan, was brought into the mix. It hosts approximately 30 to 40 events per season.[9]

Pinnacle of Success

In 1999, Palace Sports and Entertainment bought the National Hockey League's Tampa Bay Lightning and the leasehold rights to its home, the St. Pete Times Forum, formerly known as the Ice Palace in Tampa, Florida.[10]

After years of hard work, in 2003–2004 Davidson became the only professional sports team owner to have three championship teams in one year when the NBA Detroit Pistons, NHL Tampa Bay Lightning, and WNBA Detroit Shock all captured crowns.

Guardian architectural glass was used in the company's Auburn Hills, Michigan, headquarters building.

CHAPTER SEVEN

GUARDIAN ENTERS THE NEW MILLENNIUM

After decades of success, Bill Davidson was able to generate a new focus, a new mission. He wasn't resting on his laurels or only looking backward. While Guardian was not exactly reinventing itself, we were coming up with some very powerful new goals and ways of identifying ourselves. Not every leader is able to do that after being at the helm for 40-plus years, and that's what separates Bill Davidson from the non-Bill Davidsons.

—Bob Gorlin, vice president and general counsel, 2001

AS GUARDIAN ADVANCED toward the year 2000 and the onset of the new millennium, Bill Davidson and his management team took time to assess what had been accomplished and what direction Guardian should take in the future. Guardian had never lived by long-range strategic plans or blueprints and was not about to start adopting such methods. However, in light of the headlong rush toward growth on virtually all continents and the expansion of the three business groups, Davidson did think it appropriate to identify a rough agenda for the company—one that would give some direction for the future but not be contrary to the Guardian precepts of flexibility, opportunism, and common sense. The result was a decision to define a strategic focus for the company that was built on four simple cornerstones: enhance core competencies; exploit existing capital asset base; create new competencies; and develop the next generation of leadership.

As Jeff Knight, Guardian's CFO, explained:

The strategic focus was not a blueprint designed to tell people what to do or how to do it. It was simply a shorthand way of describing the areas of emphasis in Guardian's overall agenda. The focus on enhancing core competencies and exploiting the capital asset base was a link to the past because

we had always been strong in these areas and we had to continue to devote resources and energy to the things that had made us successful. The focus on creating new competencies and developing new leaders was more an expression of changes required in the future. To continue to be successful, we needed to change in some fundamental ways, principally through product and process innovation, and we also needed even greater concentration on developing the cadres of people who would lead Guardian in the years to come.[1]

Consistent with Guardian's historical approach, there were no specific guidelines or instructions on how to implement any of these broad agenda items—this would be left up to the business units and determined by them in the context of particular competitive conditions. However, the strategic focus did give an overall coherence and emphasis for the period beginning with the onset of the new millennium.

Inside the Science & Technology Center, Guardian's research team can subject new glass products to a wide variety of stresses and conditions to see how they will peform in the real world.

Flat Glass Expansion Continues

Building on past successes, Guardian's operating units continued to expand their core businesses in 2000 and beyond. Leading the way was the glass division. During the 1990s, the company had built glass factories in nontraditional markets in the former Soviet Bloc, India, Southeast Asia, South America, and the Middle East, and had solidified its position in the well-established markets of North America and Western Europe. This pattern would continue unabated, with Guardian expanding its presence in old markets and moving into new ones.

Guardian's first major step in the 21st century was the announcement that it would build a float glass plant in Częstochowa, Poland, a city with a population of about 260,000 located in the south-central part of the country.[2] As European managing director Jim Moore explained, "The facility represented a continuation of Guardian's commitment to Eastern Europe that began with major investments in Orashaza, Hungary, in 1989 and Thalheim,

Germany, in 1996. The strong growth in construction and automotive glass in these regions, coupled with growing customer demand for our coated products, made Poland a high priority as we expanded."[3] Lajos Sapi, Guardian's regional managing director for Central and Eastern Europe whose responsibilities included the new plant, added: "Early on, Guardian realized that Poland had a substantial need and an ability to pay for high-quality glass for residential and commercial development. We were impressed as Poland moved quickly from a centralized, command and control economy to a market-based economy."[4]

Construction of the Częstochowa plant began in June 2001 and was completed ahead of schedule and on budget only 13 months later, even though the plant required installation of an electrical substation, natural gas pipeline, and railway connection.[5]

"One of our core competencies is the ability to build state-of-the-art float glass plants anywhere in the world, even in regions far from established equipment suppliers and lacking experienced local contractors, and to do it economically and quickly. Our capability has been enhanced over the years as we have learned and leveraged from each previous project and turned the construction process into a science. Needless to say, this competency translates into substantial value for Guardian," said Russ Ebeid.[6]

As planned from the outset, a high-speed sputter coating machine was added to the Polish float line in 2003.

The launch and start-up of the float plant and coating operation in Poland were seamless. Jim

---

Above: In September 2001, Ralph Gerson, left, and Wieslaw Maras, mayor of Częstochowa, prepare the final document to be included in the Polish plant's cornerstone, while Piotz Wojaczek, chairman of the board of Katowice special economic zone, looks on.

Right: The opening of the float glass plant in Poland was attended by Russ Ebeid, left, Bill Davidson, and Karen Davidson.

Moore confirmed that Poland quickly arrived at Guardian's volume expectations and remained there.[7] According to Rene Fiorese, who oversaw European sales, "Guardian launched Częstochowa at the right time and with the right people. Our float line and coater were running at full capacity and our prospects grew even brighter as of May 1, 2004, when Poland was one of 10 countries to join the European Union."[8]

Janos Egyud, a veteran of the Hunguard management team and managing director of Guardian Poland, expected the new plant to benefit from a more open border, ease of transportation, and less paperwork. He also saw Poland as the new Guardian frontier from which further expansion into Ukraine and Russia would eventually be undertaken.[9]

Guardian was also seizing opportunities on the Western boundary of Europe. In April 2002, Guardian announced plans to build a float glass plant in Goole, Yorkshire, England, about 40 miles from the industrial city of Leeds.[10] The announcement had tremendous commercial and symbolic significance. Only some 30 years earlier, Guardian had launched its first float plant in Michigan against strenuous opposition from Pilkington. Now Guardian was in the process of overtaking Pilkington as a float glass

Right: Janos Egyud, a veteran of the Hunguard management team and managing director of Guardian Poland

Below: Guardian opened a major float glass plant in Poland in 2002 after only 13 months of construction.

Above: Russ Ebeid, Julian Proffitt, and Ralph Gerson seal the time capsule cornerstone of the Goole, Yorkshire, England, float glass plant.

Below: The Goole float glass plant near completion.

manufacturer by building a plant on its home turf. As Fiorese expressed it, "This is a bit like parachuting behind enemy lines. We were now setting up manufacturing operations in Pilkington's backyard rather than transporting glass into the United Kingdom from our facilities in Luxembourg and elsewhere in Europe."[11]

Jim Moore elaborated on the decision to build a plant in Goole:

Goole was the perfect location for many reasons. The demand for glass was already established in the northern and more industrialized portion of England so we knew raw materials would be readily available. The infrastructure in and around Goole was suitable for a business of our size. Maybe most important, we knew having a float plant in the United Kingdom would help alleviate some of our customers' fears of potential shipping problems.[12]

After a relatively long construction period caused in part by a very tough winter season, the Goole facil-

Above: The Renault building in Paris was built with Guardian architectural glass. Guardian had been steadily expanding its worldwide capacity to produce a wide variety of architectural glass products.

Below right: Jean-Luc Pitsch, chief financial officer of Guardian Europe, joined Guardian in 1996.

ity, under plant manager Julian Proffitt, began production in November 2003.[13]

While these projects were unfolding in Europe, the flat glass group also made two very different kinds of investments in emerging markets where it already had a significant presence: the Middle East and Latin America. During 2003, a team that included Peter Walters, Jean-Luc Pitsch, and David Jaffe negotiated a joint venture agreement with the Egyptian Kuwait Holding Company to purchase the Egyptian Glass Company (EGC). In 1998, EGC had launched a float glass plant located in the Tenth of Ramadan industrial park outside of Cairo, Egypt.

An unusual feature of the 2003 transaction was that the joint venture acquired the plant through a public auction from Egyptian government agencies, which held the bulk of the plant's equity. As Pitsch pointed out, "In winning the auction, we went head-to-head with Pilkington, which had a historic interest in the Egyptian Glass Company. But Guardian's belief that the Middle East, while posing some obvious risks, was a place we wanted to be made us determined to add EGC to our family."[14]

Interestingly, some 24 years before, Guardian executive Ed Sczesny had accompanied U.S. government officials on a trade mission to investigate a possible Egyptian float glass plant.[15] In 2003, Guardian finally won the prize.

In April 2003, the joint venture appointed Firas Sakkijha, the plant manager of Guardian's Fullerton, California, patterned glass facility, managing director.

Above: Peter Walters and Ayman Laz, director of Egypt Kuwait Holding Company, seal a joint venture deal for Guardian to purchase an interest in Egyptian Glass Company.

Below: In August 2003, Guardian broke ground on a new float glass plant in the town of El Marqués, Mexico. Guardian chose the site for its strong workforce and proximity to all the major Mexican markets. Russ Ebeid and Mark Lacasse were at the groundbreaking ceremony.

As Sakkijha noted about the transition: "The staff at our Cairo plant was extremely qualified and capable. They had been producing high-quality glass products for nearly five years. Now we were building awareness about Guardian's culture of safety, growth, and production efficiencies."[16] To accomplish the transition and achieve production improvements, Guardian personnel from around the world began to work with EGC's leadership and crews while EGC's management team visited the Guardian plant in Al Jubail, Saudi Arabia, to learn best practices there. After assuming leadership of the plant, Sakkijha and his team increased flat glass output from 400 tons to 480 tons per day and generated record profits for EGC.[17]

Almost half a world away, Guardian broke ground in August 2003 on a new float glass plant in the town of El Marqués, state of Queretaro, just north of Mexico City. Guardian chose the site because of its strong workforce, cooperative state and municipal governments, and its proximity to all the major Mexican markets.[18] Mark Lacasse, managing director of Latin American operations, explained the broader

strategic significance of the new plant: "Despite some bumps along the way, Mexico has had one of the world's fastest growing economies, and we believed the future there was very bright. Mexico is also the home country of Vitro, a competitor that has been increasing its global presence, and we thought it is important to bring the fight directly to Vitro in its primary market. Finally, having a well spaced triangle of plants in Mexico, Venezuela, and Brazil allows us to serve our expanding Latin American customer base more efficiently and economically."[19] The El Marques plant was launched in August 2004 after a record-breaking construction period of about 51 weeks.

All the growth of the 1990s and later years did not distract the flat glass group from focusing on improving the company's return on existing assets. In fact, with hundreds of millions of dollars in new investments, creating efficiencies and exploiting the existing capital asset base became even more critical to Guardian's success. As Davidson explained in his 2001 annual letter to Guardian employees:

As you recall, one of the cornerstones of Guardian's business strategy has been to maximize the performance of existing assets. In other words, we want to make the most of our current operations.[20]

He reiterated this priority in his 2003 annual letter, in which he challenged all employees to "find ways to get more for less. I encourage all of you to

Guardian had made significant improvements in achieving longer furnace campaigns and technological advances in the float process to increase production and improve efficiency. In 1995, Guardian established its Hot End Audit Team, otherwise known as the HEAT Team, to focus on the development of best practices worldwide to increase production and improve glass quality.

contribute ideas about creating efficiencies and leveraging existing resources."[21]

Getting the most out of its asset base had long been one of the flat glass group's greatest strengths. This objective was reemphasized with the arrival of the new millennium. Richard Alonzo observed:

Our capital expenditures during the past two decades, and especially in the 1990s, have been incredible. With the completion of the Mexico project, we will have caught up with Pilkington in worldwide float glass production. Guardian now has 24 float lines, plus tremendous capacity in downstream fabrication, which means that the value of any efficiencies achieved in one plant can be multiplied many times over. This makes the focus on achieving efficiencies even more compelling.[22]

The company had made significant improvements in achieving longer furnace campaigns and technological advances in the float process to increase production and improve efficiency. As corporate engineer Ajit Vashi pointed out, "Guardian has successfully increased the furnace life from five years in the 1970s to a projected 17 years for the Richburg and Kingsburg furnaces. We have done this by steady improvements in furnace design, revolutionary developments in furnace maintenance and operations, and improvements in furnace refractory materials."[23]

Similarly, Guardian's Hot End Audit Team (the HEAT Team), which was established in 1995, had focused on the development of best practices worldwide to increase production and improve glass quality. HEAT Team veteran Wally Palma believed that "the program of auditing furnaces, developing solutions to problems, adopting new technologies, and sharing useful information throughout the Guardian family led to significant and tangible improvements in all aspects of the operation of our float plants. Similar approaches have also been employed for the cold end of the float plants and in our fabrication facilities."[24] Joe Bruce, who played a major role in promoting continuous improvement at Guardian's plants, pointed to significant increases in throughput, yield, and quality without new investment in numerous Guardian facilities, including the Carleton tempering line and the Llodio patterned glass line.[25]

By the end of 2003, the flat glass group had assets in excess of $3 billion invested in some 15

Left: Joe Bruce played a major role in promoting continuous improvements at Guardian's plants.

Below: The European Union Parliament building in Brussels, Belgium, relied on Guardian architectural glass. By the new millennium, Guardian Europe was a mature company with a full range of value-added glass products and a seasoned leadership team.

countries representing every major commercial region. It was recognized as the second largest float glass producer in the world. According to Chief Accounting Officer Don Trofholz, some 60 percent of Guardian's flat glass sales for 2003 came from outside the United States, quite remarkable for a company that had virtually no international presence prior to 1980. The growth of the glass group since 1990 had been particularly dramatic; over that time it had added $2 billion of assets and had built or acquired 15 of its 24 float plants. Significantly, 11 of those new plants were in less-developed regions of the world, where the obstacles to success were high but the potential rewards attractive to companies, like Guardian, willing and able to take risks. In reviewing this record of success, Ebeid said, "Our prospects for the future are even brighter. You can

expect us to strengthen our position in established markets and continue to pursue opportunities in the emerging markets where the potential for growth is almost without limit."

Guardian clearly intended to keep up its relentless pressure on its rivals in the glass industry.

Dramatic Growth for Building Products

In 2000, Guardian's Building Products Group took another major step forward, acquiring Cameron-Ashley Building Products, a distributor of a wide array of products used in new construction, remodeling, and repair work. With sales in excess of $1 billion, the company maintained a network of more than 160 branches in the United States and Canada to distribute to independent retailers, builders, contractors, and mass merchandisers. Product lines included roofing, millwork, pool and patio enclosure materials, insulation, and siding.[26]

Duane Faulkner, president of the Guardian Building Products Group, explained how the acquisition complemented and broadened the Group's existing competencies:

The Cameron-Ashley acquisition was driven by three principal considerations. First, even though BMA had been built into a billion dollar business, it could not get access to many products and programs that were only available to warehouse distribution, which is where Cameron-Ashley was

strong. We could now make these products and programs available to the BMA member-dealers. Second, the acquisition of Cameron-Ashley added over a billion dollars in buying power that we could now combine with BMA. This gave us even more ability to provide benefits to our own customers. Finally, with its distribution centers, Cameron-Ashley had built a significant fiberglass distribution business to both the dealer and insulation contractor market segments. This enabled us to sell even more Guardian fiberglass internally, which is one of our paramount objectives.[27]

After the acquisition was completed, the Building Products Group undertook significant internal rationalization and reorganization, which included the sale of a number of the Cameron-Ashley warehouse locations that did not fit into "the strategy of bundling products around fiberglass sales while helping customers build their businesses."[28]

In early 2003, another piece of the puzzle was put in place when Guardian bought out the minority shareholders of Builder Marts of America. With BMA now 100 percent owned, the focus quickly turned to fully integrating its wholesale distribution business with the Cameron-Ashley and Guardian fiberglass operations. By the end of 2003, the Building Products Group had made great progress in cutting costs, eliminating redundancies, and integrating all the recent acquisitions into one unified and strategically focused business unit headquartered in Greenville, South Carolina. Faulkner emphasized that "the objective was to have one company with one name—Guardian."[29] The Group had sales of $2 billion and was now comprised of fiberglass manufacturing, distribution, and the manufacturing operations of Ashley Aluminum.[30]

Guardian Fiberglass, which had added a fifth North American insulation facility in Kingman, Arizona, in 2000 and a second production line at Inwood, West Virginia, in 2004, was now in position to serve the entire North American market.[31] Under the direction of Bill Jacoby, those plants were all dedicated to "the low-cost production of the highest quality products with a process that stressed safety and environmental responsibility."[32] Distribution consisted of direct sales to customers where

Above: Ashley Aluminum manufactured swimming pool enclosures like the one shown here.

Right: Guardian's Building Products Group distributed lumber, insulation, windows, and other building supplies through a national network. The group expanded with the acquisition of Cameron-Ashley, a distributor of a wide array of products used in new construction, remodeling, and repair work.

Left: Bill Jacoby oversaw Guardian Fiberglass operations, which was dedicated to low-cost production and high-quality products.

Guardian acted as a broker, formerly carried out under the BMA name, and warehouse distribution, which consisted of the former Cameron-Ashley warehouse locations. The group's consolidated distribution brought the benefits of heightened purchasing power and new products and programs to an expanding customer base from a streamlined and increasingly efficient operation. Meanwhile, Ashley Aluminum, the one unit that continued to operate under its previous name, offered independent contractors a variety of building products, including pool and patio enclosure materials.[33]

Above: The Guardian Building Products Group manufactured and distributed many of the materials used in homes.

Below left: The Building Products Group's plant in Kingman, Arizona, which opened in 2000, was the fifth to produce fiberglass insulation.

Below right: The Building Products Group fiberglass plant in Inwood, West Virginia, the division's fourth, opened in 1998.

Opposite: Guardian's plant in Albion, Michigan, produced nearly 200 different fiberglass products.

Evaluating the prospects for future growth, Sales and Marketing Vice President Martin Powell exuded optimism:

> *Today we can claim less than half the dealers in North America as our customers, and we provide less than 10 percent of that group's total product requirements. We have a tremendous ability to manufacture fiberglass efficiently and get it to market. There is plenty of room to grow internal sales of fiberglass even without adding to our customer base. As we add to that base, the internal market for fiberglass insulation made at our plants will grow even more. In addition, we already have significant purchasing power*

Above: Guardian glass was used in the windows of many new housing developments across North America.

Left: Martin Powell is the head of sales and marketing for the Building Products Group.

> *and diversity of distribution for a wide range of other building products, and this is growing. So we see nothing but tremendous potential, and we intend to take advantage of it.*[34]

As Faulkner concluded, "Guardian Building Products is a very unique company because we have both a manufacturing base and a large direct selling and distribution operation. With the people and vision that we have, we expect significant growth and profitability down the road."[35]

Changes at Guardian Automotive

With the arrival of the new millennium, the automotive group also experienced dramatic changes. On July 1, 1999, Jack Sights, president of Guardian Automotive, announced his retirement after more than a decade of service. He had been instrumental in building Guardian Automotive into a highly respected OEM supplier. In 1999, *Automotive News* ranked Guardian 85th on its list of the top 100 global automotive suppliers.[36] By this time, Guardian had been named a Tier-One supplier for Ford Motor Company as well as Supplier of the Year by General Motors. As Sights observed after his retirement:

Bill Davidson is the smartest businessman I've ever worked with. He brings in good people and then gets out of their way. I can remember a conversation once where I was explaining something to him, and he stopped me in the middle and said, "Look, I didn't hire you for me to make these decisions. I hired you for you to make these decisions." That's part of his managerial brilliance.[37]

After Sights' retirement, David Clark, former vice president of corporate finance, was named president of Guardian Automotive.[38] At the same time, Guardian combined its North American automotive glass and trim operations into one unit. With the new organization, Guardian Automotive would strive to exploit the synergies of the two businesses as well as pursue cost efficiencies required in an automotive industry that was beginning to place severe pressure on suppliers' margins. As part of this agenda, Guardian bought out the minority shareholders in AMC and focused on merging the cultures of the two companies.

While much of the emphasis at Guardian Automotive after 2000 was on creating a unified and efficient organization, identifying and developing lead-

ership, and maximizing return on existing assets, selected expansion did take place. New injection-molding operations opened at the plants in Evansville, Indiana; Morehead, Kentucky; and Covington, Georgia. The plastic-chrome-plating lines at the Evansville, Morehead, and Alicante, Spain, facilities expanded. Guardian's Evansville and Morehead plants expanded their high-gloss paint capability. Finally, glass operations at Ligonier, Indiana, and Upper Sandusky and Millbury, Ohio, were upgraded.[39]

In May 2002, David Clark retired from Guardian, and leadership of Guardian Automotive was passed to D. James Davis. Around the same time the group's headquarters was consolidated at the former AMC offices in Warren, Michigan. Like Sights, Davis was a veteran of the auto industry, most recently serving as president for the Americas at TI Automotive, a manufacturer of fluid delivery systems. In announcing his hiring, Davidson praised Davis' "depth of experience" and "dynamic leadership skills."[40]

Davis immediately jumped into three areas that he regarded as critical priorities for his group:

Above: Employees celebrate Guardian's receipt of DaimlerChrysler's Gold Award for Supplier Excellence for 2001. From left are Mary West, Don Tullman, and Jeep Sieg. In 1999, Guardian also won the Gold Award for recognition of its superior performance as a supplier.

Left: Guardian received the General Motors Supplier of the Year award in 1999, placing it among an elite group of systems and parts suppliers to the world's largest automotive companies.

Left: In May 2002, Jim Davis was named to lead Guardian Automotive. A veteran of the auto industry, Davis immediately jumped into three areas he regarded as critical priorities for his group: leadership, manufacturing efficiency, and diversification of the customer base.

Below: An employee inspects a windshield.

finding the right leadership for the future, achieving manufacturing efficiencies, and diversifying the customer base. Davis recalled the ongoing challenge of finding the right people for his organization:

In the book Good to Great, *author Jim Collins stresses a people philosophy that mirrors what I've found in my own experience and that closely aligns with long-standing Guardian beliefs. In a nutshell, you first get the right people and then determine the strategy and specific direction of the company. Collins says his research shows that great companies "first got the right people on the bus, the wrong people off the bus, and the right people in the right seats—and then they figured out where to drive it.*[41]

During the months after he assumed command of the group, Davis added, "I spent much of my time meeting people from all levels of the company and evaluating their skills and personal qualities. I had to make some tough decisions about who to bring on, who to remove, and who to put in different seats on our bus." While this is an undertaking that never ends, "by 2004, despite the inevitable disruptions of such a people evaluation, we had finally developed some stability and continuity in our leadership."[42]

A critical priority for Guardian Automotive was the achievement of manufacturing excellence. According to Davis, "Today's automotive environment is fiercely competitive. The Big Three in particular—General Motors, Ford, and DaimlerChrysler—

The plating line in the Morehead, Kentucky, automotive plant. The facility expanded the high-gloss paint capability of Guardian Automotive.

are under severe cost and pricing pressures, and they are passing these burdens on to their suppliers. What this means for Guardian Automotive is that we have to accelerate our efforts to become a world-class manufacturer."[43] In the short term, achieving manufacturing excellence meant the introduction of a "zero defect" target at all plants, the turnaround of the Morehead, Kentucky, and Upper Sandusky, Ohio, facilities, and the prompt introduction of common sense manufacturing (CSM).[44]

"CSM is our approach to lean manufacturing," explained Manufacturing Vice President Kevin Myers. "In many ways we've made our business more complex than it really needs to be. We've allowed the way we do business to become encrusted with activities and tasks that do not add value and that actually waste time and money. Common sense manufacturing is a passionate commitment to identify and eliminate waste and bottlenecks while striving for simplicity. It comes about by getting all the people involved in understanding the process, not just their own tasks."[45] Myers believed that "CSM reverses the usual 'top down' approach to manufacturing and empowers everyone on the shop floor to be engaged in decision-making and problem solving."[46] The same principles—referred to as common sense administration—were being applied to nonmanufacturing processes as well. As Davis noted, "Support functions, administrative, and technical teams are utilizing the CSM tools in the office to eliminate waste and improve efficiency. For both factory and office, this is a never-ending journey."[47]

The last priority Davis emphasized after his arrival at Guardian Automotive was increasing the diversity of the group's customer base. The "Big Three," Guardian's traditional base, was losing considerable market share to the European and Asian transplants, with "obvious consequences for Guardian's business."[48] Davis noted that the Big Three's North American market share had dropped from 73 percent in 1993 to 61 percent in 2003 and that the decline was expected to continue. "While GM, Ford, and DaimlerChrysler will always be important to us, we have to diversify our customer base by winning business from the Asian and European OEMs," he added. "This means that our quality, service, and product capability have to be world class. We are making progress with very demanding customers such as Nissan, Toyota, and BMW, but we have to get better every day if we want to grow that business to significant levels."[49]

By early 2004, the emphasis on diversification was starting to show initial results. Guardian became the principal supplier of chrome-plated grilles for all Nissan vehicles manufactured in the United States, including the Maxima and Pathfinder Armada. The company also received its first two contracts to supply exterior trim parts to Toyota, for the Tundra vehicle. Around the same time, an important glass contract for the X5 lift gate was awarded by BMW. Although relatively modest in terms of sales dollars, these contracts were significant for the long-term direction of the Automotive Group. In addition, important new business was realized during this period from the Big Three, still the core of the Automotive Group's customer base. In the largest single contract ever received by Guardian,

General Motors awarded Guardian a glass supply contract for its full-size SUVs—the Yukon, Tahoe, and Suburban—as well as the full-size pickup trucks. The company also received major contracts to supply DaimlerChrysler vehicles, including the new Pacifica and the redesigned Chrysler 300. Both were examples of leveraging the group's exterior systems capabilities. Combining the competencies of its various operations, Guardian supplied more than 50 glass and exterior trim parts for the Pacifica, manufactured at eight different Guardian plants, and supplied windshields and a variety of exterior trim for the highly popular Chrysler 300.

Meanwhile in Europe, the Grevenmacher facility had finally turned the corner. Under the leadership of Albert Franck, the plant had matched its new technology and manufacturing efficiency with the requirements of selected auto manufacturers and

Guardian Automotive supplied side lites (side windows) and windshields for Chevrolet SUVs like the Suburban.

achieved consistent profitability. The plant's ability to produce first-generation IRR windshields, a feature highly desired by certain European car companies, had gained it a competitive advantage. In the United States, the Automobile Group had virtually all of its business with the Big Three. Grevenmacher enjoyed a far more diverse customer base. The facility was a key supplier to Audi, BMW, and PSA. An important new contract was awarded by PSA that included a significant component of next generation IRR windshields for its D23 vehicle. At Guardian Valencia (formerly known as the Lab Radio trim operation), the new millennium presented new challenges. Under the direction of Luc Theis and his team, a major restruc-

turing necessitated by a serious decline in the plant's competitiveness had begun in 2002. By 2004, the plant had achieved stability once again.

During this period, one thing was clear throughout the Automotive Group—it was engaged in an extraordinarily tough business that was not getting any easier. The car manufacturers' relentless pressure on cost reduction was continuing to squeeze profitability even as the operations became

Above: Guardian supplied glass and exterior trim components for the Chrysler Pacifica.

Right: The Grevenmacher facility was a key supplier to such automakers as Audi, BMW, and PSA.

more productive. The challenges were great for the Automotive Group, but according to Davis, "With the right people leading our efforts and with the empowerment of every single individual in our offices and factories, I truly believe we can make Guardian Automotive a major contributor to Guardian in the years to come. It will take blood, sweat, and tears. But I wouldn't have taken on the job if I didn't firmly believe in our future."[50]

Creating New Competencies at Guardian

While Guardian's operating philosophy was always innovative, indeed revolutionary, within the glass industry, Guardian had never invested significantly in product innovation or organized research and development. Most of the company's technical advances were the result of refinements made inside the individual plants directed at solving a particular problem or achieving a defined commercial solution. Consequently, the company's advances tended to be episodic and specific, such as press bending and the encapsulation of windshields, rather than continuous and programmatic. In the late 1990s, this traditional approach to innovation would begin to give way to the imperatives of changing competitive conditions.

As at so many other critical moments in Guardian's history, it was Davidson who had the vision to direct and lead change. In his 1999 letter to Guardian employees, Davidson not only looked back, but more significantly also shared his view of the future:

For the last 20 years, Guardian has been in a capital expenditure phase, building float plants at a

Opposite: Guardian's Science & Technology Center in Carleton, Michigan, used specialized laboratories to conduct research. In the glazing lab, Dave Orleans, senior development technician, tests an improvement in the laminating process by loading a windshield into a material baking oven. The oven will bond polyvinyl laminate between two pieces of glass.

Right: Scott Thomsen was chosen to lead the Science & Technology Center initiative. His responsibility was to unify and coordinate critical aspects of product and process innovation.

rate of nearly one every year. As we move into the final year of this century, we need to begin looking at the plants we have and finding ways to make them more profitable. We can only become more profitable through change, and that is the direction in which this company is headed. Therefore, I have two challenges for each of you. First, continue to be the low-cost producer of your products. Second, pursue the development of further downstream operations and more new products. As a company, we need to exploit our current capabilities and competitive advantage, while at the same time, develop new capabilities. It is these new capabilities that will see Guardian through the inevitable moment when our old capabilities no longer provide an advantage. We must either evolve as a company or fall behind. In 1999 and beyond, you'll begin to see a shift toward this way of thinking within Guardian.[51]

The cornerstone of Guardian's new direction was the establishment of a Science & Technology Center to unify and coordinate critical aspects of product and process innovation. The individual recruited to lead the initiative was Scott Thomsen, a former Honeywell aerospace engineer who had joined OIS in 1995 and eventually was given responsibility for its engineering and manufacturing. After OIS shut its doors, he was heavily recruited by many high tech companies but was attracted to Guardian by the unique opportunities it offered.

I came to Guardian in 1999 with a little trepidation and lots of excitement. I was used to companies that were high tech to the core, such as Honeywell and even OIS, and Guardian was just at the earliest stages of making science and technology part of the fabric of the company. This was also a big part of the attraction since I would have the chance to be there at the very beginning and have a big impact. One of the first tasks I had was to define what R&D should look like at Guardian because there really was very little activity in that area. It was a tough position because Guardian made its money by being very lean, having good quality, and being

Above: The Science & Technology Center was one of the most sophisticated and-comprehensive glass laboratories in the world.

Left: Bill Davidson christens the Science & Technology Center in 2001. Designed to coordinate all of Guardian's research, the center didn't take long to roll out new products.

decentralized. Having a central R&D center could be viewed as counter-culture.[52]

Thomsen's arrival did create some culture shock. In Ebeid's view, this was a good thing. "Scott and I spent many hours talking together both before and after he joined us. He had to get comfortable with Guardian being a place where his talents and vision could be realized. Bill Davidson felt our company needed the new perspectives, skills, and disciplines that Scott could bring. We also needed to be sure that Scott would shake things up but still work to the strengths of Guardian's culture. He signed up

and was given plenty of room to operate, so obviously all of us were satisfied."[53]

An outgrowth of the early discussions was the decision to build a new, state-of-the-art facility to house a dedicated science and technology function. "That's one of the things I love about Guardian," Thomsen said. "If they have confidence in you, they let you do the job. It's what you make of it, and you're held accountable. I was given a lot of freedom to define what the R&D function would be and what it would look like."[54]

While Thomsen and the team he was assembling initially worked out of the Carleton glass plant, in June 2000, a 50,000-square-foot facility was opened across the street from the glass plant. The location was selected because "we did not want to grow out of touch with the realities of day-to-day operations," Thomsen recalled. The Science & Technology Center housed specialized labs and employed some 50 scientists, engineers, and technicians from a variety of disciplines. The facility had the resources to simulate a production line. It also could test the effects of the environment on glass; study how coatings were applied; analyze the chemical composition of glass and plastic products; and develop new glass, plastic, adhesive, and sealant products.[55]

The center had two overriding objectives: provide Guardian innovative products for Guardian plants to offer their customers and develop efficient manufacturing processes that increase quality while reducing customer costs. According to Thomsen, "By coordinating the research and development [R&D] for various technologies—in effect, applying technologies across product lines—Guardian will reduce development costs and the time it takes to bring new products to market."[56] However, the new center was definitely not intended to be the source of all ideas and all innovations. "We needed strong talent at our plants to complement activities at the Center," Thomsen explained. "A proper balance must exist to make our R&D efforts successful. The S&T Center enables us to try ideas 'offline' while continuing to work closely with plant R&D efforts. It's all about thinking globally, yet acting locally."[57]

It did not take long for Guardian's new team to roll out innovative products. One of the first advances in 2000 was the development of improved infrared reflective (or IRR) glass, the next generation of solar control glass. While first developed in Europe, essential new refinements in IRR were the result of a group effort among the Science & Technology Center, the Thalheim Germany float glass plant, which housed an advanced high-speed glass coater, and the Grevenmacher automotive glass fabrication facility.[58] Albert Franck, Grevenmacher's managing director, explained the benefits of IRR coated glass: "First, and most importantly, IRR blocks the sun's damaging infrared rays. Second, it reduces the heat load in vehicles, enabling manufacturers to downsize the air conditioners in their vehicles. Guardian was the first company to manufacture IRR glass in Europe."[59]

While commercializing and efficiently manufacturing IRR would prove extremely challenging and costly, it presented a major potential growth area for Guardian's automotive business in Europe.

In the architectural market, Guardian developed the Sun-Guard series of coated glass products for use in skyscrapers, office complexes, and other buildings. This solar-control, low-E product offered architects and builders a unique combination of pleasing aesthetics, energy efficiency, durability, high performance, and fabrication flexibility.[60] Another important technological breakthrough featured the application

of multiple layers of microscopic coatings through chemical vapor deposition or ion beams to give a diamond-like hardness to glass. "With this groundbreaking project, consumers won't have to worry about scratching their tabletops and businesses can save money from fewer glass component replacements," observed Tony Hobart, head of North American sales.[61] Other promising product innovations would include improvements in performance and durability of low-E glass, hydrophobic and hydrophilic glass for improved visibility and easy maintenance, ultraviolet blocking glass to help protect photos and artwork from the sun's damaging rays,[62] "first-surface mirrors" for use in projection TVs and ultimately for scanners[63]

The Burrard building in Vancouver, British Columbia, Canada, used Guardian's Sun-Guard technology.

and other business machines,[64] chemically coupled materials created by the automotive group,[65] and novel glass designs developed at the Fullerton, California, patterned glass plant.[66] In 2002, Guardian further enhanced its technical base by investing in Engineered Glass Products, a leader in the development of heated glass technology.[67]

Much of the new emphasis on product innovation at Guardian was aimed at developing sophisticated value-added coated products made on high-speed glass coating machines. Guardian had entered the business in 1977 with its first coater located near the Carleton float glass plant. Additional coaters were installed in Corsicana, Texas, in 1982, and Bascharage, Luxembourg, in 1984 (with later expansions and upgrades). Despite its early entry and coating experience, Guardian was still a relatively small factor in the business, especially in North America, until Davidson made developing new products a critical priority. An early sign of this was the installation of a sophisticated high-speed coater in Thalheim, Germany, in 1997. After that, manufacturing capacity and competencies grew at a staggering rate to support the new products being developed by the science and technical teams.

In 2000, Guardian installed a new coater in Corsicana to run Sun-Guard and other products. It was followed in 2002 by the launching of a coater in Geneva, New York, and the start-up of the world's largest glass coater in Bascharage, Luxembourg. In 2003, Guardian installed an R&D coater in DeWitt, Iowa, which plant manager Pat Tuttle would use to develop products with local market value and appeal, and a high capacity line in Częstochowa, Poland. In 2004, the Kingsburg plant, under the direction of plant manager Jeff Booey, launched a coater to serve markets in the western United States and a full-scale coater was in the planning stages for DeWitt.

This immense growth in coated glass manufacturing capacity in such a short time was remarkable.

Above: Guardian's high-performance residential glass regulates the effects of external environmental conditions to ensure that interiors stay comfortable and safe from harmful UV rays.

Opposite: The Main Tower in Frankfurt, Germany, was built with Guardian architectural glass.

Thomsen considered it "phenomenal to think that in five years you can go from number six or seven in the world to number one."[68] It should not be thought that this growth came without growing pains. "Recruiting technically sophisticated people to run all these machines had been extremely difficult," recalled Bruce Cummings. "We had tremendous help from people like Joe Bruce and Scott Thomsen who went outside of their usual disciplines to find and hire talented technicians and operators."[69]

Product and process innovation have had a profound ripple effect on other disciplines within Guardian that have added new competencies as a response to the call for product and process innovation.

"We all have lots to learn, but we're making progress," said Bob Gorlin. "One example is that our legal function had to adapt to the change in direction that our business was taking. We needed to build up our capabilities for patent prosecution and managing intellectual property. In each year since 2000, Guardian has filed an average of 10 times as many patents as it did in 1998 and prior

Guardian has accounted for a number of breakthrough technologies and innovations to improve performance and durability of glass. Developments include ultra-mirror, left, which contains an ultraviolet coating for superior performance. Patterned glass, right, offers a unique combination of pleasing aesthetics, durability, high performance, and fabrication flexibility. An important technological breakthrough was the application of mulitple layers of microscopic coatings through chemical vapor deposition or ion beams to give a diamond-like hardness to glass. The DiamondGuard process has been used for glass countertops (below right), Humvee windows (below left), and on the windows of the Washington, D.C., Metro (below).

years, so the lawyers absolutely had to be ready to support this company initiative."[70]

Similarly, other business functions needed additional competencies and an adjustment in focus. "We're trying to get ahead of the curve," said Mike Morrison, director of North American Business Development. "When you're the first one in the market with a new product you have a distinct advantage because you can more readily command your own price if the product hasn't yet become a commodity. However, now all our people need to employ far greater sophistication in understanding value-added products and in defining and targeting specialized markets. We've basically had to build up a marketing function from scratch, and it hasn't been easy. Business development, marketing, and sales have had to work closely with Science & Technology and manufacturing to jointly determine what needs to be developed, how proposed new products can be exploited in the marketplace, and whether they can be produced in a commercially feasible way."[71]

One of the consequences of developing value-added products in the global marketplace was a new emphasis on branding. Ebeid explained:

Above: The largest coating line in the world was installed at Bascharage, Luxembourg.

Right: Michigan Governor John Engler toured Guardian's Science & Technology Center in 2001. Here, Scott Thomsen, chief technology officer, demonstrated a hydrophobic windshield coating.

We are bringing our products closer to the consumer rather than to the fabricator or distributor. The consumer will go for a brand rather than ask the technical competency of the product. Now we have to change our mindset by looking ahead at branding so we can use pull-through advertising or strategies rather than push through.[72]

In what would be a multiyear initiative, noted Peter Walters, Guardian began to take steps to increase the trademark protection for its logo and other names and symbols, "establish greater harmony in the use of its names and products, and project an association between global Guardian and the value-added products it was putting into the market."[73]

The Science & Technology Center represented a new era for Guardian Industries that Davidson had launched in his call to action several years before. "It was very energizing," recalled Gorlin:

After decades of success, Bill Davidson was able to generate a new focus, a new mission. He wasn't resting on his laurels or only looking backward. While Guardian was not exactly reinventing itself, we were coming up with some very powerful new goals and ways of identifying ourselves. Not every leader is able to do that after being at the helm for 40 plus years, and that's what separates Bill Davidson from the non-Bill Davidsons.[74]

It would now be up to the thousands of Guardian's employees worldwide to demonstrate the drive, initiative, intelligence, and creativity to act on Bill Davidson's vision.

Navigating Through Difficult Years

Guardian continued to grow and prosper in the new millennium against a backdrop of very difficult economic conditions. The American economy, which had been significantly fueled by technology investment in the late 1990s, slipped into recession in early 2001, in large part the result of a stock market bubble that began to collapse in 2000. During the 2000–2002 period, the S&P 500 stock market index dropped by almost 50 percent and the technology weighted NASDAQ index fell almost 80 percent. The manufacturing sector was particularly hard hit by the recession and would take much longer to recover than many experts initially predicted.

Then, just as the country was coming to grips with recession, an international tragedy made everything else seem inconsequential. On September 11, 2001, terrorists hijacked four jetliners in the United States. Two were crashed into the Twin Towers of the World Trade Center in New York City, one into the Pentagon in Washington, D.C., and the last into a Pennsylvania field after an apparent passenger revolt. The attacks claimed nearly 3,000 lives and represented the worst terrorist assault in history.

The effects of September 11 were immediate and monumental. Money and goods poured into the stricken cities as America pulled together in a spontaneous burst of patriotism and anguish. The rest of the world reached out to America with sympathy and support. While the country was still reeling from the loss of life, the economic effects began to spread. For three days after the attack, air travel in the United States was suspended. The stock markets closed, and for almost two weeks economic activity virtually ground to a halt.

Gradually the U.S. economy began to regain its footing, but it would soon be jolted again with the high profile collapse of industry icons Enron and Worldcom, and the subsequent investigations that would reveal rampant accounting irregularities at many companies. Soon, the global war on terror and the imminent Iraq war would take over the headlines and dominate the news throughout a jittery world.

As always, Guardian took a patient, long-term view during this time, and the company was rewarded for the scope of its investments during the preceding decade. Although the U.S. economy would take considerable time to recover fully, the recession-

As a global company, Guardian realized the benefits of its geographic diversification after the negative economic effects of the September 11, 2001, terrorist attacks on the United States.

ary impacts on the company were mitigated because housing construction continued strong throughout the period, the result of historically low interest rates driven by a federal reserve policy designed to stimulate the economy. More significantly, as a global company, Guardian realized the benefits of its geographic diversification, with some regions, particularly Asia, the Middle East and South America, doing well despite the world's uncertainties.

Reflecting on its History

As Guardian faced the challenges and opportunities of the new millennium, the company also reached key milestones that made it look back with pride on its history. In 2002, it celebrated the 70th anniversary of its start in the modest St. Jean Avenue plant and Bill Davidson's 45th year of extraordinary leadership. Davidson had taken over a small bankrupt company in 1957 and had built it into a respected global power. Remarkably, even as the company grew very large and complicated over those decades, he had continued with fierce determination to foster a special environment where what began as a family business "still thinks, acts, and feels like a family business."[75]

In the best-selling book, *Good to Great*, author Jim Collins describes the characteristics of extraordinary leaders who build enduring greatness in companies. These individuals have a unique "paradoxical blend of personal humility and professional will." On the one hand they are "modest, shunning public adulation, never boastful, acting with quiet, calm, determination," yet at the same time they demonstrate a "ferocious resolve, an almost stoic determination to do whatever needs to be done to make the company great." Anyone who has known and worked with Davidson or reviewed his career knows that these words could easily have been written with him in mind.

In the early years of his leadership at Guardian, Davidson had espoused a philosophy that was frequently quoted:

At Guardian Industries, our philosophy is that a company, like people, should grow a bit each year in vision, in performance, in accomplishments.

And grow it did. In the 35 years following its 1968 combination of Guardian Glass and ABC Photo, Guardian sales had grown in each and every year, starting at a modest $22 million in 1968 and reaching close to $5 billion 35 years later. By the end of 2003, the company had operations in dozens of locations in some 15 countries, representing virtually all regions of the world. Each of its businesses was respected as a leader in its respective industry. As Davidson put it with typical understatement, "We plan to grow from where we are today. We think we have a very, very solid base for the future."[76]

Doing it the Right Way

The transformation and growth of Guardian during the years 1968 through 2003 were impressive, but the secret formula behind Guardian's success had been people living the Guardian culture. CFO Jeff Knight stressed, "The company's story cannot be represented exclusively by the numbers found in its financial statements. From the very beginning, Guardian has stood for valuing and respecting people and its growth has been based on those values."[77] Bruce Cummings, Guardian's vice president of human resources, agreed: "Guardian is a bottom line company. No one would say that we are particularly 'warm and fuzzy.' But while stressing results, we have also embedded into our genetic code a concern for safety, health, the environment,

The graph shows Guardian's steady and significant growth since 1968. The unusual spike in revenues for 2001 reflects Guardian's purchase of Builder Marts of America (BMA) and Cameron-Ashley (CA).

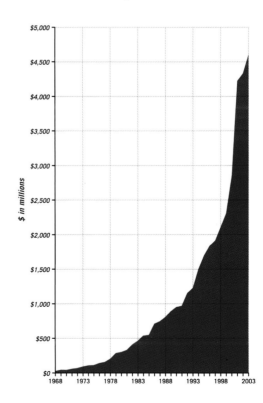

community involvement, and educational opportunity. Good operating results and those concerns go hand in hand."[78]

Safety Comes First

Guardian's commitment to safety at its facilities has deep and powerful roots. Unlike many other manufacturing companies, Guardian realized early on that safety was everyone's responsibility. Don Tullman, plant manager at Kingsburg until 1998 and at Carleton thereafter and "Employee of the Year" in 2000, explained the Guardian philosophy that "no one person or one committee could assure a safe environment in our plants. It could only be achieved with a concerted effort by every employee and complete dedication of every manager."[79]

According to Tullman, "The high priority attached to safety is shown in our words and our actions. In many facilities, every incident that would or even could cause a doctor visit is immediately reported to

senior plant leaders. This is done no matter where in the world we are and what we might be doing."[80]

Consistent with the overriding Guardian value of personal responsibility, individuals are held accountable for their own safety as well as that of others. "An employee who created a hazard must be asked to make a personal commitment to work safely in the future."[81]

At their locations around the globe, the people of Guardian find their own distinctive ways to practice safety. At Gujarat Guardian in India, the plant's local newsletter referred to "Safety—Our Way of Life" and proudly described passing the incredible safety milestone of 5 million hours without a loss time accident.[82] *Guardian World* has a regular feature called

---

Above: A world map depicts Guardian plants and many distribution centers.

Right: The Gujarat, India, plant celebrates 3.5 million man hours without a lost-time accident. The plant members later went on to reach 4.5 million, then 5 million hours.

Guardian is committed to safety at its facilities worldwide, and it expects every employee to take responsibility for their own safety as well as that of others. Plants are highlighted in *Guardian World* for their milestones and accomplishments. Al-Jubail, Saudi Arabia, above, celebrates 3 million hours without a lost-time accident. The Nong Khae plant in Thailand, below left, is honored for being accident free for 5 million hours. And the Fullerton, California, shipping department, below right, was honored for its outstanding safety record.

"Safety News" that highlights milestones and accomplishments, from the 100 safety ideas developed by operators at the Auburn, Indiana, automotive glass plant,[83] to the Morehead, Kentucky, auto trim plant's Team Safety Basketball, a program that audits safety equipment, procedures, and federal compliance,[84] to the Rayong Thailand float plant's capture of a prestigious national safety award,[85] to the adoption by Guardian Building Products of a rigorous loss control program for its distribution branches.[86] These and hundreds of other examples underscore the passion with which safety is always in the news at Guardian.

While implemented locally, safety was organized around a comprehensive loss control program that began in the mid-1970s. Nancy Sivy, who followed Wally Lutz and Tom Boss as Guardian's global risk manager, said that, "While the program has undergone some changes, the basic elements have remained essentially the same and have always focused on competition."[87]

Left: At their locations around the globe, the people of Guardian find their own distinctive way to practice safety. Here Gujarat employees hold a safety celebration.

Right: Nancy Sivy is Guardian's global risk manager.

In the format developed in 1999 by Sivy and a representative group of plant managers, each year members from the risk management group visit, evaluate, and assign points to all Guardian manufacturing facilities.[88] "Plants can receive awards—silver, gold or platinum—based on the final scores developed," explained Sivy. "These are presented by Bill Davidson at the annual world staff meeting held each January in Auburn Hills. The platinum award is given to plants that achieve three consecutive years of gold level loss-control performance. We also have an award for "most improved plant" as well as the infamous spike award given to the plant with the worst performance. This award is a hunk of glass with a railroad spike sticking out of it and it is presented to a very unhappy plant manager amidst a chorus of boos and catcalls. No plant has ever won the spike twice."[89] The program's success and the commitment of thousands of Guardian employees worldwide were underscored by OSHA safety statistics that showed Guardian to be three times better than the industry standard.[90]

Health and Physical Fitness

Guardian's commitment to the health of its employees was as firmly entrenched as safety. For many years after he joined the company in 1969, former human resources director Ken Battjes was the strongest advocate for physical fitness and health maintenance programs. Sports competitions and tournaments within and between facilities, organized for many years by longtime employee Tim Bolinger, became fixtures and were enthusiastically supported by hundreds of employees. Weight loss and seat belt campaigns were actively promoted.[91]

In 1983, Guardian introduced the HealthGuard Program, a far more ambitious and focused effort to elevate the well-being of its employees and control healthcare costs. It rolled out a seven-step program for better living, concentrating on exercise, diet, limiting use of alcohol, avoidance of smoking and illegal drugs, blood pressure awareness and control, use of seat belts and developing positive attitudes. Guardian also introduced a health promotion manager to advance the program and rolled out various action plans to stimulate participation by employees.[92] The company's innovative approach was recognized in a *CNN News* special. The "President's Award" and the "Winner's Circle" became ways to recognize employees who out-competed their colleagues in maintaining sound health practices.

Davidson enthusiastically supported Health Guard and outlined his views shortly after it was introduced:

I believe Health Guard is one of the best programs we've ever offered Guardian employees. Encouraging people to take charge of their health and reduce health care costs is a worthy objective. I have personally believed in the value of physical fitness for many years. HealthGuard does not tell employees how to live. It encourages them to consider the effects of lifestyle on their well-being. The decision to accept those recommendations and to act on them is up to each person.[93]

Healthy competition between employees and plants thrived at dozens of Guardian locations, involving thousands of employees. A quick review of the pages of *Guardian World* can only touch the surface: from the annual squash tournament at Auburn Hills

Above: Guardian Europe sales manager Rene Fiorese (number 19007) finishes the New York City Marathon in the wake of the 2001 attack on the World Trade Center.

Below: In 1983, Guardian created the HealthGuard Program to focus on the well-being of its employees and control healthcare costs. The wellness program encompasses seven steps for better living. From left: The Al-Jubail, Saudi Arabia, team gathers for a group photo; employees of the Porto Real, Brazil, plant stretch before work; and the first-place basketball team from Al-Jubail proudly displays its trophy.

in which more than 40 employees participated in 2003,[94] to the DeWitt float glass plant's four-month long "healthy living competition" in which dozens of employees lost weight, lowered cholesterol or stopped smoking,[95] to the 2003 Annual Basketball & Volleyball tournament in which some 600 Guardian employees, friends, and families from 18 facilities competed for trophies,[96] to Guardian Al Jubail's health-conscious nutrition program,[97] to the conquest of Brazil's Pedra Selada summit by 100 hikers from Guardian Porto Real,[98] to inspiring individual achievements such as Rene Fiorese's completion of the New York Marathon in November 2001, just weeks after the tragic events of September 11.[99] These and innumerable other activities exemplifed the values of competition, caring and assumption of personal responsibility that are fundamental to Guardian.

Environmental Responsibility

Guardian's commitment to the environment was inseparable from its dedication to safety and health. Richard Alonzo, looking back to the period when Guardian first entered glass manufacturing, recalled:

We knew from the beginning that the more efficient our operations, the more environmentally friendly we would be. The two objectives are not inconsistent; they go hand in hand.[100]

Ebeid observed that "cost-effective manufacturing uses less energy, creates less waste, maximizes natural resources and breeds a culture that thrives on efficiency." He added that, "With the launch of our Kingsburg, California, plant, we shocked the industry by producing quality glass with fewer people in a facility that ran cleaner than all other float glass plants on the planet."[101]

Above: HealthGuard activities like this beach volleyball game in Al-Jubail, Saudi Arabia, are an important part of life for employees at Guardian.

Below: Wind turbines similar to these were built near the Gujarat, India, facility in 2003 and supply about 45 percent of the plant's electrical requirements.

Guardian's environmental commitment "goes beyond compliance with government regulations," noted Peter Walters. "We are dedicated to compliance but the spirit of our activities is actually even more connected to the Guardian value of protecting the health and safety of our employees, customers, and communities. There are hundreds of examples that demonstrate this point."[102]

Guardian's environmentalism was concentrated in three areas: the introduction of energy-saving processes, the production of ecologically friendly products, and recycling. A dramatic example of an energy-saving process can be observed on the plains of western India, where 14 windmills were constructed by the Gujarat India facility in 2003. This wind power project churned out some 8,400 kilowatts of pollution-free power and supplied the plant with about 45 percent of its electricity requirements. It was motivated by the desire to gain stability of energy supply, reduce costs, and in the words of Gujarat plant manager Dinesh Mukati, "to thank Mother Earth."[103]

In the area of product development, Guardian's scientists were developing an array of solar control products designed to help conserve energy, reduce

auto emissions, and keep interior temperatures consistent. Products like Guardian's IRR glass allowed vehicle manufacturers to use smaller air conditioning units that were easier on the engine, required less fuel, and lightened the overall vehicle weight—all of which meant less fuel consumption.[104]

Recycling probably had greater participation around the world than any other environmental initiative. The Ligonier, Indiana, automotive glass fabrication plant became a leader in 1996 when it joined the Environmental Protection Agency's WasteWise Program, which committed participants to achieving concrete results in waste management and recycling.[105] In 2003, Ligonier was named a Program Champion for annually recycling 1 million pounds of materials otherwise destined for landfills.[106] Dozens of other facilities worldwide joined the effort, including the world headquarters in Auburn Hills, Michigan, which annually recycled more than 100 tons of office materials; the Rayong, Thailand, plant, which reclaimed water and used it for irrigation; the Covington, Georgia, trim plant, which recycled phosphoric acid from its operations for conversion into fertilizer,[107] and many Guardian locations worldwide that collect unused cullet from customers and

use it at their plants. As Environmental Manager Mike Turnbull summarized, "From the receipt of raw materials to the use of our products, Guardian is a steward of the environment."[108] Efficient manufacturing and environmental responsibility were twin objectives that at Guardian have not been mutually antagonistic.

Serving the Community

Guardian's concern for safety, health, and the environment carried over to a passion for community involvement and social responsibility. In remarks given to the Council of Michigan Foundations upon his being named Philanthropist of the Year in 1997, Davidson said:

My commitment to philanthropy stems from a number of beliefs I hold true. First, I believe we should each try to repay society as much as we can for the education and the success we have enjoyed

Top: Guardian architectural glass adorns the Fresno City Hall in Fresno, California. The Kingsburg, California, plant produced quality glass in an environmentally sound manner.

Left: *Guardian World*, the company newsletter, provides company information to all Guardian employees. This edition concentrated on Guardian's worldwide enviornmental efforts.

and from which we have benefited. Second, we each have a responsibility to do all we can to provide a better world for future generations. Third, we should each try to contribute to finding solutions for the problems in our communities and our world. And fourth, one of the secrets to a fulfilling life is to be able to do things for other people.[109]

Davidson's personal beliefs generated major philanthropic and educational gifts by Guardian and encouraged and supported thousands of Guardian people in their efforts to give something back to the dozens of communities where they worked and lived. Guardian's largest single educational endowment came in 1992 with a contribution of $30 million to establish the William Davidson Institute at the University of Michigan School of Business Administration. The primary purpose of the Institute was to assist students, business leaders, policy makers, and research scholars involved in the transformation of the world's former centralized economic systems into free market economies. Davidson's passion for promoting education in this area had been fueled by Guardian's own experiences in Hungary. Guardian followed this contribution with an additional grant in 1997 to help fund housing for the Institute. The Institute demonstrated Davidson's commitment to assist students, entrepreneurs, and scholars in addressing and tackling real world problems and in making a difference.

Closer to home, as an outgrowth of Davidson's belief in educational opportunity, in 1986 Guardian created a merit-based college scholarship program to assist the children of U.S. employees faced with the rising cost of advanced education, and established the Guardian Educational Foundation to administer the program.[110] By the end of 2003, some 610 students had been beneficiaries of this program.[111]

Guardian also gave back to the community through major contributions in the areas of health, recreation, and culture. These included gifts to the Karmanos Cancer Institute, the Children's Hospital of Michigan, and the Hermelin Brain Tumor Research Center at the Henry Ford Hospital in Detroit. In cooperation with the Detroit Pistons, in the early 1990s Guardian executives helped create the PARKS Program to reconstruct and revitalize many of Detroit's aging parks. In 1998, Guardian began a series of gifts to the Detroit Symphony Orchestra for

Bill Davidson's belief in and commitment to educational opportunity have generated philanthropic and educational gifts by Guardian around the globe. In 1986, Guardian created the Guardian Educational Foundation, a merit-based college scholarship program to assist the children of U.S. employees faced with the rising cost of advanced education.

the purpose of funding multinational tours by that renowned cultural institution.[112]

While Guardian as a company showed its commitment to education, health, and culture over the years by making very large contributions, thousands of its employees were also reaching out to their communities around the world. In Porto Real, Brazil, the plant sponsored a program to promote adult education for those in the community who did not have access to publicly funded resources.

"We could have spent our time and money in ways that might have made a bigger splash and been more visible. But with over 200 adults now able to read and countless others having learned basic preventive health measures to combat dengue fever and sexually transmitted diseases, we at Guardian Brazil can be proud of our small contribution to the community's well-being," said Mark Lacasse.[113]

The Porto Real plant's service to its community was replicated in countless similar activities of Guardian employees around the world. In Maturin, Venezuela, people from the plant cleaned and painted a local elementary school, installed a potable water tank, donated clothes and toys, and sponsored a field trip for the students.[114]

During a very tough business downturn, the Ligonier, Indiana, automotive facility avoided layoffs by loaning its employees, who still received their Guardian paychecks, for various public service jobs in the community.[115] Employees at the Millbury, Ohio, plant, through their GIVE (Guardian Industries Volunteer Employees) program, raised money for the Salvation Army, mentored elementary school students, and took responsibility for keeping miles of local roads litter free.[116]

Members of the Building Products team in Greenville, South Carolina, celebrated the holidays with a giving tree, providing food, clothing, and toys to benefit local families.[117]

In unique contributions having significance that transcended their local communities, Guardian Navarra served as the exclusive sponsor to restore the high altar of the historic cathedral in Tudela,[118] while the automotive group helped restore the city bus on which civil rights heroine Rosa Parks had refused to give up her seat in 1955.[119] These few illustrations represented the activities of thousands of Guardian

employees who volunteer to give something back to their communities.

Developing the Next Generation of Leadership

As Guardian entered the new millennium, its people were intensely occupied with the need to fuel growth by developing the next generation of leadership. In an article published in the glass industry's principal trade journal, Ebeid reflected on what he thought was the key to successful growth:

We believe a strong record of growth depends more on how a company develops its leaders than on the pace of housing starts or some other economic measure. With the right people to lead it, most companies can prosper through any economic cycle. In fact, the best sailors are made in stormy waters.[120]

Ebeid then described Guardian's recent focus on refining the process by which "it finds and keeps the strong leaders. We hire excellent people, put them in an environment where they can take as much responsibility as they can handle, then challenge them to their fullest."[121]

The process Ebeid was referring to was known at Guardian as "Recruit-Develop-Challenge-Retain." While these elements are found in one form or another in most sophisticated companies, "at Guardian," recalled Bruce Cummings, "they have become a bit like a religion." The key at Guardian, however, was that, "this religion would not be practiced solely by human resources professionals."[122] The

Guardian's Automotive Group helped restore the city bus that civil rights heroine Rosa Parks rode in 1955.

GUARDIAN INDUSTRIES GETS INVOLVED IN THE COMMUNITIES

GUARDIAN INDUSTRIES IS DEEPLY COMmitted to making meaningful contributions to the communities in which it has facilities. It recognizes and appreciates the correlation between quality of life, employee morale,

high-quality production, and customer satisfaction. That is why Guardian companies around the world continually reach out to their communities in an effort to improve the lives of those who contribute to the company's success.

Guardian's community outreach initiatives include:

- In locales from Rayong, Thailand, to Pontiac, Michigan, Guardian employees have volunteered their time to the Habitat for Humanity program to build homes for people in need.

- Employees from Luxembourg, England, and Poland in Europe to the state of Texas in the United States have done their part to

help raise funds and awareness for cancer research.

- Facilities from Porto Real, Brazil, to Fullerton, California, and Morehead, Kentucky, have hosted blood drives for the Red Cross.

- Employees in the United States, Germany, Saudi Arabia, India, Thailand, and Venezuela have reached out to local schools in an effort to nurture the local youth who may someday work for Guardian as well.

While health, shelter, and education receive significant support through the efforts of Guardian's global facilities, local cultural programs have hardly been neglected. In Texas, the Corsicana facility raised funds to restore the community's historic opera house and cinema. In Spain, the Tudela facility contributed to the restoration of the 500-year-old high altarpiece at the local cathedral.

Guardian facilities have also gone above and beyond expectations by aiding communities struck by disaster. When record rainfall in Indiana caused rivers to overflow, the Auburn facility pitched in with shovels and sandbags. The Galax facility also provided relief when a flood wreaked havoc in West Virginia. And several facilities volunteered for fundraising efforts in the aftermath of 9-11.

Guardian recognizes that environmental efforts are an important part of maintaining a healthy community. Whether it was the park rehabilitation project in Michigan, Arbor Day tree plantings in Ohio, or a recycling program for the mutual benefit of the environment and school programs, Guardian's "green" initiatives are making a difference.

Although a great deal of Guardian's outreach efforts are initiated and implemented at a local level, the corporation and its leader, William Davidson, have made significant contributions to cancer research, education, and the arts. Among the organizations that have benefited are the Karmanos Cancer Institute and Children's Research Center of Michigan; the University of Michigan; the Weizmann Institute of Science in Rehovot, Israel; the Jewish Theological Seminary of America in New York City; and the Detroit Symphony Orchestra.

Regardless of the dollar value, Guardian recognizes that nurturing the communities in which it does business is an important investment in the future of its success.

Guardian has a worldwide commitment to helping the communities in which it has a presence. The company's outreach extends to education, building homes, fundraising, blood drives, and more.

urgent need to support the massive growth of the 1980s and 1990s and supply leaders for the next wave of growth was a company-wide imperative. It transcended any particular departmental boundaries.

To drive the point home that responsibility for human resources extended to all managers and supervisors, Guardian created the "CHAMPS" program, an assessment process designed to evaluate and improve the human resources function at plants around the world. "CHAMPS" stood for "Challenge And Make People Successful" and was one of the cornerstones of developing leadership. During a CHAMPS assessment, a team consisting of a cross-section of production personnel, corporate staff, and HR professionals met with local management and reviewed in detail all facets of the plant's operations that involved people. They then jointly developed specific recommendations that became the responsibility of the local management team. One of the most important consequences of a successful assessment, said frequent team participant Bill Valk, was "the creation and implementation of a disciplined approach to recruiting, developing, challenging, and retaining leaders at all levels. Just talking about these things isn't enough."[123]

Key to the Future — Preserving the Culture

Another response to Guardian's explosive growth began to take shape at the start of the new

millennium with an initiative directed toward identifying and promoting the key elements of Guardian's culture. As Cummings observed, "One of Guardian's greatest strengths is its unique culture, and we had to make sure that as Guardian expanded into new countries and businesses, we did not lose the values that made us successful in the first place."[124]

The culture initiative had gained steam as part of the strategic focus agenda that Davidson introduced in the late 1990s. The emphasis on enhancing historical competencies had prompted an objective examination of those attributes that had made the company so consistently successful over many years. It did not take long for those involved to realize that the most important and enduring drivers of Guardian's success were not related to technical competencies but rather flowed from the core values embodied in the company's operating philosophy and reflected by the attitudes and behaviors of its key employees—in other words, "The Guardian Way."

Guardian had always prided itself on the uniqueness of its culture. From the image of a "raging bull" smashing the establishment and going its own way, to the many stories that had been handed down depicting the accomplishments of Guardian "heroes," Guardian's culture was always acknowledged as something special, particularly among those who had been with the company from the early days. However, as the years passed, there was a growing danger that the strength of the culture might begin to erode. Gorlin observed:

As Guardian's culture evolved it was communicated primarily through action and observation. People at all the plants learned and refined the Guardian

Opposite: Guardian Flachglas supplies glass to Germany and Central Europe. Its glass has been used for many buildings, including the Sony Center in Berlin, Germany.

Above: Bruce Cummings is Guardian's vice president of human resources. He was instrumental in the company's efforts to build new leadership for the 21st century.

Right: Guardian has created a number of programs to reward plants and employees for their hard work and dedication. Here, Russ Ebeid presents employees of the Gujarat, India, plant with an award.

Left: The Time Warner building in New York is another example of Guardian-supplied glass. *(© John Slaughter/Emporis.com)*

Right: Bob Gorlin is vice president and general counsel. He joined Guardian in 1989 and oversees the company's legal function.

Way directly from Bill Davidson, Russ Ebeid and other architects of the culture. These "founders" led by example and were frequently seen and heard by employees even at new facilities. The culture was also transmitted when people who had absorbed Guardian values were sent to different places around the world. The problem is that we are victims of our own success. As the number of new locations and employees mushroomed in the 1990s through internal growth and acquisitions, the informal methods of communicating the culture became inadequate. We were in danger of losing touch with what had made us a special company to begin with.[125]

As senior leaders began examining the Guardian Way, they were careful to separate those attributes that represented core Guardian values from business practices and strategies that needed to continually evolve as business conditions warranted.

"In a fast-paced world of change, we definitely did not want to fixate on the past and be stuck with out-of-date ways of doing business. But on the other hand, it would be a huge mistake to abandon those attributes that have formed the foundation of 'The Guardian Way' and that should be as much a driver of success in the future as they were in the past," said Ralph Gerson.[126]

In his March 2001 letter to Guardian employees, Davidson shared some of his thoughts concerning the challenge of preserving Guardian's culture:

Guardian's growth has created the new and larger challenge of maintaining and expanding those elements of our culture that have enabled us to grow as individuals and as a company. Size alone tends to work against some of our more treasured values—a lean and flat organization with individual responsibility and accountability. This challenge is made all the more complex with the introduction of cultural and business characteristics from throughout the world where we maintain facilities. We must preserve core Guardian values in all operations while drawing strength from fresh approaches reflecting different environments and changing business conditions.[127]

The culture initiative received a boost of energy that started with Ebeid's attendance at a leadership conference conducted by Disney World in Orlando, Florida. One of the themes of the conference was the importance of culture to the success of the organization. "While Disney's particular culture is not at all like Guardian's," Ebeid recalled, "I was very impressed by the focused way that Disney defined and used its culture to advance the objectives of the business. The general approach was something Guardian could use. I remember calling Bruce Cummings from Florida and telling him to come down and look this over."[128]

Eventually, numerous Guardian managers from throughout the world would attend Disney conferences to experience first-hand the benefits of promoting culture in their organizations.

The culture initiative was in essence a focused and broad-based drive to articulate and communicate core Guardian values so that future generations of Guardian people could continue to live by them. "One of the first things we needed to do," recalled Cummings, "was come up with a written statement of the Guardian Way. There had been several informal versions, but it was time to give real thought and attention to a statement we could all live with."[129] Such a document was created through the efforts of senior leaders from around the world. In a few short paragraphs, the Guardian Way stated the underlying themes that made Guardian unique: commitment to people, belief in entrepreneurial spirit, emphasis on results, focus on individual responsibility and opportunity, hatred of bureaucracy, and dedication to winning.[130]

"Articulating the values is only the beginning of the journey," said Jeff Knight. "The next stage is more

difficult and has no end to it. Each Guardian facility will figure out how to use the Guardian Way as a tool for understanding, teaching, and living the values that made this company great."[131] Throughout the world of Guardian—from Ligonier, Indiana, where plant manager Tim Morrow took the culture to a new level by driving decision-making to the shop floor, to Gujarat, India, where the people lived and breathed Guardian values, and back to Carleton, Michigan, where open channels of communication made everyone feel they could contribute, hundreds of people in dozens of facilities mobilized to maintain, enhance, and teach the culture. "This process is critical to the growth and development of the next generation of Guardian's leaders and needs to be one of our highest priorities," said Ebeid.[132]

Perhaps no event demonstrated the link between Guardian and its people better than the World Staff Meeting held in Auburn Hills in January 2004. Ordinarily this meeting was a time for Guardian's most senior global leaders to share performance data and discuss plans for the coming year. For the first time ever, Guardian facilities from around the world selected a total of 88 special representatives from their locations to visit Auburn Hills and learn what really took place at the World Staff Meeting. Many of the representatives had been chosen through vigorously contested competitions at their facilities.

As Davidson explained his motivation for this extraordinary gathering, "I've always felt it important that you help people understand where we are, where we want to be, and that we all share the responsibility for getting there. It also was critical that we remove any mystery associated with senior staff meetings."[133] The representatives participated side-

Guardian believes in maintaining and expanding the elements of its culture as it pays special attention to the individuals and the cultural nuances within the Guardian world. Employees gather at the 2004 staff meeting reception (below left), and Dave Rose was dressed as Maharaja by the Gujarat plant staff after being named 2001 "Employee of the Year" by Bill Davidson.

by-side with regular attendees at a week of group meetings, tours, individual conferences, dinners, and receptions. The week ended with a unique panel session at which the 88 representatives asked candid questions of Russ Ebeid, Duane Faulkner, Jim Davis, and Scott Thomsen.[134]

In keeping with a Guardian function, the representatives were not just passive onlookers. Not only did they engage senior leaders at the panel and other events, they also participated in evaluations of the week's activities and had to prepare presentations to deliver at their home facilities. A sampling of the representatives' comments underscored the significance of the event:

"...the World Staff Meeting shed a greater light on who Guardian is. I don't think a lot of the workers realize Mr. Davidson is a people's man and what he means to society as a whole."

—Raymond Balfour, Rexdale, Canada

"We are from different countries, but we speak the same language and we have the same culture."

—Emilio Alvarez Gonzalez, Llodio, Spain

"...Now I can tell what the difference is between knowing...the Guardian Way ...and feeling it. We, Guardian, are much more than glass and glassmakers. You can take my word for it."

—Henryk Arciszewski, Częstochowa, Poland

"I came away with a bigger picture on how global Guardian has become over the years. Everyone was very approachable and eager to learn about me and what division I work in."

—Ralph Truax, Albion, Michigan

"I was surprised how friendly, open, and frank the members of top management were with us."

—Zoltan Borbely, Oroshaza, Hungary

"I now have a better understanding of the Guardian Way and Guardian culture. I understand where I am and what I need to do next."

—Jerdpong Nakasuwan, Rayong, Thailand

"I truly felt like I was part of a big family."
—Jean-Francois Tacconi, Bascharage, Luxembourg

"Guardian is a successful company because of the people... Everyone knows what they have to do... At Guardian we find people who want to learn, work hard, and grow."

—Jesus Rodriguez, Maturin, Venezuela

The January 2004 World Staff Meeting was an extraordinary event because it brought everyone in the company together and acknowledged his or her individual and collective importance. "What I've seen consistently throughout all the years is what I call the power of individual contributions," said Knight. "Guardian's success stories are built on a multitude of individual contributions. We have succeeded by bringing good people into the organization and letting them contribute, and when you add up all the contributions, the result is more than the sum of the parts."[135]

Davidson highlighted a week of recognition and surprised virtually everyone assembled at the World Staff Meeting by naming "All Guardian Employees" as the 2003 "Employee of the Year." In his 2004 letter to fellow Guardian employees, Davidson pointed to some recent growth milestones for the company, such as surpassing Pilkington as a float glass producer, and explained his choice for "Employee of the Year:"

How did we do it? In short: Guardian people. Success is the result of dedication, commitment and courage to take risks. It is the result of imaginative thinking, lean operations and localized decision-making. But, at the end of the day, we could not have done any of this without talented, hard working people. And, Guardian has the best. You have demonstrated your value and helped Guardian to prosper. This year's award honors all the people who are the foundation of Guardian; who work so hard each day to produce, sell and deliver the products we make. It is for the people who maintain our furnaces, work on our production and fabrication lines and load our trucks. It is for those that embrace and believe in what we do.[136]

The 2003 "Employee of the Year" Award was an expression of Davidson's focus on "developing our next generation of leadership," and his recognition that, while this was an ongoing process that would require tremendous work, "our efforts are paying off."[137]

Guardian employees gather at the company's 2004 world staff meeting. Special representatives from around the world were also present.

The Legend Continues

The legend of Guardian Industries is a success story for the ages. It is a tribute to the hard work, dedication, and creativity of Guardian's people, beginning with the 20 employees at St. Jean Avenue on Detroit's Lower East Side and growing by 2003 to more than 19,000 people at dozens of facilities on every continent. It is a saga of economic productivity and expansion, as Guardian has evolved from a producer of fewer than 100 windshields per day and sales of about $130,000 in 1932 to become the world's sec-

ond-largest float glassmaker and one of the world's largest distributors of building products, with total sales in 2003 near the $5 billion mark. It is a vision of endless horizons, as Guardian has transformed itself from a Michigan company to a truly global enterprise where people representing dozens of nationalities and cultural traditions contribute to a common mission. Perhaps above all, it is a testament to the determination, courage, optimism, and vision of a man who believed in Guardian and what its employees could accomplish. The legend continues to be written by the people of Guardian because the best is yet to come.

NOTES TO SOURCES

Chapter One

1. Frank Coffey and Joseph Layden, *America on Wheels: The First 100 Years: 1896-1996. Companion to the PBS Special* (Los Angeles: General Publishing Group, 1996), 23-24.
2. Ibid., 39–40.
3. Ibid., 47-51.
4. Phillip Applebaum, *The Wetsmans: Odyssey of an American Family,* (William Morse Davidson, 1994), 148.
5. Ibid., 148-149.
6. Ibid., 149.
7. "Safety Glass!" *Guardian World,* October 1972.
8. Applebaum, *The Wetsmans: Odyssey of an American Family,* 149.
9. William S. Ellis, Glass: *From the First Mirror to Fiber Optics, The Story of the Substance That Changed the World,* (New York: Avon, 1998), 137.
10. Ibid., 149.
11. "Looking Back..." *Guardian World,* July/August 1982.
12. Applebaum, *The Wetsmans: Odyssey of an American Family,* 150.
13. Ibid., 146-147.
14. Ibid., 208.
15. Ibid., 149.
16. "Looking Back..." *Guardian World,* July/August 1982.
17. "50 Years of Growth," *Guardian World,* July/August 1982.
18. Applebaum, *The Wetsmans: Odyssey of an American Family,* 150-151.
19. "Barney H. Hertzberg Celebrates Forty Years of Service with Guardian Industries," *Guardian World,* October/November 1978.
20. "60 Years in Glass Industry," *Guardian World,* October 1971.
21. "Barney H. Hertzberg Celebrates Forty Years of Service with Guardian Industries," *Guardian World,* October/November 1978.
22. Ibid.
23. "Guardian Industries A Brief History—1932-1978," *Guardian World,* October/November 1978.
24. Applebaum, *The Wetsmans: Odyssey of an American Family,* 151.
25. Ibid., 185.
26. Ibid.,179-183.
27. Ibid.,186-187.
28. Ibid., 187.
29. Ibid., 188-189.
30. Ibid., 209.
31. Ibid., 197.
32. Bill Davidson, interview by Jeffrey L. Rodengen, tape recording, 15 February 2001, Write Stuff Enterprises.
33. Applebaum, *The Wetsmans: Odyssey of an American Family,* 209.

34. Ibid., 197-198.

35. Ibid., 208-211.

36. Ibid., 208.

37. Charlie Vincent, "Davidson's Pistons: Up From Scrap Pile," *Detroit Free Press*, 25 March 1984, 8D.

38. Ken Battjes, "William M. Davidson Trouble Shooter-Doctor-Healer," *Guardian World*, October 1975.

39. Applebaum, *The Wetsmans: Odyssey of an American Family*, 209.

40. Vincent, "Davidson's Pistons: Up From Scrap Pile," *Detroit Free Press*.

41. Applebaum, *The Wetsmans: Odyssey of an American Family*, 209.

42. Ibid., 210.

43. Ibid., 211.

44. "A Look Back at The 1950s," *Glass Magazine*, January 1998.

45. Applebaum, *The Wetsmans: Odyssey of an American Family*, 211, and "Looking Back," *Guardian World*, July-August 1982.

46. Coffey and Layden, *America on Wheels: The First 100 Years: 1896-1996*, 163.

47. Ibid., 144-145.

48. Applebaum, *The Wetsmans: Odyssey of an American Family*, 197.

49. Coffey and Layden, *America on Wheels: The First 100 Years: 1896-1996*, 144-145.

50. "Detroit Plant Announces $250,000 Capital Expenditures Program," *Guardian World*, October 1972.

51. Applebaum, *The Wetsmans: Odyssey of an American Family*, 225.

52. Ibid., 211.

53. Ibid., 211-212.

54. Ibid., 212.

55. Ibid.

56. Ibid.

57. Ibid., 212-213.

58. Ann Newman, interview by Jeffrey L. Rodengen, tape recording, 1 March 2002, Write Stuff Enterprises.

59. Applebaum, *The Wetsmans: Odyssey of an American Family*, 212.

60. "Guardian Glass in Earlier Days," *Guardian World*, June 1976.

61. Applebaum, *The Wetsmans: Odyssey of an American Family*, 225.

62. Marie Chestney, "Guardian's Most Senior Employee: Barney Hertzberg," *Guardian World*, July/August 1982.

63. "How Glass-Strike Deadlock Broke," *U.S. News & World Report*, 27 February 1959.

64. John Gallager, "The Piston Nobody Knows," *Detroit Free Press*, 22 September 1991, 6.

65. Chestney, "Guardian's Most Senior Employee: Barney Hertzberg," *Guardian World*, July/August 1982.

Chapter Two

1. "Photographic Processing Selects Guardian Photo Photofinisher of the Year," *Guardian World*, August/September 1985.

2. Warren Coville, interview by Jeffrey L. Rodengen, tape recording, 11 February 2002, Write Stuff Enterprises.

3. "Who Will Process Color Film?" *Business Week*, 30 July 1955, 50-51.

4. Davidson, interview.

5. "Photographic Processing Selects Guardian Photo Photofinisher of the Year," *Guardian World*, August/September 1985.

6. Ibid.

7. Ibid.

8. "Guardian Photo Inc. New Northville Plant," Guardian Industries Annual Report, 1968.

9. "Photo/Glass Facility Opens in Chicago," *Guardian World*, June 1971.

10. "Guardian Photo News," Guardian newsletter, January 1971.

11. "Photo Division Sees Bright Future," *Guardian World*, April 1972.

12. "Guardian Photo Division" Guardian Industries Annual Report, 1972.

13. "Turning to Borderless," *Photo Marketing*, July 1973, 4.

14. "Technical Advancements Highlight Record Year," Guardian Industries Annual Report, 1974, 21.

15. Dave Bundy, "Photo Flashes," *Guardian World*, October 1974.

16. "Photo Having 'Super Summer,'" *Guardian World*, August 1973.

17. Ibid.

18. "Photo Division Sees Bright Future," *Guardian World*, April 1972.

19. "Will Photo Kiosks Overtake Stores in Photofinishing?" *Photo Marketing*, August 1975, 6.

20. "Photo Division Focuses on 24 Million Dollar Sales Year...," *Guardian World*, August 1976.

21. "Will Photo Kiosks Overtake Stores in Photofinishing?" *Photo Marketing*, August 1975, 6.

22. Ibid.

23. "Photo Flashes," *Guardian World*, June 1976.

24. "Photo Division Focuses on 24 Million Dollar Sales Year...," *Guardian World*, August 1976.

25. "Photo Moves into New Facility in Allentown, Pa.," *Guardian World*, December 1978-January 1979.

26. "Photo Processing," Guardian Industries Annual Report, 1977, 14.

27. "GAF's 'Best Interests' Say 'Get Out of Photofinishing,'" *Photo Marketing*, March 1978, 112.

28. "What's Ahead for Guardian?" *Photo Marketing*, July 1979, 32-34.

29. Ibid.

30. Ibid.

31. Ibid., and Guardian Industries Annual Report, 1979.

32. Guardian Industries Annual Reports, 1979 and 1980.

33. "Photo Plant Integration Progressing Smoothly," *Guardian World*, June/July 1978.

34. Ibid.

35. "What's Ahead for Guardian?" *Photo Marketing*, July 1979, 32-34.

36. "Photographic Processing Selects Guardian Photo Photofinisher of the Year," *Guardian World*, August/September 1985.

37. "Photo Introduces New Film Services," *Guardian World*, February/March 1985.

38. "Guardian Photo Leads National Awareness Drive," Guardian Industries news release, 1 May 1985.

39. Guardian Industries news release, 16 January 1984.

40. "Photographic Processing Selects Guardian Photo Photofinisher of the Year," *Guardian World*, August/September 1985.

41. Greg Bowens, "Guardian Photo to be Sold; Pistons Owner Reaches a Deal With Rival Firm Qualex Inc." *Detroit Free Press*, 19 July 1991.

42. Davidson, interview.

Chapter Three

1. "Looking Back," *Guardian World*, July/August 1982.

2. "Glass Distribution Centers," Guardian Industries Annual Report, 1969.

3. "This is Guardian Industries: Distribution Centers," Guardian Industries Annual Report, 1968.

4. "Guardian Distribution Centers," Guardian newsletter, September 1969.

5. Harold E. Simpson, "The Glass Industry 1967," *The Glass Industry*, February 1968, 71.

6. Harold E. Simpson, "The Glass Industry 1964," *The Glass Industry*, February 1965, 72.

7. Harold E. Simpson, "The Glass Industry 1969: Flat Glass," *The Glass Industry*, May 1970, 228 and Harold E. Simpson, "The Glass Industry 1968," *The Glass Industry*, March 1969, 131.

8. "Architectural Glass Division," Guardian Industries Annual Report, 1969, 11.

9. Harold E. Simpson, "Ten Years of Progress in The Glass Industry: Flat and Structural Glass," *The Glass Industry*, November 1959, 614.

10. Davidson, interview.

11. Oscar Feldman, interview by Jeffrey L. Rodengen, tape recording, 15 February 2001, Write Stuff Enterprises.

12. "Deuteronics' Glossary of Science, Engineering and Technology Terminology," http://www.etscience.co.za/inv_jzz.htm, citing M. Shukla, Competing Through

Knowledge, (New Delhi: Response Books, 1997), 103.

13. Ibid.

14. Davidson, interview.

15. "Float Glass Plants Around the World," *The Glass Industry*, June 1969, 302.

16. Guardian Proxy Statement, 7 November 1968.

17. Davidson, interview.

18. Guardian Industries, Annual Report, 1967.

19. Guardian Industries, Annual Report, 1968.

20. "Glass Terms: Automotive Glass Repair, Replacement, and Installation Terms," Glass Facts.com: The One Place for Flat Glass Industry Information, http://GlassFacts.com, 8 January 2001.

21. Davidson, interview.

22. Ibid.

23. "Permaglass Merges With Guardian Corp.," Guardian Industries Annual Report, 1969, 7.

24. Ibid.

25. "Permaglass Merger," Guardian newsletter, 10 December 1969.

26. "The Piston Nobody Knows," *Detroit Free Press*, 22 September 1991, 6.

27. Richard Alonzo, interview by Jeffrey L. Rodengen and Richard Hubbard, tape recording, 29 March 2001, Write Stuff Enterprises.

28. "The Man With the Camera," *Guardian World*, Summer 1998.

29. "Float Glass Plants Around the World," *The Glass Industry*, June 1969, 302.

30. Davidson, interview.

31. Feldman, interview.

32. Ibid.

33. Davidson, interview.

34. Guardian newsletter, 1969.

35. H. Samuel Greenawalt, interview by Jeffrey A. Knight, January 2004, Guardian Industries.

36. Ibid.

37. Applebaum, *The Wetsmans: Odyssey of an American Family*, 229.

38. Davidson, interview.

39. Guardian newsletter, 1970.

40. Gwen Kinkead, "The Raging Bull of Glassmaking," *Fortune*, 5 April 1982, 58-64.

41. "Float Glass Dedication," *The Glass Industry*, November 1970, 484.

42. Davidson, interview.

43. Feldman, interview.

44. Kinkead, "The Raging Bull of Glassmaking," 58-64.

45. Davidson, interview.

46. Kinkead, "The Raging Bull of Glassmaking," 58-64.

47. Ibid.

48. Davidson, interview.

49. Kinkead, "The Raging Bull of Glassmaking," 58-64.

Chapter Four

1. Alonzo, interview.

2. Davidson, interview.

3. "Celebrating 30 Years of Glassmaking at Carleton,"

Guardian World, September 2000, 6-8.

4. "4:30 p.m., August 20th," Guardian newsletter, 11 September 1970.

5. "Celebrating 30 Years of Glassmaking at Carleton," *Guardian World*, September 2000, 6-8.

6. Ibid.

7. "4:30 p.m., August 20th," Guardian newsletter, 11 September 1970.

8. "Campbell Plant News," Guardian newsletter, 15 October 1970.

9. "New Flat Glass Plant Dedicated in Carleton," Guardian Industries Annual Report, 1970, 7.

10. Guardian newsletter, December 1970.

11. "Plant Works to Keep Workers Happy," *Detroit Free Press*, 21 January 1973, reprinted in *Guardian World*, February 1973.

12. Guardian newsletter, March 1971.

13. Guardian newsletter, December 1974.

14. "Plant Works to Keep Workers Happy," *Detroit Free Press*, 21 January 1973, reprinted in *Guardian World*, February 1973.

15. Ibid.

16. "Plant Celebrates Second Anniversary," *Guardian World*, August 1972.

17. Ibid.

18. Ibid.

19. Ibid.
20. "Plant Works to Keep Workers Happy," *Detroit Free Press*, 21 January 1973, reprinted in *Guardian World*, February 1973.
21. Guardian 1970 annual report.
22. "New Float Line Nears Completion," *Guardian World*, April 1973.
23. "Carleton Plant Expansion Underway," *Guardian World*, October 1971.
24. "Safety Glass!" *Guardian World*, October 1972.
25. "Carleton Plant Expansion Underway," *Guardian World*, October 1971.
26. "3rd Expansion for Carleton Announced," *Guardian World*, April 1973.
27. "Architectural Glass Division," Guardian Industries Annual Report, 1972, 13.
28. "Guardian Buys Sitelines Incorporated," *Guardian World*, April 1974.
29. "New Lines, Acquisitions Account for Sales Gain," Guardian Industries Annual Report, 1974, 15.
30. "Employee of the Year Award Winners," *Guardian World*, February 1976.
31. "New All-Electric Plant Now Operating in Ohio," Guardian Industries Annual Report, 1974, 13.
32. "Automotive Glass Division," Guardian Industries Annual Report, 1971, 11.
33. "President's Message," Guardian Industries Annual Report, 1975, 7.

34. "Glassmakers Reflect Detroit's Troubles," *Business Week*, 24 February 1975, 82.
35. Ibid.
36. "U.S. Production and Factory Sales of Passenger Cars, Trucks, and Buses," Motor Vehicle Facts & Figures 1997, American Automobile Manufacturers Association, 1997.
37. "Annual Value of Construction Put in Place in the United States 1970-1979," United States Census Bureau, http://www.census.gov/const, 1 February 2001.
38. "Carleton Rebuilds No. 1 Float Line," *Guardian World*, February 1975.
39. "Capital Expansion Retrenched but Modernization Continues," Guardian Industries Annual Report, 1975, 23.
40. "Guardian Enters Reflective Glass Market," *Guardian World*, August 1976.
41. Karl Straky, interview by Barb Koch, tape recording, 7 February 2001, Write Stuff Enterprises.
42. "Guardian Enters Reflective Glass Market," *Guardian World*, August 1976.
43. "Reflective Glass Program Stepped Up...," *Guardian World*, October 1977.
44. *Guardian World*, February 1972.
45. *Guardian World*, February 1973.
46. *Guardian World*, February 1972.
47. *Guardian World*, April 1972.

48. *Guardian World*, February 1973.
49. Ibid.
50. Davidson, interview.
51. *Guardian World*, February 1977.
52. Russ Ebeid, interview by Jeffrey L. Rodengen, tape recording, 15 February 2002, Write Stuff Enterprises.
53. *Guardian World*, February 1977.
54. Jeff Knight, interview by Jeffrey L. Rodengen, tape recording, 29 November 2001, Write Stuff Enterprises.
55. Alonzo, interview.
56. Guardian Industries Annual Report, 1974.
57. "Guardian Forms Insulation Division," Guardian Industries press release, 4 January 1978.
58. Ibid.
59. "Guardian to Make Insulation," *Guardian World*, January/February 1978.
60. "A Letter From Your President," *Guardian World*, December 1979.
61. "Huntington Insulation Plant Begins Operation," *Guardian World*, April/May 1978.
62. "Glass Manufacturing," Guardian Industries Annual Report, 1977, 6.
63. Ron Nadolski, interview by David A. Patten, tape recording, 16 February 2001, Write Stuff Enterprises.
64. *Guardian World*, February/March 1980.
65. *Guardian World*, January/February 1978.

66. Ebeid, interview.

67. *Guardian World*, February/March 1980.

68. Ebeid, interview.

69. Alonzo, interview.

70. *Guardian World*, February/March 1980.

71. *Guardian World*, August/September 1978.

72. Ebeid, interview.

73. Ibid.

74. Ibid.

75. "Kingsburg Plant Management Team Selected," *Guardian World*, January/February 1978.

76. Ibid.

77. Ibid.

78. "Guardian to Build New Glass Plant," *Guardian World*, October 1976.

79. Alonzo, interview.

80. Ebeid, interview.

81. Guardian Industries Annual Report, 1981, 7.

82. "Wally Palma Named Corsicana Plant Manager," *Guardian World*, December 1979.

83. Ajit Vashi, interview by Jeffrey L. Rodengen, tape recording, 6 December 2001, Write Stuff Enterprises.

84. Lu Rimar, interview by Jeffrey L. Rodengen, tape recording, 3 December 2001, Write Stuff Enterprises.

85. "Guardian Industries Launches Fourth Float Glass Line," Guardian Industries press release, 23 December 1980.

86. "Corsicana Glass Plant: Coming on Strong," *Guardian World*, October/November 1981.

87. Guardian Industries news release, 27 December 1982.

88. "Low-E Glass: Keeping the Heat In!" *Guardian World*, October/November 1983.

89. "Ft. Lauderdale Plant to Get New Furnace and Building Addition," *Guardian World*, July/August 1980.

90. Guardian Industries Annual Report, 1981, 2.

91. "Guardian's Raw Glass Sales Soar," *Guardian World*, December 1979.

92. Guardian Industries Annual Report, 1980, 5.

93. Alonzo, interview.

**Chapter Four Sidebar:
Glass Saves Energy**

1. H. E. Simpson, "The Glass Industry—1966," *The Glass Industry*, February 1967, 78.

2. H. E. Simpson, "The Glass Industry—1964," *The Glass Industry*, February 1965, 74.

3. H. E. Simpson, "The Glass Industry—1966," *The Glass Industry*, February 1967, 78.

4. H. E. Simpson, "The Glass Industry—1961," *The Glass Industry*, February 1962, 65.

5. "Reducing Carbon Dioxide Emissions and Energy Consumption With High-Performance Glass," Primary Glass Manufacturers Council, Topeka, Kansas, 2001.

6. H. E. Simpson, "Ten Years of Progress in the Glass Industry: Flat and Structural Glass," *The Glass Industry*, November 1959, 614-617.

7. "Reflective Glass Program Stepped Up..." *Guardian World*, October 1977.

8. H.E. Simpson, "The Glass Industry—1967," *The Glass Industry*, February 1968, 74.

9. "Reflective Glass Program Stepped Up..." *Guardian World*, October 1977.

10. "Buildings that Mirror the Sky," *The Glass Industry*, June 1971, 196-198.

11. "Reducing Carbon Dioxide Emissions and Energy Consumption With High-Performance Glass," Primary Glass Manufacturers Council, Topeka, Kansas, 2001.

12. Ibid.

13. Ibid.

14. "Low-E Glass: Keeping the Heat In!" *Guardian World*, October/November 1983.

Chapter Five

1. Davidson, interview.

2. Ebeid, interview.

3. "A Cozy Arrangement Shatters," *Financial Times*, 25 January 1982, 13.

4. Ibid.

5. Ibid.

6. Jim Moore, interview by Jeffrey L. Rodengen, tape recording, 29 March 2001, Write Stuff Enterprises.

7. Ebeid, interview.

8. "Guardian to Build Float Plant in Luxembourg," *Guardian World*, June/July 1979.

9. Robert Goebbels, interview by Jeffrey L. Rodengen, tape recording, 25 January 2002, Write Stuff Enterprises.
10. Davidson, interview.
11. Howard Benedict, interview by Jeffrey L. Rodengen, tape recording, 6 December 2001, Write Stuff Enterprises.
12. Davidson, interview.
13. "Employee of the Year," *Guardian World* January-March 1988.
14. Moore, interview.
15. Rimar, interview.
16. "Guardian in Europe," *Guardian World*, October/November 1982.
17. Guardian Industries Annual Report, 1983, 7.
18. Ebeid, interview.
19. Franky Simoens, interview by Jeffrey L. Rodengen, tape recording, 6 December 2001, Write Stuff Enterprises.
20. Guardian Industries news release, 18 March 1982.
21. Alonzo, interview.
22. Paolo Scaroni, interview, "Speaking in One Voice," *U.S. Glass Magazine*, Volume 36, Number 9, September 2001.
23. Guardian Industries press release, 17 November 1982.
24. Knight, interview.
25. Ibid.
26. "Guardian Acquires Interest in Spanish Glass Company," *Guardian World*, February/March 1984, and "Villosa—Glassmaker of Llodio, Spain," *Guardian World*, October/November 1986.
27. "U.S. Glass Maker to Acquire 48% Stake in Spanish Group," *Financial Times*, 12 January 1984, 17.
28. Guardian Industries news release, 10 January 1984.
29. "Villosa Launches New Float Line," *Guardian World*, October/November 1985.
30. "Guardian Expands in Europe," *Guardian World*, April/May 1986.
31. "Guardian Announces European Glass Expansion," Guardian Industries news release, April 1986.
32. Nadolski, interview.
33. Knight, interview.
34. Paul Rappaport, interview by Richard Hubbard, tape recording, 29 March 2001, Write Stuff Enterprises.
35. Knight, interview.
36. Ibid.
37. Guardian Industries Annual Report, 1981.
38. Guardian Industries news release, 27 December 1982.
39. Guardian Industries news release, 1 September 1982.
40. "Double Seal Glass Purchased," *Guardian World*, July/August 1982.
41. Ebeid, interview.
42. "Guardian at a Glance," *Guardian World*, April/May 1984.
43. "Guardian Buys Buchmin Industries," *Guardian World*, April/May 1985.
44. Nadolski, interview.
45. Ibid.
46. "Floreffe Plant to Make Tint Glass," *Guardian World*, October/November 1984.
47. Ibid.
48. "Guardian Transportation Starts Operations," *Guardian World*, December 1983.
49. "Automotive Glass Group," *Guardian World*, December 1985.
50. "New Automotive Glass Plant Starts Operation," *Guardian World*, April/May 1985.
51. Duane Faulkner, interview by David Patton, 8 February 2001, Write Stuff Enterprises.
52. Guardian Industries news release, 26 January 1981.
53. Knight, interview.
54. Ibid.
55. "Guardian Enters Leasing Business," *Guardian World*, February/March 1981.
56. "Guardian Acquires Windsor Plastics," *Guardian World*, July-September 1988.
57. Knight, interview.
58. Ibid.
59. "Dear Fellow Employees," *Guardian World*, December 1984.
60. "Detroit Plant Closes its Doors After Many Years of Service," *Guardian World*, October/November 1981.
61. Ibid.
62. Alonzo, interview.
63. "Carleton Employees Reject Union Organizing," *Guardian World*, October/November 1979.

64. Don Tullman, interview by Barbara Koch, tape recording, 7 February 2001, Write Stuff Enterprises.

65. "Union Voted Out; Carleton Strike Ends," *Guardian World*, December 1986.

66. Ebeid, interview.

67. Bill Valk, interview by Jeffrey L. Rodengen and Richard Hubbard, tape recording, 29 March 2001, Write Stuff Enterprises.

68. "Union Voted Out; Carleton Strike Ends," *Guardian World*, December 1986.

69. Valk, interview.

70. Ibid.

71. Monroe Evening Times, various articles, May and June 1986.

72. Ebeid, interview.

73. "Tear Gas Used at Guardian," Monroe Evening News, 8 August 1986.

74. Kerry Kerrigan, WJBK News, 8 August 1986.

75. Valk, interview.

76. Ibid.

77. "Decertification Vote at Guardian Carleton Plant," Departmental Correspondence, 17 October 1986.

78. "Guardian Chief to Buy All Stock," *Detroit News*, 10 July 1984.

79. "A Letter from the President," *Guardian World*, August/September 1984.

80. Davidson, interview.

81. "Ask the President," *Guardian World*, February/March 1986.

82. Ibid.

83. *Guardian World*, August/September 1986.

84. "A Letter from the President," *Guardian World*, August/September 1984.

85. "Ask the President," *Guardian World*, February/March 1986.

86. Knight, interview.

87. "Automotive Glass Group," *Guardian World*, December 1985.

88. "Guardian to Build Two New Float Lines," *Guardian World*, June/July 1987.

89. "Guardian to Spend $250 Million on New Plants & Equipment," *Guardian World*, August/September 1987.

90. Ebeid, interview.

91. Benedict, interview.

92. "Guardian to Build Two New Float Plants," *Guardian World*, June/July 1987.

93. Ibid.

94. "Richburg Float Glass Plant Launched," *Guardian World*, October/November 1988.

95. "Guardian to Spend $250 Million on New Plants and Equipment," *Guardian World*, August/September 1987.

96. "Guardian to Build Two New Float Glass Plants," *Guardian World*, July-September 1988.

Chapter Six

1. Robert H. Gorlin, interview by Jeffrey L. Rodengen, tape recording, 8 November 2001, Write Stuff Enterprises.

2. "Guardian to Build Plant in Venezuela," *Guardian World*, September/October 1980.

3. *Guardian World*, September/October 1980.

4. "Guardian to Build Two New Float Glass Plants," *Guardian World*, July-September 1988.

5. Knight, interview.

6. "Vimosa Plant Nears Completion," *Guardian World*, June 1990.

7. Mark Lacasse, interview by author, 2002.

8. "Venezuela Plant Under Construction," *Guardian World*, September 1989.

9. Lacasse, interview.

10. "Guardian Industries Corp., Harvard Business School N9-292-083," June 5, 1992, 4-5.

11. Peter Walters, interview by Jeffrey L. Rodengen, tape recording, 15 February 2001, Write Stuff Enterprises.

12. "Hunguard Plant Under Construction," *Guardian World*, March 1990.

13. Ibid.

14. Ebeid, interview.

15. Ralph Gerson, interview by Jeffrey L. Rodengen, tape recording, 15 February 2001, Write Stuff Enterprises.

16. "Hunguard Glass Plant Started," *Guardian World*, September 1989.

17. Harvard Business School, 8.

18. "Guardian Signs Joint Venture With Hungarian Glassmaker," PR Newswire, 20 July 1988.

19. Gerson, interview.

20. Harvard Business School, 6.

21. "Hunguard Plant Under Construction," *Guardian World*, March 1990.
22. "Hunguard Glass Plant Started," *Guardian World*, September 1989.
23. Benedict, interview.
24. Mike Morrison, interview by Jeffrey L. Rodengen, tape recording, 10 December 2001, Write Stuff Enterprises.
25. "Hunguard Plant Successfully Launched," *Guardian World*, March 1991.
26. Moore, interview.
27. "1998 Employee of the Year," *Guardian World*, January 1999.
28. Lajos Sapi, interview by Robert H. Gorlin, 20 January 2004, Guardian Industries.
29. "1998 Employee of the Year," *Guardian World*, January 1999.
30. Sapi, interview.
31. *Guardian World*, March 1990.
32. "Guardian to Build Float Glass Plant in Thailand," *Guardian World*, June 1991.
33. Walters, interview.
34. Dusit Nontanakorn, interview by Jeffrey L. Rodengen, tape recording, 24 February 2002, Write Stuff Enterprises.
35. "Thailand Finally OKs Joint Glass Venture," *Journal of Commerce*, 28 June 1990.
36. Charles Smith, "Asahi Launches Expansion Drive in Asia: Overseas Focus," *Far Eastern Economic Review*, 28 September 1989, 149.

37. Gerson, interview.
38. Thailand Finally OKs Joint Glass Venture," *Journal of Commerce*.
39. Gerson, interview.
40. "Guardian to Build Float Glass Plant in Thailand," *Guardian World*, June 1991.
41. "New Thailand Plant Up and Running," *Guardian World*, December 1992.
42. Benedict, interview.
43. Tullman, interview.
44. Benedict, interview.
45. John Bedogni, interview by Jeffrey L. Rodengen, tape recording, 13 February 2001, Write Stuff Enterprises.
46. Nontanakorn, interview.
47. "Thailand II Now on Stream," *Guardian World*, June 1997.
48. Ibid.
49. Chuck Croskey, interview by Jeffrey L. Rodengen, tape recording, 13 February 2001, Write Stuff Enterprises.
50. "Guardian Purchases Partner's Equity in Siam Guardian," *Guardian World*, March 2000.
51. Marcia Berss, "Nice Guys Finish Last," *Forbes*, 6 July 1992, 92.
52. "Comments of Ralph J. Gerson Before the U.S.-Japan Export Symposium," 19 October 1992.
53. Gerson, interview.
54. Walters, interview.
55. "Guardian Selected for Japan Corporate Program," PR Newswire, 4 April 1991.
56. "Guardian Steps Up Efforts to Expand Japanese Market,"

American Glass Review, 1 June 1992.
57. Alan L. Adler, "The Glass Wall: Auburn Hills' Guardian Industries Chips Away at Barriers to the Japanese Glass Industry," *Detroit Free Press*, 29 January 1996, 6F.
58. "Guardian Executive Vice President Tells CEO's Japan Still Not Doing Enough," Guardian Industries news release, 14 July 1993.
59. "U.S. Glass Industry Seeks Japan Access; Earlier Pact Made Little Headway," *Journal of Commerce*, 25 January 1994, 4A.
60. Croskey, interview.
61. "Guardian to Build Plant in India," *Guardian World*, December 1990.
62. Joe Bruce, interview by Jeffrey L. Rodengen, tape recording, 15 February 2001, Write Stuff Enterprises.
63. Walters, interview.
64. Gerson, interview.
65. Vinay Kumar Modi, interview by Jeffrey L. Rodengen, tape recording, 12 February 2002, Write Stuff Enterprises.
66. Walters, interview.
67. Ann Waichunas, interview by Robert H. Gorlin, 20 January 2004, Guardian Industries.
68. Gerson, interview.
69. Vashi, interview.
70. Ibid.
71. Ibid.
72. "Asia Plants Nearing Completion," *Guardian World*, June 1992.

73. Modi, interview.

74. Dave Rose, interview by Robert H. Gorlin, 20 January 2004, Guardian Industries.

75. Gerson, interview.

76. "Guardian Steps Up Efforts to Expand Japanese Market."

77. Walters, interview.

78. Ibid.

79. Ibid.

80. "Four Float Plants Under Construction," *Guardian World*, March 1996.

81. Croskey, interview.

82. "Gulfguard Successfully Launched," *Guardian World*, December 1996.

83. Croskey, interview.

84. "Guardian to Build Float Glass Plant in Brazil," *Guardian World*, June 1996.

85. Ibid.

86. Lacasse, interview.

87. "Customer Service and Logistics as Marketing Tools," *Guardian World*, June 2000.

88. Lacasse, interview.

89. Wilson Farhat Jr., interview by Jeffrey L. Rodengen, tape recording, 8 January 2002, Write Stuff Enterprises.

90. Lacasse, interview.

91. Don Trofholz, interview by Robert H. Gorlin, 20 January 2004, Guardian Industries.

92. "Construction Underway on Second Float Plant in Spain," *Guardian World*, September 1992.

93. Guardian Industries news release, 24 May 1991.

94. Knight, interview.

95. Luc Theis, interview by Robert H. Gorlin, 20 January 2004, Guardian Industries.

96. Ibid.

97. Moore, interview.

98. "Four Float Plants Under Construction," *Guardian World*, March 1996.

99. "Guardian Europe Celebrates Expansions: Guardian Flachglas Inaugurated," *Guardian World*, December 1997.

100. Ibid.

101. Ibid.

102. "Guardian Europe Celebrates Expansions: New Laminating Line at Lux II," *Guardian World*, December 1997.

103. Ibid.

104. Ibid.

105. "Guardian Europe Celebrates Expansions: Mirror Line Inaugurated at Hunguard," *Guardian World*, December 1997.

106. "Guardian Europe 15 Years of Progress 1981-1996," *Guardian World*, September 1996.

107. *Guardian World*, June 1996.

108. "Guardian Acquires Interest in Industries Cover," *Guardian World*, December 1990.

109. "Guardian Buys Interest in Canadian Glass Company," *Guardian World*, June 1991.

110. "Guardian Buys Walker Atlantic Glass," *Guardian World*, December 1991.

111. "Falconer Glass Industries Purchased by Guardian," *Guardian World*, September 1991.

112. Ibid.

113. "Guardian Expands Mirror Manufacturing Capacity," *Guardian World*, March 1993.

114. "DeWitt Launched," *Guardian World*, June 1996.

115. Guardian to Expand Worldwide Coating Capabilities," Guardian Industries news release, 10 February 1998.

116. Rich Rising, interview with Jon VanZile, tape recording, 13 March 2002, Write Stuff Enterprises.

117. "Guardian to Build Float Glass Plant in New York," *Guardian World*, September 1996.

118. Jeff Green, "Guardian Moving Next Door to Palace," *Oakland Press*, 23 June 1993.

119. Jack Sights, interview by Jon VanZile, tape recording, 6 March 2002, Write Stuff Enterprises.

120. "New Automotive Fabrication Plant Under Construction," *Guardian World*, September 1990.

121. "Guardian at Mid-Year," *Guardian World*, September 1990.

122. Sights, interview.

123. "New Automotive Fabrication Plant Under Construction," *Guardian World*, September 1990.

124. "New High-Tech Products Developed," *Guardian World*, September 1990.

125. "Ligonier Automotive Fabrication Plant A Success Story!" *Guardian World*, June 1997, and "Ligonier Gets Advance Look at New Chrysler LH Cars," Guardian Industries news release, 28 August 1992.

126. "Ligonier Automotive Fabrication Plant A Success Story!" *Guardian World*, June 1997.

127. Glenn Longardner, interview by Jeffrey L. Rodengen, tape recording, 1 March 2002, Write Stuff Enterprises.

128. "Guardian Industries Announces Technological Breakthrough," Guardian Industries news release, 4 June 1993.

129. "What is SMG®?" *Guardian World*, September 1992.

130. Albert Franck, interview by Jeffrey L. Rodengen, tape recording, 3 January 2002, Write Stuff Enterprises.

131. Sights, interview.

132. "The Transformation of Evansville," *Guardian World*, December 1997.

133. "Automotive Moulding Company Joins the Guardian Team," *Guardian World*, March 1996.

134. Ibid.

135. David Clark, interview by Jeffrey L. Rodengen, tape recording, 29 March 2001, Write Stuff Enterprises.

136. Sights, interview.

137. Steve Markevich, interview by Robert H. Gorlin, 20 January 2004, Guardian Industries.

138. "Guardian Automotive Acquires European Trim Company," *Guardian World*, Spring 1998.

139. Markevich, interview.

140. John Couretas, "Guardian Automotive to Build Kentucky Plant,"*Crain's Detroit Business*, 14 October 1996, 47.

141. "Commercial Production Begins at Morehead," *Guardian World*, Spring 1998.

142. "Guardian Morehead Expansion Creates 100 New Jobs," *Guardian World*, December 2000.

143. "Fiberglass Focuses on the Future," *Guardian World*, June 1990.

144 "Guardian Buys Canadian Fiberglass Plant," *Guardian World*, June 1994.

145. "Guardian Fiberglass to Build New Plant in West Virginia," Guardian Industries, June 1997.

146. Jeffrey McCracken and Robert Sherefkin, "Guardian Considers Investing in Materials Biz," *Crain's Detroit Business*, 20 July 1998, 3.

147. Martin Powell, interview by Robert H. Gorlin, 20 January 2004, Guardian Industries.

148. Ibid.

149. McCracken and Sherefkin, "Guardian Considers Investing in Materials Biz."

150. "BMA Our Company," www.buildersmarts.com, 10 April 2001.

151. Faulkner, interview.

152. "Ace Hardware and Builder Marts of America Create Largest Lumber, Building Materials, and Millwork Buying Group," www.ace-hardware.com, 10 April 2001.

Chapter Six Sidebar: Davidson's Folly

1. "Talk of the Town: The Palace of Auburn Hills," *Guardian World*, January/February 1988.

2. Claire M. Hinsbert, "Business Arena: Using the Auburn Hills Palace as a Template, CEO and President Tom Wilson Took Two Ailing Venues—Pine Knob and the Meadow Brook Music Festival—And Parlayed Them Into Part of his Thriving Empire. How Did He Do It?" *Corporate Detroit*, November 1995, p. 8.

3. "Talk of the Town: The Palace of Auburn Hills," *Guardian World*, January/February 1988.

4. "Ilitch & Davidson: The Rival Kings of Entertainment," *Detroit Free Press*, 8 August 1992, 1A.

5. Jeff Corey, interview by Barbara Koch, tape recording, 8 May 2001, Write Stuff Enterprises.

6. Eric Whisenhunt, "Pumping Up the Profits," *Business Detroit*, November 1990, 21.

7. Tom Wilson, interview by Robert H. Gorlin, 1 June 2004, Guardian Industries.

8. "About Us," http://www.palacenet.com, 8 May 2001.

9. Whisenhunt, "Pumping Up the Profits."

10 "Palace Sports and Entertainment, Inc.," PS&E press release.

Chapter Seven

1. Knight, interview.

2. *Guardian World*, March 2001.

3. Moore, interview.

4. "Expanding Europe," *Guardian World*, second quarter, 2004.

5. *Guardian World*, third quarter, 2002.

6. Ebeid, interview.

7. "Expanding Europe," *Guardian World*, second quarter, 2004.

8. Rene Fiorese, interview by Robert H. Gorlin, 5 August 2004, Guardian Industries.

9. Expanding Europe," *Guardian World*, second quarter, 2004.

10. *Guardian World*, second quarter, 2002.

11. Fiorese, interview.

12. "Expanding Europe," *Guardian World*, second quarter, 2004.

13. "Production Under Way at Goole," *Guardian World*, first quarter, 2004.

14. Jean-Luc Pitsch, interview by Robert H. Gorlin, 5 August 2004, Guardian Industries.

15. "Guardian Participates in Egypt Development Talks," *Guardian World*, October/November 1979.

16. "Guardian Partners with Egyptian Float Glass Plant," *Guardian World*, fourth quarter, 2003.

17. Ibid.

18. "Mexico Home to Guardian's 24th Float Glass Plant," *Guardian World*, fourth quarter, 2003.

19. Lacasse, interview.

20. *Guardian World*, March 2001.

21. *Guardian World*, first quarter, 2003.

22. Alonzo, interview.

23. Vashi, interview.

24. Wally Palma, interview by Jeffrey L. Rodengen, tape recording, 3 April 2001, Write Stuff Enterprises.

25. Joseph Bruce, interview by Robert H. Gorlin, 10 August 2004, Guardian Industries.

26. "Cameron Ashley Announces Acceptance of Offer From Guardian Industries," Business Wire, 1 May 2000.

27. Faulkner, interview.

28. Ibid.

29. Ibid.

30. "GBPG: Customer Focused, Growth Oriented," *Guardian World*, second quarter, 2003.

31. *Guardian World*, September 2000.

32. Bill Jacoby, interview by Robert H. Gorlin, 5 August 2004, Guardian Industries.

33. *Guardian World*, second quarter, 2003.

34. Powell, interview.

35. Faulkner, interview.

36. "Guardian Consolidates Automotive Group for Innovation and Growth," Guardian Industries news release, 14 July 1999.

37. Sights, interview.

38. "Guardian Consolidates Automotive Group for Innovation and Growth," Guardian Industries news release, 14 July 1999.

39. "Guardian Automotive: A Global Leader in Exterior Systems Innovation," *Guardian World*, June 2000.

40. "Guardian Industries Names D. James Davis President and CEO of Automotive Products Group," press release, 6 May 2002, Guardian archive.

41. Jim Davis, interview by Robert H. Gorlin, 15 August 2004, Guardian Industries.

42. Ibid.

43. Ibid.

44. Ibid.

45. Kevin Myers, interview by Robert H. Gorlin, 15 August 2004, Guardian Industries.

46. Ibid.

47. Davis, interview.

48. Markevich, interview.

49. Ibid.

50. Davis, interview.

51. *Guardian World*, Winter, 1999.

52. Scott Thomsen, interview by Jeffrey L. Rodengen, tape recording, 14 December 2001, Write Stuff Enterprises.

53. Ebeid, interview.

54. Thomsen, interview.

55. "Science & Technology Center Provides a Cornerstone for Innovation," *Guardian World*, September 2000.

56. *Guardian World*, September 2000.

57. "A Cornerstone...," *Guardian World*, September 2000.

58. "Guardian Europe: Update 2000," *Guardian World*, December 2000.

59. *Guardian World*, December 2000.

60. "Product Profile," *Guardian World*, second quarter, 2002.

61. "Product Profile," *Guardian World*, fourth quarter, 2002.

62. "Technology Profile," *Guardian World*, first quarter, 2002.

63. "Product Profile," *Guardian World*, June 2001.

64. Thomsen, interview.

65. "A Marriage Made in Heaven," *Guardian World*, first quarter, 2003.

66. "Product Profile," *Guardian World*, Fall 2001.

67. www.egpglass.com

68. *Guardian World*, first quarter, 2004.

69. Bruce Cummings, interview by Robert H. Gorlin, 10 August 2004, Guardian Industries.

70. Gorlin, interview.

71. Morrison, interview.

72. "Questions and Answers," *Guardian World*, first quarter, 2004.

73. Walters, interview.

74. Gorlin, interview.

75. Jeffrey A. Knight, interview by Robert H. Gorlin, 20 August 2004, Guardian Industries.

76. Davidson, interview.

77. Knight, interview.

78. Cummings, interview.

79. Tullman, interview.

80. Ibid.

81. Ibid.

82. *Reflections*, second quarter, 2004.

83. *Guardian World*, third quarter, 2002.

84. Ibid.

85. *Guardian World*, December 2000.

86. *Guardian World*, second quarter, 2004.

87. Nancy Sivy, interview by Robert H. Gorlin, 20 August 2004, Guardian Industries.

88. *Guardian World*, second quarter, 2003.

89. Sivy, interview.

90. *Guardian World*, second quarter, 2003.

91. "Bolingers Win War Against Waistlines," *Guardian World*, October/November 1985; "Guardian Employees Buckle Up," *Guardian World*, December 1988.

92. "HealthGuard 'Better Living' Goals Defined," *Guardian World*, February/March 1986.

93. "Ask the President," *Guardian World*, February/March 1986.

94. *Guardian World*, third quarter, 2003.

95. *Guardian World*, June 2001.

96. *Guardian World*, second quarter, 2003.

97. *Guardian World*, second quarter, 2004.

98. *Guardian World*, second quarter, 2002.

99. *Guardian World*, first quarter, 2002.

100. Alonzo, interview.

101. Ebeid, interview.

102. Walters, interview.

103. "The Greening of Guardian," fourth quarter, 2003.

104. Ibid.

105. *Guardian World*, March 2000.

106. *Guardian World*, first quarter, 2004.

107. "The Greening of Guardian," *Guardian World*, fourth quarter, 2003.

108. *Guardian World*, fourth quarter, 2003.

109. Davidson, interview.

110. "Guardian Announces New College Scholarship Program," *Guardian World*, June/July 1986.

111. Cummings, interview.

112. Walters, interview.

113. Lacasse, interview.

114. *Guardian World*, third quarter, 2003.

115. *Guardian World*, June 2001.

116. *Guardian World*, third quarter, 2003.
117. *Guardian World*, first quarter, 2003.
118. *Guardian World*, March 2001.
119. *Guardian World*, second quarter, 2003.
120. *Glass Magazine*, January 1999.
121. Ibid.
122. Cummings, interview.
123. Valk, interview.
124. Cummings, interview.
125. Gorlin, interview.
126. Gerson, interview.
127. *Guardian World*, March 2001.
128. Ebeid, interview.
129. Cummings, interview.
130. Cummings, interview.
131. Knight, interview.
132. Ebeid, interview.
133. *Guardian World*, first quarter, 2004.
134. Ibid.
135. Knight, interview.
136. *Guardian World*, first quarter, 2004.
137. Ibid.

INDEX

Page numbers in italics indicate photographs.